Faith Transformed

Christian Encounters with Jews and Judaism

Edited by
John C. Merkle

Essays by
Walter Harrelson
Alice L. Eckardt   *Alice L. Eckardt*
Eva Fleischner
Franklin Sherman
Norman A. Beck
Clark M. Williamson
John T. Pawlikowski, o.s.m.
Eugene J. Fisher
Michael B. McGarry, c.s.p.
Mary C. Boys, s.n.j.m.
John C. Merkle

Afterword by
Irvin J. Borowsky

A Michael Glazier Book

THE LITURGICAL PRESS
Collegeville, Minnesota

www.litpress.org

Published in cooperation with
The American Interfaith Institute

A Michael Glazier Book published by The Liturgical Press

Cover design by David Manahan, O.S.B. Cover photo by Francisco Schulte, O.S.B. Western Wall of the Temple Mount, Jerusalem.

1	2	3	4	5	6	7	8

Library of Congress Cataloging-in-Publication Data

Faith transformed : Christian encounters with Jews and Judaism / edited by John C.
    Merkle ; essays by Walter Harrelson . . . [et al.] ; afterword by Irvin J. Borowsky.
        p. cm.
    "A Michael Glazier book."
    Includes bibliographical references and index.
    ISBN 0-8146-5117-8 (alk. paper)
        1. Christianity and other religions—Judaism. 2. Judaism—Relations—Christianity.
    I. Merkle, John C. II. Harrelson, Walter J.

BM535.F26 2003
261.2'6—dc21

                                                                    2003041634

"The essays of the more senior contributors to *Faith Transformed* provide a valuable entrée to an important part of the developing history of Christian-Jewish relations over the past half-century. We need to keep that story and that memory alive. . . . The book as a whole offers a rich diversity of the 'results' of interfaith encounter. To read how these results emerged and how they differ is sheer delight!"

David P. Efroymson
Professor Emeritus, Religion
La Salle University

"This book courageously explores the crucial areas of theological and personal transformation. Readers will find themselves moved by the stimulating accounts of how Christian thinkers were changed through their encounters with Jews and Judaism. It is an excellent text for seminary courses and adult education classes alike, opening the door to an essential dialogue that Christianity must have."

Linda Mercadante
Professor of Theology, B. Robert Straker Chair
The Methodist Theological School in Ohio

"*Faith Transformed* sets forth a series of inspiring stories that trace the development of the rapprochement between Jews and Christians since the end of the *Shoah*. The essays by these Catholic and Protestant theologians reveal how it is possible to engage in the time-honored quest for 'faith seeking understanding' with intellectual rigor and a profound commitment to the service of the Church. Jews and Christians who read these essays will find the patience and fortitude to forge ahead with the new relationship between their communities. They will discover narratives of faith strengthened and renewed rather than weakened or diluted."

Michael A. Signer
Abrams Professor of Jewish Thought and Culture
University of Notre Dame

Contents

Acknowledgements   vii

Contributors   ix

JOHN C. MERKLE
Introduction   xi

one
WALTER HARRELSON
**What I Have Learned about Christian Faith
from Jews and Judaism**   1

two
ALICE L. ECKARDT
Growing into a Daring and Questioning Faith   17

three
EVA FLEISCHNER
Encountering Anew the Living God—in a Living People   37

four
FRANKLIN SHERMAN
Steps Along the Way   51

five

NORMAN A. BECK
Replacing Barriers with Bridges   71

six

CLARK M. WILLIAMSON
Blessed *Chutzpah,* Blessed Questions, Blessed *Chaverim*   90

seven

JOHN T. PAWLIKOWSKI, O.S.M.
Drawing from Jewish Wellsprings   110

eight

EUGENE J. FISHER
Enriching Christian Life Through Encounter with Judaism   130

nine

MICHAEL B. McGARRY, C.S.P.
The Path to a Journey   144

ten

MARY C. BOYS, S.N.J.M.
The Road Is Made by Walking   162

eleven

JOHN C. MERKLE
Faith Transformed by Study and Friendship   182

appendix

CHRISTIAN SCHOLARS GROUP ON CHRISTIAN-JEWISH RELATIONS
**A Sacred Obligation: Rethinking Christian Faith
in Relation to Judaism and the Jewish People**   202

IRVIN J. BOROWSKY
Afterword   207

Index   211

Acknowledgements

I am deeply grateful to my colleagues for their contributions to this volume, as I have long been indebted to them for their inspired leadership in Christian-Jewish relations; to Peter Dwyer, Mark Twomey, and their editorial staff at The Liturgical Press for their expertise and encouragement in the publication of this book; to Irvin J. Borowsky and the American Interfaith Institute, as well as Mark Conway and the Literary Arts Institute of the College of Saint Benedict, for their generous support; and to my beloved spouse, Sarah Pruett, for her abiding support of this project, her careful reading of the manuscript, and her ever-insightful suggestions that have significantly enhanced the book.

Contributors

NORMAN A. BECK
Poehlmann Professor of Theology and Classical Languages
Texas Lutheran University, Seguin

IRWIN J. BOROWSKY
Chairman
American Interfaith Institute, Philadelphia

MARY C. BOYS, S.N.J.M
Skinner and McAlpin Professor of Practical Theology
Union Theological Seminary, New York City

ALICE L. ECKARDT
Professor Emerita of Religion Studies
Lehigh University, Bethlehem, Pennsylvania

EUGENE J. FISHER
Executive Director, Secretariat for Catholic-Jewish Relations
United States Conference of Catholic Bishops, Washington, D.C.

EVA FLEISCHNER
Professor Emerita of Religion
Montclair State University, Montclair, New Jersey

WALTER HARRELSON
Distinguished Professor Emeritus of Hebrew Bible
Vanderbilt University, Nashville

MICHAEL B. McGARRY, c.s.p.
> Rector
> Tantur Ecumenical Center, Jerusalem, Israel

JOHN C. MERKLE
> Professor of Theology
> College of Saint Benedict, St. Joseph, Minnesota

JOHN T. PAWLIKOWSKI, o.s.m.
> Professor of Social Ethics
> Director, Catholic-Jewish Studies Program
> Catholic Theological Union, Chicago

FRANKLIN SHERMAN
> Professor Emeritus of Jewish-Christian Studies
> Founding Director, Institute for Jewish-Christian Understanding
> Muhlenberg College, Allentown, Pennsylvania

CLARK M. WILLIAMSON
> Indiana Professor of Christian Thought Emeritus
> Christian Theological Seminary, Indianapolis

JOHN C. MERKLE

Introduction

From early on Christians have defined Christianity in relation to the Jewish tradition from which it emerged. Unfortunately, Christians have usually misunderstood and misrepresented Judaism and have failed to appreciate the ongoing spiritual vitality of the Jewish people. Traditionally, the Christian churches have taught that the validity of Judaism came to an end with the coming of Christ and the emergence of Christianity. Christian self-understanding was built in large part upon the notion of Christianity having replaced Judaism as the one valid pathway to God. But in the last half-century, in light of a better understanding of the Jewish tradition, many Christians, including church leaders, have been rethinking and reversing the timeworn Christian teachings concerning the Jewish people and their faith. In fact, over the last four decades, numerous Christian churches have issued formal statements repudiating traditional anti-Jewish teachings and affirming the abiding validity of Judaism. Since traditional Christian self-understanding involved the claim that Christianity superseded Judaism, it is clear that the new affirmation of Judaism's validity necessitates a reevaluation of Christian self-understanding.

In this book eleven Catholic and Protestant biblical scholars, historians, and theologians who have been deeply involved in Christian-Jewish relations share how their encounters with Jews and Judaism have transformed their understanding and practice of Christianity. In various ways they reveal how their Christian faith has been profoundly enriched by drawing inspiration from Jews and Judaism.

xii • FAITH TRANSFORMED

The idea for this book came in the midst of my teaching a college course called "Christianity in Relation to Judaism." While there are a number of excellent texts to choose from for such a course, personal narratives recounting the experiences that generated creative rethinking of Christian faith in relation to Judaism have been scarce. Having assigned autobiographical works in other courses, I became convinced that many students learn more about subjects when they are presented in the context of personal life experiences. I therefore invited a number of Catholic and Protestant colleagues in Christian-Jewish relations to explain how their theological understanding and religious practice have been affected by their involvement with Jews and Judaism. I am deeply grateful for their contributions to this book, and I am honored to have the opportunity to add the story of my own journey to the stories of such esteemed colleagues and friends.

All eleven of us are members of the Christian Scholars Group on Christian-Jewish Relations, which began in 1969 and is currently sponsored by the Center for Christian-Jewish Learning at Boston College. Our essays in this book reveal not only a wide variety of interfaith experiences but also a significant diversity of theological perspectives. Nevertheless, along with our other colleagues in the Christian Scholars Group, we were, after extensive deliberation, able to formulate a consensus statement, "A Sacred Obligation: Rethinking Christian Faith in Relation to Judaism and the Jewish People." Since the issues raised in "A Sacred Obligation" are explored throughout this book, it is fitting to include this statement as an appendix, which may serve as a summary of what we collectively consider to be essential to a Christian faith transformed through encounters with Jews and Judaism.

Also included at the end of this book is an afterword by Irvin J. Borowsky. The story that he as a Jew shares concerning his encounter with Christianity confirms the urgency of Christians rethinking their religious self-understanding vis-à-vis Judaism and the Jewish people.

My hope in editing this book is that it will inspire other Christians to reexamine their own views of Judaism and their understanding and practice of Christian faith in relation to Judaism.

WALTER HARRELSON

What I Have Learned about Christian Faith from Jews and Judaism

How I Became Acquainted With Judaism

My earliest engagement with Judaism came, I believe, in 1937 or so when I was working in Washington, D.C., at the Justice Department as a teen-aged messenger boy and attending various night classes. One of these was a semester-long class on Josephus (first century C.E. Jewish historian), taught at one of the Bible Institutes in Washington. Josephus fascinated me, for he introduced me to the world of Judaism at the time of the beginning of Christianity and told stories not found in the Bible. From that class I turned to the reading of the so-called "Lost Books of the Bible," available then in an edition the name of which I have long forgotten. I read Jubilees, Enoch, the Testament of the Twelve Patriarchs, and other esoterica. But it was never suggested to me by my teachers that I read the Mishnah (the first comprehensive post-biblical book of Jewish law, formulated about 200 C.E.) or any of the rabbinic literature that carries on from the Mishnah. Judaism was clearly alive, but to my Christian teachers of that time Judaism was of no real interest, save as a reminder of an additional group that was in need of conversion to Christianity.

My next engagement with Judaism was at the end of the Second World War, when at Chapel Hill, North Carolina, I worked with my professor of philosophy, a refugee with his Jewish wife from Germany, preparing packages for German refugees and incidentally learning about Dietrich

Bonhoeffer and other Christian resisters to Hitler. The Holocaust was frequently mentioned, but the professor and his wife were by now Christians, and their special concern was with the rebuilding of German life and institutions on democratic grounds. Soon after I left Chapel Hill, the professor and his family returned to Germany and worked valiantly for years thereafter in that endeavor. The relations of Jews and Christians did not, however, come into focus for me during those undergraduate years at Chapel Hill, despite the fact that I spent much of my classwork in philosophy dealing with St. Augustine, St. Thomas Aquinas, Spinoza, Kierkegaard, and some of the twentieth century existentialist philosophers, in the process beginning to learn how Christians often had misunderstood Judaism and mistreated Jews.

Encounters During Graduate Study

A serious exposure to living Judaism first came at Union Theological Seminary in New York City when I was engaged in my first formal theological work. In a class in beginning Hebrew I worked with a young Jewish student, now a professor at Princeton University, trying to come to terms with the biblical language. My Jewish colleague knew how to pronounce Hebrew fluently, and he understood in general what the text said. But he had no knowledge at all of the grammar and syntax of biblical Hebrew, and he marveled that we Christians could understand the intricacies of the language while being laughably unable to pronounce the words. He said on one occasion, "I never knew that there was a Southern way to pronounce Hebrew."

More importantly, my real knowledge of Judaism began to come during those seminary years. It came in three or four distinct ways: through the study of the Hebrew Scriptures with my Christian teachers; through marvelous encounters with professors of the Jewish Theological Seminary and professors of Near Eastern studies at Columbia University, including Abraham Joshua Heschel, H. L. Ginsberg, and Isaac Mendelssohn; and through the sessions of the "Fellowship of Socialist Christians," which had a number of Jewish members, including Will Herberg, as well as its major Christian founders, Reinhold Niebuhr, Eduard Heimann, and Paul Tillich. I will never forget a session dealing with human sexuality and the Bible. On that occasion, Herberg gave a paper in which he argued, not entirely seriously, I am sure, that the biblical Israel considered premarital sexual relations to be no really serious moral problem; the community was forceful in demanding sexual fidelity in marriage, but it may even have expected men and women to come to know one another sexually prior to marriage, thereby avoiding many problems. The family of course had to exercise oversight and see that promiscuity was avoided.

Reinhold Niebuhr warmly criticized the Herberg paper, saying that too much was being claimed. What Herberg should have said, said Niebuhr, was that sexual activity during betrothal, prior to the actual marriage ceremony, might well be condoned so long as the conventions of marriage were then observed. But Niebuhr agreed with Herberg that Jews had never had the sexual hangups that characterized most of the history of the Christian community.

My late friend and colleague, Rudolf Mach, was a student at the University of Basel in Switzerland when I went there in 1950 for a year of study with the theological faculty, a faculty that included Karl Barth as well as the people in biblical studies with whom I most wanted to work—Eichrodt, Baumgartner, Cullmann, and Karl Ludwig Schmidt. Barth was a world celebrity, not least for his well-known emphasis on the centrality of the Jewish Scriptures for Christian life and faith. Schmidt too was a famous anti-Nazi who had left Nazi Germany for Switzerland, as Barth had done, to avoid punishment by the Nazis. But it was Rudolf Mach, my student colleague and new friend, who began my serious introduction to Talmud (the Mishnah plus commentaries on the Mishnah, compiled from the third to the seventh centuries, constituting the most famous collection of Jewish teachings) and Midrash (a collection of rabbinical commentaries on the Bible). He helped me with the study of rabbinic Hebrew and with the Aramaic of the Talmud, and he said that I helped him a bit with the study of Assyro-Babylonian, which he was starting at the time. Mach was the first person in my hearing to characterize Judaism as a religion for life in this world, whereas Christianity was strictly speaking a religion of redemption from this world. I argued against that characterization of Christianity, even as I silently accepted its close approximation to the reality of much actual Christian practice.

Teaching in Boston and Chicago

During my four years at Andover Newton Theological School, located in the Boston area, I did much work on the newly discovered Dead Sea

Scrolls, lectured widely on the subject in order to support my family, and also developed a special interest in English translation of the Hebrew Scriptures. Lectures on the newly published Revised Standard Version of the Bible began to make me much more sensitive than I had been before to infelicities in translation that did harm to readers, including Jewish readers of the New Testament. But I did not have any really close associations with Jewish colleagues during those years, except at meetings of the Society of Biblical Literature and the American Schools of Oriental Research.

One momentous event during the Andover Newton days was the visit of the great Jewish philosopher Martin Buber to the area. A public lecture at Brandeis University was electrifying for all in attendance, and a later opportunity to meet with him personally at Columbia University in New York, on his same trip to the United States, was even more touching and rewarding. From that meeting, I knew myself to have been, in some sense, a part of the Jewish people all along—as a Christian believer.

My move to the University of Chicago in 1955 changed many things in my life, including my approach to the study of religion generally and certainly my ways of relating the texts of the Hebrew Scriptures to the Christian community. Important in the occurrence of these changes was my work with my close friend and colleague, the late Ralph Marcus, a long-time student of Hellenistic Judaism and a specialist in Josephus, Philo, and the Greek translations of the Bible. Ralph had an office in the Divinity School, was a regular participant in faculty affairs, and became a warm friend.

In addition, my Christian colleague in the field of Hebrew Bible, J. Coert Rylaarsdam, was a champion of conversations between Jews and Christians, knew the Jewish liturgy very well, and was an ardent friend and supporter of the state of Israel. His eloquent way of relating Judaism and Christianity helped me immensely.

Beyond that, my classes in Arabic and Assyro-Babylonian at the Department of Oriental Languages put me in closest touch with specialists in the ancient Near Eastern world who were also devout Jewish believers. I think of Moshe Held and Stanley Gewirtz, in particular, and my teachers, Ignace Gelb and Gustave von Gruenebaum, both escapees from Nazism in Europe who had lost many family members in the Holocaust, though they were not at all religious, were deeply steeped in the rabbinical traditions as well as learned in ancient Semitic languages and literatures. The class in Akkadian was especially valuable, for the students included two immensely learned and devout Jews and one equally learned and devout Jesuit, working together on pre-Jewish and pre-Christian religious and legal texts from the biblical world.

The Vanderbilt Years

Other major changes occurred during the long stay at Vanderbilt University. In Nashville for the first time I was plunged immediately into the struggle for racial justice, in which local rabbis and other Jewish leaders were centrally involved. These interfaith struggles for a better community brought deepened respect for Jews, brought close personal friendships between my family and several Jewish families, and began my personal effort to enrich my understanding of Judaism—living Judaism. Work with a Jewish colleague who was a member of the Divinity School faculty helped immensely. So also did the struggles in support of the State of Israel in 1967 and again in 1973, struggles in which Jewish leaders found virtually all of their Christian colleagues and partners simply silent and unaware, it seemed, of what to the Jewish community was so clear: Israel and the Jewish people were once again facing the possibility, if not indeed the prospect, of utter annihilation.

During these years at Vanderbilt—indeed, early on in my stay there—Vanderbilt began its annual summer conferences on Judaism and the Jewish people, greatly assisted by the work of Rabbi Solomon S. Bernards and the American Jewish Committee. We regularly invited college and university teachers of religion, plus some campus chaplains, to join us for an intensive week of orientation to Judaism: its history, thought, liturgical life, and contemporary reality. Jewish and Christian leaders provided the faculty, scholarships helped cover the expenses, and much of value was accomplished. I still meet faculty members regularly who were a part of those seminars and who speak affirmatively of their importance for their teaching, their research, and their life in association with Jews.

At Vanderbilt, our university chaplain, Beverly Asbury, joined with the Divinity School in the sponsorship of what was to become the oldest continuous lecture series devoted to the Holocaust at a major university (or so we are told). Asbury continued as the prime mover, along with the local Jewish community, in the sponsorship of the series, which continues to thrive today. Asbury also served as chair of the State Commission on the Observance of the Holocaust and, in that capacity, had much to do with the coming of the Anne Frank Exhibit to Nashville, which brought tens of thousands of Tennessee citizens and many visitors to the state to see the exhibit—the most visited exhibit ever.

The Vanderbilt years included the incorporation of solid work on Judaism and the Jewish people into the Divinity School and the graduate religion curricula and the buildup of library holdings that soon included an entire wing of the divinity library devoted to Judaica. Additions to the library holdings, made possible by a major gift from the chairman of Service Merchandise in memory of his parents, enabled the school to secure the library of the late Nahum Glatzer, a marvelous collection that includes a number of letters and other items from Franz Rosenzweig and Martin Buber.

It was at Vanderbilt that my association with Rabbi Randall M. Falk and his wife, Edna, and their family began. Rabbi Falk was first my clergy colleague in the struggle for public justice in the city, then my student in a doctoral program, and after that my colleague on the faculty, and later (and still today) co-author and co-lecturer on the relations of Judaism and Christianity. His gifts to me are beyond counting and beyond measure.

Scholarly Societies and Workshops

It would be a mistake not to mention how much I have learned through the work of the scholarly societies to which I have belonged, and through various workshops and conferences. One of the major factors shaping my exposure to Judaism and to Jewish scholarship has been my long association with a total of about three dozen Christian scholars who have held membership in the group now called the Christian Scholars Group on Christian-Jewish Relations. Such sustained attention to the subject has been invaluable for a person with my training and specialties. It has enabled me to read and discuss papers and books regularly, specifically on Christian-Jewish relations, written by group members that include specialists in virtually all of the theological disciplines, and by invited Jewish scholars. This forum, like the regular National Workshop on Christian-Jewish Relations, the many Holocaust conferences worldwide, and the monumental Holocaust Memorial Museum in Washington, with its great research collection, continues to deepen my appreciation of Judaism even as it informs and illuminates my grasp of Christian faith.

Also, when one thinks of the place that Jewish-Christian dialogue has had in the American Academy of Religion, the Society of Biblical Literature, and the American Schools of Oriental Research, to name just three, one can imagine the life-transforming value such encounters have had. It is of course possible to be a member of one or more of these groups and never give thought to the presence and work of Jewish colleagues, to form close friendships with Jews, or consciously to set out to become acquainted with the work of such colleagues just because they are Jewish. But it has not been possible for me to engage in the work of these societies without conscious reflection, over and again, on how marvelous it has been to pursue our studies "scientifically," without direct regard to religious affiliation, while all the while learning more and more about the religious and moral world of our associates through their papers and their lives. I think of the late Harry Orlinsky, a giant of biblical and Jewish learning and one of my dearest friends.

What Have I Learned from Jews and Judaism?

Before citing some of the most important things I have learned from Judaism and from my friendship with Jews, I must first point out that it is impossible to distinguish fully between what I have learned from the study of Tanakh, what Christians call the Old Testament, and what I have learned from Talmud, Midrash, other Jewish writings ancient and modern, and from study and work with Jewish scholars and the Jewish community generally. But the Christian Old Testament (though larger than the Jewish Tanakh and arranged in a different order) is Jewish Scripture too; thus, what we Christians learn there, we also learn, humanly speaking, from Jews and Judaism.

I say "humanly speaking" because there is one other distinction that is impossible to make, due to the nature of divine revelation. To put it directly, I don't know how to distinguish between *what I have learned through my own initiative* and *what has been disclosed to me by God.* We can all acknowledge this impossibility, can't we? Human interchanges are regularly the medium of divine disclosures. Thus, all that I write about here relates to the mystery of how any one of us can know anything. Paradoxically, we could say that *everything is learned through our efforts,* and we could also justly claim that *nothing is learned only through our efforts.*

I must, therefore, speak about what I *think* I have learned from my encounters with Jews and Judaism. What follows are some examples.

A Deeper Understanding of the Reality and Mystery of Incarnation

First, I believe that I have learned from the study of Tanakh and from work with Jewish scholars and other Jews just how deeply Jewish faith is rooted in history, how important land and family and peoplehood are, and how close to the struggles and joys and pains of human life the one we call God actually is. For a Christian that cannot help but underscore the reality and the mystery of the incarnation of the Son of God in the Jew Jesus. Some Christians may feel the need to draw back from classical Christian understandings of incarnation as a result of the Jewish-Christian encounter. For me the nearness of God in Jesus is only underscored through the recognition of how God the Creator is also intimately and continuingly involved in the creation, and especially (or so it seems) in human life, and most especially (or so it seems) in the life and struggles and sufferings and joys of the people of God. That has to do with what we call incarnation, the presence in human form of the God of Jewish and of Christian faith, present not only in the people of the covenant but present too, and supremely, in this fully human Jesus. God takes the side of struggling humankind in the midst of the world's struggles and sufferings and pain and death.

As Paul puts it in 2 Corinthians 5:21, "The one who knew no sin became sin for us, that in this one we might become God's righteousness." That is, in my words, a way of saying that there is no distance, not any at all, between the sovereign and loving and demanding God, on the one side, and the struggling and yearning and creative human one whom God has sent. On the human side, there is no distance between this one sent by God and the human community to whom he is sent. In him, God is present as Immanuel, "God with us," present to the whole of creation.

Background for this way of seeing Jesus as the Incarnate One is surely to be found in the pictures of Wisdom present with God at the creation, rejoicing in the world of God's creation as God's very first created being (Prov 8), then as first creative act that touches every other creation, like a mist (Sir 24), and then as a pervasive presence in the whole of the universe (Wis 7–9), and finally, in Christian form, as the Incarnate Word (John 1). The John text suggests a difference between the Wisdom theme and the Word made flesh, but is the latter not clearly traceable to the former?

This does not mean that there is anything inevitable in the incarnation of God within the world. But it is surely no accident that later Jewish thought will speak of the Torah in ways quite similar to this picture of Wisdom, and also will speak of the Sabbath in similar terms. These are finally viewed, not as creations of God, but (according to some lines of Jewish thought) as eternally with God, just as the Church came to speak of Jesus. My point is that there is a kind of plurality in the Godhead in Judaism, just as there is a Trinity in the Christian understanding of deity. And it is that plurality that allows a way of better explaining, I believe, what the Church came to mean by the incarnation of the Son of God—the second person of the Holy Trinity as fully God and fully human.

Now I would not claim at all that the full meaning of incarnation for the Christian believer is traceable to these developments. My point is rather that my own struggles to understand Judaism, and especially later texts in the Hebrew Bible and the literature of Apocrypha, Pseudepigrapha, and Talmud and Midrash, have led me the better and (I believe) more faithfully to affirm the Christian claim that in the Jew Jesus, born to Mary, the fullness of Godhead was pleased to dwell.

The Social Character of Human Sin

I have also been helped greatly by the study of Judaism and by conversations and discussions with Jewish scholars and friends to gain, I believe, a better and a deeper understanding of what Christians unfortunately came to call "original sin." Original sin is best comprehended, I believe, as the buildup and continuing influence of a given generation's misdeeds upon the next generation. While the prophet Ezekiel rightly demands that each generation accept responsibility for its own sins and exercise the freedom God grants to live responsibly in God's world, the truth surely is that the Bible's vivid picture of the spread of sin and of consequent death throughout God's good universe portrays how weighty human misdeeds become in the culture within which they occur—as well as in the following generations to which a given generation carries those misdeeds. The most graphic biblical picture, of course, comes prior to the great flood: "The LORD saw that the wickedness of humankind was great in the earth, and that every inclination of the thoughts of their hearts was only evil continually" (Gen 6:5). That is a grim picture indeed. Later generations are not viewed as having gone so far. Why? Because a people of God's own possession has entered the world, charged to be a blessing in the world. Evil surely comes and spreads, but so also does God's intervening actions to check evil, and so also do human deeds of justice and acts of mercy check the spread of evil.

The Qumran community (also called the Essenes, a first-century C.E. sect of Jews) spoke of two spirits in conflict within the universe, on the cosmic plane, and also within every human heart: the spirit of Light and the spirit of Darkness. Rabbinic discussions, building on Genesis 6, spoke of the *yetser ha-tov,* the impulse to good, and the *yetser ha-ra,* the impulse to evil. These both portray a world that is in need of, and in process of, redemption by the good Creator God who will never be content with destruction but demands that the world, and certainly the people of the Covenant, move and be drawn forward toward redemption. But neither the Qumran picture of two spirits nor the rabbinical teaching about two impulses denies the fundamental goodness of God's creation. True, the creation is damaged, twisted, and wounded; but it is God's creation, for which human beings bear a major responsibility, under God.

As a Christian I relate this understanding directly to Paul's picture of a world suffering under the power of sin and death, groaning and yearning to find freedom from "this body of death." Some have mistakenly associated this view with forms of Jewish apocalyptic thought that seem to have given up on this world and whose adherents therefore yearn for cataclysmic divine intervention to bring to birth a new world. But other Jewish thought, including Christian thought like that of Paul, rather refers to the radical transformation of life on *this* earth. The study of Judaism and conversations with Jews have helped me to see that this is the more likely way to read first century talk about the presence and power of sin and evil in the world. It is still God's world, under the ultimate direction of God, but God's very own spirit labors along with the people of God toward the birth of that coming new day.

Redemption as the Consummation of God's Purposes for this World

This brings me to the theme of redemption or salvation, another affirmation central to both Judaism and Christianity. Here it is the study of the prophets of Israel and of some themes in rabbinic and contemporary Jewish thought that have helped me to understand what I believe is an essential feature of Christian redemption or salvation: the consummation of God's promises and purposes for this world. A Christian view of redemption inspired by Jews and Judaism must be about the transformation of this world; it cannot simply be about personal salvation in the next world— which is all too often the only theme in Christian preaching about salvation.

A feature of redemption that has been prominently underscored for me through the study of the Jewish Scriptures and through work with Jewish scholars, rabbis, and laypersons has to do with the future, with human hope, with the question of whether the world is moving toward some cosmic purpose. The answer to this question is a matter of faith, and I grant that my Christian way of understanding hope and cosmic purpose is not identical with a Jewish way. But I surely have been helped to this Christian vision through my dealings with Jewish faith and the Jewish community.

The first point to stress is that "Messiah" is a term for an earthly deliverer who would be God's agent in the redemption of Israel. Redemption on that score is often said to be earthly redemption, and redemption in the sense of the restoration of the fortunes of the people of God, enabling them to live in their own land and bear their distinct witness before the nations of the earth. My studies lead me to say that that is not quite the whole picture. Messianism at Qumran, for example, involved a hope in the coming of two messiahs, both expected to be a part of the cosmic struggle mentioned above. The Jews of Qumran seem to have been more concerned about a faithful life, lived in obedience to God's Torah, in which the community was able to await the day when God would dwell on a transformed *earth,* with Jerusalem as its center. Their hope for the messianic age was tied to the holy land and it involved the holy center where true worship of God prevailed. But its character certainly had less to do with the restoration of some ruler from the line of David than it did with the mysterious and powerful presence of God among a faithful and worshiping people of God.

I believe that the early Christians shared much of this outlook. They too looked for the coming of God's triumph, already brought very near in the person of the Messiah who was God's beloved Son, God's gift to earth for earth's redemption and transformation. But their emphasis fell on the existence of a new form of community life, where the commitment was indeed to God's Torah, God's demands, but it was most of all a commitment to live and walk in the light of God's presence among them in the person of the divine Spirit, and that Spirit was the Spirit of Jesus the Messiah whom God had raised from death to new life. It was a community of the resurrection, where the claim was made over and again that the promises of God were finding their realization, here in this world, and in the midst of the community of Israel. Before long, the message of Christian faith was understood to be a message for all the earth, with an invitation to all the earth to join in this new community of the Resurrected One.

When I try to size up what this confidence in the nearness of the day of consummation must have meant for Jews and Christians in the first century, I am struck over and again with the remarkable similarities and with one or two decisive differences. For both communities, it must surely have involved judgment upon a society that, despite believing in a coming transformation of life on earth, was unwilling to act in ways that would help bring about that transformation. Think, for example, of the pictures of the Jerusalem that was to come to be—as depicted in prophetic texts such as Isaiah 35, one of the great texts speaking of consummation for the entire universe. To the holy center, Zion, would come streaming all those who were fearful of heart, hard pressed to believe in God's triumph. They would now hear the command "Behold your God." The eyes of the blind would be opened, the ears of the deaf unstopped. Those unable to speak would be given voice, and even the lepers, the outcastes of society, along with those who suffered from mental illness or were simple-minded— all these would come marching to Zion on God's highway, laid out in the desert of human failings and human degradation. And finally, at long last, sorrow and sighing would flee away.

Such a picture of what God is bringing must surely have been recognized to be a judgment upon both the Jewish community that accepted Jesus and the community that did not. How awful, people must have thought and said, for our world to resemble this coming world so poorly, so imperfectly! Any city, and certainly Jerusalem, the center of God's plans for earth, must have felt the sting of judgment when such a text portraying Zion's future was read or heard, and pondered.

But these pictures of the day of consummation also offered hope and consolation in times of failure and distress and loss. Israel and the Church might fail, but God would not fail. The day of consummation might be delayed, and we might be doing too little to help bring the day to birth, but in God's promise lay the confidence that the day would indeed dawn. So along with the judgment came hope—hope born of confidence in the truth of God's promises. For the Christian, the experience of Christ's resurrection from the dead, Christ's active presence within the community of believers, gave additional weight to the truth of these promises.

Such a hope must have brought a fresh dynamism into the life of those Jews who accepted Jesus as Messiah as well as among those Jews who did not. There is drawing power in the promises of God, for they encourage and indeed demand that we fall into step with divine purposes, let ourselves be drawn toward that coming day when Zion will welcome into its life and arms all the broken and troubled and aching human beings awaiting redemption.

And can we deny that within both early Judaism and early Christianity the communities believing in these divine promises recognized that what was promised was already being realized, before the day of consummation? Such a confidence in God brings much of what it promises for the future. Therein lies the glory of Jewish and Christian visions of the coming reign of God, the future consummation of God's promises and purposes for this world. The promises of God are not just about some chronological time or day to come. They are promises that, in faithful and believing communities, bring into being much of what they promise—for there is no mistaking that these communities, Jewish and Christian alike, knew the divine presence promised for the end of days right then in their midst. The reign of God is always, for the faithful, to some extent being actualized in the now.

Torah as Grace

Another important thing I learned from Jews and Judaism, as one might expect, is about the inner meaning of God's law, God's teaching, what Jewish Scripture calls "Torah" and what is so central to Jewish life and faith in all times. Why should it have taken Christians so long to learn the value of Torah for their lives? A part of the problem was Paul's sharp contrasts between what he called *nomos,* by which he seems to have meant oppressive demands that stifled creativity, and what he called *charis* or grace, God's free gift of forgiving love that could never be earned but invited the binding of oneself inseparably to God, the giver of love and grace. It was easy to equate oppressive *nomos* with a Torah or law that some texts in the New Testament associate with the Scribes and Pharisees of Jesus' day. Forgotten in such sharp contrasts is that set of texts that show just what God's gift of the Torah atop the sacred mountain meant to Israel and continued to mean to the generations of Jews living centuries after Moses' death.

Think, for example, of Moses' return from Mount Sinai with the rewritten Ten Commandments (Exod 34). Moses' face glistened so that he had to put on a mask to prevent the people from being blinded by seeing this man who had received the Torah from God and was even then carrying it in his hands! God's Torah was sheer gift of divine grace, violated even as it was being given, and even so given afresh and pressed upon the people as the good gift of a loving and gracious and forgiving God. Think also of Psalm 119 with its repeated extolling of the glory and beauty and power of God's gift of Torah. Small wonder that Jews were taught to rehearse the gift of Torah by reciting the *Shema* (Deut 6:4-9), affirming the oneness of God and also affirming the blessedness of God's gift of Torah. In later Jewish texts, Torah becomes, like Wisdom, one of God's most precious gifts of all. It can even be spoken of as having never been created but rather as being eternal, just as God is eternal.

As a "free church" Christian, I find this meaning of Torah has been of critical importance. We Baptists and others insist on God's having called us as individuals to accept the free gift of divine grace, to affirm before the congregation what that gift means to us, and thereafter to live out the Christian life without the constraints of an authoritative hierarchical church. The Spirit guides us into all truth, enables us to read the Scriptures aright, and offers the guidance we need for life's journey. But we too have the Torah, the Torah of Christ, that body of scriptural guidance and teaching that points out the way in which Christ, by the Spirit, wants us to walk. We too can sing "Make me a captive, LORD, and then I shall be free." We all know that Torah as a gift of divine love can be transmuted into Torah as an oppressive burden laid upon the community by its leaders, who believe that in doing so they are fulfilling the commandment of God. Torah can be perverted into an instrument of enslavement, but then it is no longer the Torah that the author of Psalm 119 sang about. And how can the Christian fail to see that the Torah of the Sermon on the Mount in Matthew's Gospel is precisely the kind of Torah that worshipers can sing about, take delight in, thereby finding the inner core of meaning for their lives through meditation upon that Torah/Gospel!

Conclusion

When I am pressed, I might have to say that, by the Holy Spirit, God no doubt could have helped me to claim all of the central meanings of Christian faith sketched above even if I had not been a lifelong student of Tanakh and even if I had not sought to enter ever more deeply into the life and thought and faith of the Jewish community. But "What if?" speculations help us little. The truth is that I came to understand much of Christian faith ever so much more clearly and powerfully, I believe, as a result of encounter with Judaism and friendship with Jews.

In addition to coming to understand Christian faith more clearly, there is much more that I believe I have learned because of my work with Jewish literature and with Jewish colleagues and friends. I think, for example, of the wholesome understanding of human sexuality that has been much more fully maintained and affirmed within the Jewish community than it has, at least until very recently, among Christians. I think of the value of family and community for Jews, and how easily individualism damages Christian life and faith and thought.

Given how indebted I am to Jews and Judaism, do I feel myself more Jewish than Christian or more Christian than Jewish? The question has to be faced, for much of my life is certainly shaped by what I take to be Jewish concerns. But for me (and, I believe, for the Christian community), those cardinal affirmations that have been so markedly deepened through confronting Judaism and the Jewish people are affirmations that inseparably tie me to the Jew Jesus and to his divine mission in the world. That means I am a Christian drawn strongly and closely to Judaism.

Even if I had not learned more about Christian faith through associations with Jews and the study of Jewish Scripture and Jewish life and history and tradition, I would still be glad that I have had those associations, formed those friendships. Why? Because they have brought such pleasure, such delight, such opportunity to share fundamental human concerns with beloved colleagues and friends. But thank God, the learning and the deepening of the mystery of Christian existence could be called a welcome bonus, one that may have made my life and work more useful. And to do useful things while having fun—that is special.

ALICE L. ECKARDT

Growing into a Daring and Questioning Faith

After more than fifty years of giving thought to the effects that traditional church teachings have had on Jews, on Christians, and on Christian-Jewish relations, is it now possible for me to recall how my own faith and theology have developed? To be sure, since 1967 I have a collection of publications and lectures attesting to much of what I have said publicly. Prior to that, there were the publications of my late husband, A. Roy Eckardt, which frequently dealt with Christianity and the Jewish people, writings with which I was both familiar and often intimately involved. Even so, time of publication does not necessarily indicate just when the change in thinking occurred, nor how. For the background years of childhood and adolescence I can only rely on fragmentary memory.

Perhaps I should state where I stand at present before retracing the journey.

A fundamental principle for me is the conviction that "good theology cannot be based on bad history."[1] Yet much of traditional Christian theology, I am convinced, has been based on misunderstandings and distortions of history. This is particularly true regarding Christian claims in relation to Judaism and the Jewish people.

Down through the ages Christian theologians have almost always misrepresented the historical context of Jesus' ministry and crucifixion. They have made their case for Jesus over against a caricatured Judaism; they have misrepresented Jesus as standing apart from rather than within the world of Jewish faith and hope; and they have blamed the crucifixion on Jews (and not only on some Jews but on "the Jews") when, in fact, the crucifixion was a Roman execution. Moreover, Christian theologians have almost always ignored or distorted post-biblical Jewish history, thereby fooling themselves into thinking there was something to their claim that the Church displaced the Jews as God's people. Blissfully ignorant of the moral and spiritual vitality of post-biblical Jewish life, these theologians claimed that Christianity replaced Judaism as the one true religion. Along with a growing number of Christian theologians in our time, I am committed to promoting the more historically accurate portrait of Christianity as one way, alongside "the Jewish way," of responding to God.

This brings me to a second preliminary remark about where theologically I stand today. I do not believe that Christianity or any other religion captures a full comprehension of Divinity or of God's truth despite whatever "revelations" have come to us. This is not to say that we cannot grasp something of divine truth, for I do believe that God reaches out to human beings and wishes to be known by them. In my view, there is awareness of God to be found in many religions, but this hasn't prevented any of them, including Christianity, from misrepresenting God and God's will alongside whatever truths they teach.

This pluralist perspective does not keep me from committing myself to a particular religious tradition. I have remained within the Protestant faith in which I was raised and with which I am most familiar, even though I am frequently more persuaded by Jewish perspectives than traditional Christian ones. I am more hopeful about new, post-*Shoah* understandings of Christian faith, and I find them more compatible with the Jewish insights to which I am drawn. I believe we are given intelligence so that we may use it, and doing so will often lead us to question some ideas (no matter how long established) and to consider and conceive new ones. Mine has been and remains a questioning faith, and amidst the questioning my commitment is to newer formulations of Christian faith that affirm the ongoing validity of Judaism.

How did I get to where I am now?

Early Experiences

The one teaching from my church school years that has remained firmly with me is the emphasis put on the fact that *all* people are God's children and that God loves them all *equally*. In my mind's eye I can still see a picture of children of different races (including Blacks, Asians, Native Americans) who represented all those whom God loves. I cannot say whether Jews were specifically depicted, yet the intent (or at least my response to it) was meant to be inclusive.[2]

I grew up in the Methodist Episcopal Church that in the 1930s and 1940s, at least in the Northeast, was very much committed to the Social Gospel movement. And the ministers with whom I was acquainted focused their reading of, and preaching about, the Scriptures in line with that emphasis. I do not recall any anti-Jewish renderings of the Scriptures, not even in the Holy Week-Easter season, which I later learned was often rife with anti-Jewish content in many Christian churches.[3] I now know all too well the dreadful effects that unenlightened liturgies and sermons can have in forming anti-Jewish attitudes (even when unintended). I don't know just what our various pastors did with the more challenging biblical texts, but it cannot have been very noticeably pejorative or I think it would have affected me either by making me have a negative attitude toward Jews or by making me rebel against the preaching.

The first awareness I had of antisemitism was in the late 1930s—probably 1938 at the time of *Kristallnacht* in Germany and all that followed from that. In a conversation about this my mother mentioned that the mother of a friend of mine (a woman originally from Bavaria) enthusiastically applauded Hitler's "putting the Jews in their place!" I was shocked and remember protesting against such an attitude. I think I was even somewhat shocked that my mother would tell me about it, for I had never heard anything at home negative about any other people.

In the all-critical years of fall 1940 to the summer of 1944, I was at Oberlin College where many Black and Jewish students were my friends and a number of professors were refugees from Germany. Yet it wasn't until after the attack on Pearl Harbor that the war moved more to the foreground for us, especially, of course, for the male students. Most of us still focused primarily on our studies and on enjoying the dormitory and social life. I cannot recall knowing much about the worsening situation for Jews in Europe (the imposed ghettos, the concentration and death camps) in spite of the campus being very attuned to the military situation. But, of course, in 1945 I read about the horrors the Allied liberators discovered. By then I had left Oberlin, was married, and was working at Time Inc.

where one could not escape being tuned in to news events even if one tried.

Discoveries with Roy

From fall 1944 to 1947 my husband, Roy Eckardt, was studying for his Ph.D. at Columbia University and Union Theological Seminary, working closely with Dr. Reinhold Niebuhr, a long-time hero of his. "Reinie" (as his students spoke of him) was enthusiastic about Roy's proposed thesis topic: an analysis and evaluation of the various church theologies concerning Judaism and its people. Roy's first task was to learn the history of both that theology and the actions to which it had led. That was when we both discovered the centuries-long path of anti-Judaism and antisemitism and the terrible injustices perpetrated against the Jewish people over the many Christian centuries. I cannot leave my husband out of this account because in these early years it was his work that brought both of us face to face with the *adversus Judaeos* history. Moreover, so much of what each of us did over the subsequent decades were joint endeavors. We were genuine partners, even though each of us had a particular emphasis: in my case, history and theology; in Roy's case, theology and ethics.

Neither Roy's nor my secular and religious education (not even Roy's divinity school courses) had taught us any of this Christian anti-Jewish tradition.[4] Learning about the theological foundation of this tradition did nothing to convince either of us that there was any justification for the anti-Jewish attitudes and actions it fostered, and we called into question the theology itself.

Having just now reread Roy's thesis in its published form,[5] I can see the very firm basis on which we carried forward our earlier social concerns and rooted them within our new thinking. For we were now more aware of the traps into which traditional theology could lead us, aware of new questions which had to be asked, and new ideas explored. We would never forget that.

In his thesis Roy gave some attention to the issue of Zionism and the attempt to create a new Jewish state, and certainly agreed with Reinhold Niebuhr's endorsement of the Jewish right to a homeland there. But the State of Israel had not yet been proclaimed, or its struggle to attain independence consummated, by the time the thesis was submitted and defended. While I have to confess to my memory failing me as to how closely I followed that terrible struggle, I do know that already in the late 1940s Roy and I developed our undying concern for the State of Israel and its survival. Even so, in these early years our emphasis was largely in the theological arena. I say "our emphasis," even though through the 1950s and into the early 1960s, it was Roy and not I who did the teaching and the writing. While I was at home raising our two children, and in the latter portion of that time doing part-time graduate work at Lehigh University in the department of history, I did, all along, remain deeply interested and involved in Roy's professional work. In truth, our professional partnership began in the early days of our marriage, long before we published together or published separately on related topics.

In August 1963 Roy and I, along with our children, embarked (literally, on the Queen Mary) for Cambridge, England, on a year's sabbatical leave for Roy from Lehigh University. This was an opportunity to expand our knowledge of what was happening in the field of Jewish-Christian relations in Europe. Particularly valuable was the opportunity to work in Dr. James Parkes' impressive library, talk with him, and meet others concerned with the same subject. Roy focused on re-examining theologies about Judaism and on rethinking how Christians might cease behaving as "upstarts" and instead relate anew to their "elder brothers" in the covenant.[6]

I not only read widely in Parkes' own writings (as well as others') and worked with his wife, Dorothy, on various Parkes projects but also had the pleasure of working with Elsbeth Rosenfeld to expand her BBC radio talks into a book.[7] Elsa was, in Nazi terminology, a German "non-Aryan" (by virtue of her Jewish father and Christian mother, plus her marriage to a Jew) who had been trapped inside the Reich by the outbreak of war. She voluntarily threw in her lot with the Jewish community of Munich, utilizing her social work skills to help them cope, but eventually was persuaded, first, to go into hiding with friends, and then to cross into Switzerland by night. Elsa became our close friend and we had the pleasure of visiting at her reestablished summer home in southern Germany later in 1964.

This was only one of a number of personal contacts that year with both Christians and Jews who had experienced and survived that terrible period, and it reinforced my determination to learn even more about the *Shoah*. We traveled extensively in western Europe on two occasions that year, visiting not only some of the camps and memorials in Germany,

France, and Holland, but meeting with numerous individuals and groups committed to reconstituting both Church and society so that such a mass crime could never happen again. Survivors of the *Shoah* have had a tremendous impact on me and their friendship has been a continuous source of encouragement and strength.

I was absolutely convinced that the churches had to face up to the consequences of the centuries of their wrong teachings, especially with regard to Judaism and its people, and therefore change their proclamation of the gospel. While working on my graduate degree in the field of history, on my own I was reading theology and Church history (not usually covered in traditional history courses). So when in 1972 I was asked by the dean at Lehigh to teach a course (initiated by Roy) on the centuries of Christian-Jewish encounter, I was fairly well prepared. Within a few years I introduced two new courses: "The Holocaust: Its History and Meaning" and "Literature of the Holocaust."

Our horizons had been so stretched mentally as well as geographically by our first year abroad that we continued making overseas trips in subsequent years—to conferences of the International Council of Christians and Jews (ICCJ), to meetings of the World Council of Churches' Committee on the Church and the Jewish People (to which Roy had been appointed in 1963), to the Parkes Library now situated at the University of Southampton, and to the Oxford Centre for Postgraduate Hebrew Studies for further research, writing, and teaching. At the Oxford Centre we, as Christians, were in the minority, and consequently met and learned from quite a number of Jews—Israelis as well as North American and British Jews—utilizing the study opportunities.

Focus on Israel

In April 1966 Roy had a whirlwind tour of Israel under the auspices of the Ministry for Religious Affairs—a trip that was to help focus our attention for some years in a new direction. To be sure, by this time Israel had come to have a major place in our thinking, though it was not yet very evident in our publications.

The following year, 1967, set the seal on that. It was a critical year—for both Jews and for us. It was critical to Israel's survival, for it was the year of "the Six Day War" when Israel had to contend with Egypt, Jordan, and Syria. In the weeks preceding, during the Egyptian closing of the Straits of Tiran, the removal of United Nations troops from the Sinai, and endless threats of extermination blaring forth from neighboring Arab countries, Jews everywhere recognized the second threat to Jewish existence within a short span of years. And we agonized over what might happen to the people already so decimated by the Nazi onslaught. Despite recent years of Christian-Jewish dialogue, Christians largely remained silent, and they continued to remain silent during that war. Worse, after the Israeli victory some Christian voices suddenly were heard accusing Israel of aggression. One prominent Christian, Dr. Henry P. Van Dusen, dean at Union Theological Seminary, charged Israel with "violent, ruthless . . . aggression" aimed "not at victory but at annihilation." In *The New York Times* letters' column Roy denounced Van Dusen's outrageous accusation and was soon overwhelmed by more than three hundred letters of gratitude, to each of which he replied. Further responding to Christian voices criticizing Israel, including those in *The Christian Century,* we jointly wrote a two-part article in that journal titled "Again, Silence in the Churches."[8]

Why had the burgeoning Christian-Jewish dialogue of the 1960s not produced more outspoken sympathy and support for the Jewish state and recognition of the terrible fear of Jewish people who were neighbors? While there doubtless were hidden antagonisms (as the voices of criticism demonstrated), and a long history of Christian missionary presence in Arab countries, I think a major factor in the Christian silence was that the dialogues had focused on the theological aspects of the new relationships and had ignored the peoplehood aspect of being Jewish. A change of direction was called for.

In mid-September Roy and I made a trip to Israel, the first of many. A few months later Association Press asked if we would consider expanding our two-part article in *The Christian Century* into a book about Israel. With a leave of absence from Lehigh in the following year, we undertook this major enterprise, immersing ourselves in every aspect of the country, including its influx of Jews from many countries of East and West, its Druze and Palestinian Arab residents, its political and economic systems, its varied religious communities, its conflicts with the Arab world. During an eight-week stay in Israel and brief visits to Beirut, Amman, and a refugee camp in Jordan, we talked with as many individuals as possible—scholars, government officials, members of the press, religious figures, Palestinian citizens of Israel, kibbutzniks, lawyers, hitchhiking soldiers, Palestinian refugees, as well as U.N. personnel, American diplomats, and foreign residents of Beirut—more than fifty individuals in all. In the process, we were struck by the "tragic unity" of "common grief, common accusations, common fears, common distrust, common determination, common foreboding" linking the two peoples—but linking them in hostility. The last section of the book focused on our affirmation of Israel, and concluded with Fr. Edward Flannery's words: "It is the Christian above all who is expected to react most strongly to attacks on Jews. It is especially the Christian who is expected to rejoice at the upturn in the fortune of Jews that Zionism, or any other agency, has brought about in our own time."[9]

From July 1967 through 1974 most of my publications focused on the issue of Israel. I was very concerned with the question of the churches'—and in particular the Vatican's—opposition to the Jews' right to their own nation, and how that opposition is connected to the deep theological roots of Christian anti-Judaism. In an article published in 1972, I pointed out that what had happened in Judea, Samaria, and the Galilee centuries before—namely, the Roman defeat of two Jewish rebellions and the crushing of any possibility of a renewed Jewish commonwealth, followed shortly by Jewish exclusion from much of the Land (especially Jerusalem), and then by its becoming the Church's "Holy Land"—embodied for Christians "the church's presumed supersedence over ancient Israel."

The Church believed that God had cast Jews out from their ancestral homeland because they had rejected the Messiah (Christ) whom God had sent to them. Like Cain, they thus became eternally homeless (hence, the "wandering Jew" legend). While in the immediate post-*Shoah* years this theological view still prevailed in much of the Christian world, at least in subliminal form, it was not usually voiced. Rather, the opposition refused to recognize the Jews' need for a "country of their own as a refuge from antisemitism, as an international defender, and perhaps even as a last chance for survival." Above all, it seemed to me the vehemence with which some Christians denied that such a need existed reflected "a refusal to admit the moral indictment of Christian civilization that [was] thereby implied."[10]

My articles on Israel always dealt as much with theology as with history—and what in a 1973 article I called "the unnecessary Christian predicament." I suggested that we might look at "the newly gathered Israel" as a "sign that God is faithful to his promises and that the call of

God to the people of Israel is irrevocable," that Israel is a sign that "history still belongs to God."[11]

In a 1986 article I suggested that, while the State of Israel demonstrates Jewish courage "to embody the hopes of two thousand years in the fragile and vulnerable vessel of a state,"[12] it nevertheless lessens Jewish vulnerability and thereby makes possible the preservation of the Jewish people's covenant with God. Going one step further, I later urged Christians to "acknowledge that this reborn nation is, or at least can be, a *beginning* of *tikkun*, . . . healing of the world, even though fragmentary. For it offers the Jewish people as a collectivity some control over their lives and destiny, and offers a new possibility of survival to the people so decimated and dismembered. [It is] the only practical step taken so far to protect Jews from another genocidal attack."[13]

The Impact of the Shoah

Even more than my focus on Israel, it was the *Shoah* that compelled me to question and rethink fundamental issues of faith. This I did along with many in the Jewish, and, to a lesser extent, Christian communities. Research on the *Shoah* became a re-orienting experience for me, close to a conversion, determining the way I respond to events, look at the world, and evaluate words, actions, policies, and decisions. It led me in 1974 to write an extensive article focusing on the ways a number of Jewish and Christian thinkers have been rethinking their faith in response to the *Shoah*. I saw "a church in vast apostasy, . . . still linked to a supersessionist theology that bears the genocidal germ . . . [and] without credibility because of its failure to understand that everything has been changed by Auschwitz." I saw the Jewish people as having "experienced resurrection in history through the rebirth of the State of Israel and a new vitality in its various Diaspora communities." At the same time I saw "a Christianity that continues to insist that the world's redemption has already occurred" [and] "that by and large maintains a triumphalism which strives for a religious genocide [of Jews] through conversion."[14]

Teaching about the *Shoah* and religious responses to it pushed me steadily toward the need for a "radical reconstruction" of Christian faith. In 1975–1976 Roy and I spent a sabbatical year exploring this revolutionary renewal process (to the extent it existed at all) in West Germany, East

Germany, France, Holland, Sweden, Norway, Denmark, the United Kingdom, and Israel. That year we greatly increased our international acquaintances with other people of faith, and our thinking was challenged and expanded by them. For example, we met Christians in Germany who firmly rejected the Christian triumphalism that created a religiously-based social atmosphere of contempt for the Jewish people, and thereby helped make the *Shoah* possible or perhaps even inevitable. Among them was a Christian theologian in Darmstadt, Hans-Jochen Gamm, who identified the Nazi "Final Solution of the Jewish Question" as the singular culminating point of a centuries-long denial of Jewish integrity by the Christian world. There was also a pastor in Schwäbisch-Hall, Rudolf Pfisterer, who rejected Christian mission to the Jews as a "spiritual final solution." Similarly, Rolf Rendtorff, a professor at Heidelberg, insisted that Jews were not to be treated as potential Christians, for they possessed their own spiritual integrity.

But we found failures as well, especially the failure to fully recognize the world-changing and faith-changing event of the *Shoah.* This was particularly evident in West Germany (East Germany as well, though we did not have full exposure to that scene). There was, for example, Friedrich Greunagel and his small book *Die Judenfrage* ("The Jewish Question"). After beginning his book by calling for Jewish-Christian reconciliation, Greunagel proceeds to fault Christian churches for their failure to convert Jews to Christ. There was also the renowned Protestant theologian Jürgen Moltmann. Despite having written about Christian complicity in the *Shoah,* and calling for an end to Christian triumphalism in relation to Jews and Judaism, he nevertheless continued to present Christianity as the fulfillment of Judaism.

Also disappointing was the official statement on Christians and Jews, issued in 1975 by the Evangelical Church of Germany. Even though this statement acknowledged the deep challenge the *Shoah* posed for Christian faith, and recognized Christianity's Jewish roots and the abiding integrity of Judaism, it still continued to affirm the Church's duty to bear witness to Jews that Christ is "the salvation for all mankind." Nor did it deny Jewish responsibility for Jesus' crucifixion.[15]

In *Long Night's Journey into Day,* which grew out of our sabbatical trip to Europe and Israel during that academic year, Roy and I dealt with the *Shoah* as, among other things, "a Christian event, of fateful significance, as much as a Jewish or German event." We pointed out that in response to the

Shoah Jews naturally grapple with questions about God, suffering, and the covenant. While Christians ought to attend to these questions as well, nevertheless "in the Christian community the primary question [has to be] that of the culpability of Christians for the denigration and agony of Jews." We asked, "Is there any real hope that Christian teachings and behavior respecting the Jewish people and Judaism may be altered in any morally telling way?" After arguing at length the need for such an altering, we concluded the following: "It is clear that the world and especially the Jewish people, not to mention Christians themselves, will be infinitely better off if triumphalist Christianity can be overcome. . . . In this direction are to be found wholeness and justice and love. . . . We are persuaded that a reformed Christian faith—one that is empowered by revolutionary ferment and chastened by relativization (but not subjected to reductionism)—can be a great ally of the Jewish people, as of human beings everywhere."[16]

Confronting the Question of God

Concerning the *Shoah,* as troubling for me as the question of Christian culpability was the question of God. If God is the caring and loving God in whom we have been taught to have faith, how do we account for the terrible evils and sufferings in the world? Where is God when they are happening, or what is God doing? Are the traditional answers to these questions (many as they are) sufficient?

Since some time in the late 1960s I had been reading Elie Wiesel's writings and they had a great impact on me, not only because of the camp inmates' terrible sufferings and their struggles to endure, but because of the impact on the deeply-rooted faith of the youthful Wiesel. Despite my never having experienced such evil directly, but only vicariously, I too felt an increasing need to question God, or to question what I had been taught about God. At least I had to wonder: Is the question of this suffering and abandonment sufficiently answered by the Christian belief that God's Son also suffered and experienced abandonment, and that his resurrection holds out the hope of resurrected life for others?

I became convinced that we Christians should stop asserting that the crucifixion of Jesus constitutes the ultimate in human suffering and the sense of godforsakenness. For by such an assertion, I believe, the Church has been responsible for presenting and perpetuating a historical falsehood that has helped to sustain its triumphalist theology. Many others have known as much or more suffering and abandonment as Jesus did, as was horribly evident in the *Shoah.* There, in the "kingdom of night," some Jews had to choose which of their family members would receive the work permits, preserving life for awhile. Others had to engage in a "race of death" in which winning meant sentencing the losers to death. Mothers had to decide whether to abandon children to the gas chambers alone or to accompany them there. While the traditional claim about the ultimacy of Jesus' suffering could have been challenged before the *Shoah,* it was clearly indefensible afterward.

Would belief in Jesus' resurrection have been sufficient for Jews to overcome the despair of seeing their entire families and communities annihilated? Is it sufficient for any of us who know of the million-fold agonies? Just consider this: If Jesus had been alive or had returned at that time, he would have been killed as just one more of the six million.

Where was God in the midst of that massive suffering? Where is God when anyone suffers? Is God really omnipotent while nonetheless permitting suffering to occur? Or is there a sense in which God is helpless in the face of suffering? Whether helpless or not, does God perhaps suffer when creatures themselves suffer?

In pondering these questions, I have turned repeatedly to Hans Jonas' "tentative myth" about God's role in the world, for I find it to be one of the more provocative resolutions of these troubling questions. Drawing on the Kabbalistic myth of divine withdrawal, Jonas (whose mother was killed at Auschwitz) suggests that perhaps when engaging in creation, God "consented . . . to be absolute no more" and underwent "the contraction of divine being as a condition for the being of the world." As he reflects on his recasting of the Kabbalistic myth, Jonas says, "First, and most obviously, I have been speaking of a *suffering God.*" God suffers because God is "affected by what happens in the world," which means God is "altered, made different" because of creation. Thus, "the myth suggests the picture of a *becoming God,*" says Jonas. "If God is in any relation to the world—which is the cardinal assumption of religion—then by that token the Eternal has 'temporalized' . . . through the actualization of the world process."[17]

Related to the belief in a suffering and becoming God is the belief in a *"caring God,"* which Jonas points out is "among the most familiar tenets of Jewish faith." But Jonas' myth "stresses the less familiar aspect that this caring God is not a sorcerer who in the act of caring provides the fulfillment" of divine concern. No, this God "has left something for other agents to do" and thereby made that fulfillment "dependent upon them." Thus, "this is not an omnipotent God." From a purely logical standpoint, the idea of omnipotence is "senseless" because the very existence of another agent "limits the power of the most powerful agent." Moreover, from a theological standpoint, omnipotence is also untenable. "Surely, goodness is inalienable from the concept of God and not open to qualification." Also, however mysterious, God is not unintelligible. "There has been revelation. . . . Thus a completely hidden God is not an acceptable concept by Jewish norms." Since there is evil in the world that must be resisted, "only a completely unintelligible God can be said to be absolutely good and absolutely powerful, yet tolerate the world as it is." Thus, concludes Jonas, "After Auschwitz we can assert with greater force than ever before that an omnipotent deity would have to be either not good or totally unintelligible." Since goodness and intelligibility are necessary attributes of God, "and since we have found the concept of omnipotence to be doubtful anyway [on logical grounds], it is this which has to give way."[18]

With Jonas I am convinced that *only* a suffering God, One who *continues* to suffer with human beings, can speak to us since the *Shoah's* whirlwind of destruction, and that we mortals, empowered by God, have the obligation to help each other overcome suffering and thereby "help the suffering immortal God."[19]

As I continued to wrestle with these questions, I explored multiple efforts to supply satisfying answers within both Judaism and Christianity. Again I could only conclude that suffering is not part of God's will for creation and therefore we must give up trying to find God's beneficent action, or anything salvational, in events of suffering. Furthermore, a recognition that God suffers with human beings may also show us that there is a continual threat of destruction and dissolution against which we must fight.[20]

Increasingly I became convinced that we Christians are naive when we speak of Jesus' resurrection as the definitive answer to human suffering. Truth be told, we know that Easter does not represent the *final* victory over evil and death, just as Passover does not celebrate a *finally definitive* event. Each is an opening, an opportunity to begin again and to live with

God and for life. We cannot forget or ignore the fact that the *Shoah* occurred centuries after both the Exodus and the resurrection, just as *Yom HaShoah* (Holocaust Remembrance Day) occurs after both Passover and Easter in the calendar year. We are called to remember that the rejoicing at Passover and Easter are for happenings that, while awesome, did not stop history, nor hate. They are, at best, signs of God's ultimate hoped-for victory. They point to God's desire for goodness, justice, and harmony. Therefore we must continue to do our part as God's partners in working toward these goals—an affirmation that resonates with my Social Gospel beginnings.

The Dilemma of Forgiveness

Among the other issues that the *Shoah* and its aftermath compelled me to face is the issue of forgiveness. I recall a number of instances in the 1980s in which avowed Christians expressed their irritation, and even anger, at Jews for not "forgiving and forgetting" with regard to the *Shoah*. While repenting and asking forgiveness and being forgiven are themes central to both Judaism and Christianity, the question of forgiveness ironically has been a source of continuing misunderstanding, hurt, and recrimination. Why have numbers of Christians expressed annoyance, even anger, when Jews persist in remembering the victims of the *Shoah,* and while they continue to express concern that the perpetrators be brought to justice? Are the six million brutal murders simply to be forgotten? (Consider this question: Should Christians forget the murder of one Jew approximately two thousand years ago?) Can such indifference be separated from the world's indifference while the Nazi murders were being carried out? Does this indifference reveal an unwillingness to face the culpability of the Christian world?

Some more encompassing and difficult questions confront us as well: Can and should forgiveness be extended when there is no repentance? Can or should the living forgive the murderers on behalf of the murdered?

For many years I have grappled with these questions, and I once paid particular attention to the responses of thirty-two thoughtful and informed Christians and Jews to the issue of forgiveness as it was raised by Simon Wiesenthal's book *The Sunflower.* Wiesenthal recounts how a dying Nazi soldier told him, then a Jewish prisoner, about the soldier's participation in a massacre by fire of several hundred Jewish civilians. The killing left the soldier psychologically scarred. He regretted his actions and sought the forgiveness of a Jew—one anticipating his own death at Nazi hands. What should Simon have done? Should he have extended the forgiveness that the dying Nazi requested? Did he have the right to do so?

Of the nine respondents arguing that the Jew, Simon, should have forgiven the Nazi, eight were Christians and one was another non-Jew. Of the twenty respondents deciding *against* forgiveness, four were Christians, fourteen were Jews (all of those participating), and two were undesignated. Three respondents were indecisive. The Jewish responses reflect Judaism's affirmation that God forgives sins against God, but for sins against other persons one should seek forgiveness from them, and in that way be reconciled. But what if the sin against others is murder? Who, if anyone, has the right to extend forgiveness to the murderer?

Christians often believe that they have an obligation to forgive under any and all circumstances (though this does not mean that most Christians actually do this), and it seems that many or most Christians expect Jews to do just that with regard to those who were involved in the Nazis' attempt to annihilate the Jewish people. Thus Jews all too often are told to forgive, to forget, or are accused of being uncharitable and vengeful if they insist on remembering. Can or should the murder of millions of people be set aside this easily? Will forgiving the perpetrators, if indeed anyone has a right to forgive them, provide better security for potential victims of bigotry or hate, or will it do the opposite? Where do justice and the rule of law enter the picture?

Jesus' teachings as recorded in the Gospels are often cited by Christians as the basis for insisting on forgiving in every situation. Yet Jesus always spoke only of person-to-person wrongdoing and responses, of how one should respond to being sinned against by another. Jesus urged almost endless willingness to forgive the wrongs done to oneself as long as the other repents and asks for forgiveness. At the same time Jesus insisted that one should be reconciled with any person to whom one had done harm before approaching the altar with a gift to God. In none of these situations did Jesus speak about how anyone should respond to an attack on someone else.

So what do we make of the Christians who, in response to Wiesenthal's story, advocated forgiveness? When I read the many responses, I found myself agreeing with those who opposed forgiving because I believe that no one should forgive what has been done against another by a third party. I still hold that position. My own response would be to suggest that Simon should have told the dying German to tell his story to one or more of the other Nazi soldiers in order to try to persuade them of the need to change their actions in any comparable situation.

Repentance clearly lies at the heart of the matter of forgiveness, but it is more than merely saying "I'm sorry." It must be genuine and deep-seated, and involve a real turning around in one's intention and behavior. The turning around should also attempt to make some kind of reparation for the harm one has done, at least to those still living. Even so, there is *a time* to ask for forgiveness, and *a time* to refrain. In 1985, in another situation, thousands of South African Christians signed and issued the Kairos Document that insisted there can be "no reconciliation, no forgiveness and no negotiations . . . without repentance." I agree. Only when genuine repentance has been demonstrated should survivors of crime consider extending forgiveness, and then only for the crimes against themselves. Even those survivors, I remain convinced, are not in a position to forgive the crimes committed against others.[21]

Moreover, we cannot speak about forgiveness without confronting the issue of remembrance. Anything as evil as the *Shoah* needs to be incorporated into the collective memory so that it can help shape the future in positive and restorative ways.[22] To this end I considered the problems and opportunities involved in formulating liturgies for a Christian observance of *Yom HaShoah*. I acknowledged that such observances are burdened not only by the fact that many Christians were murderers, accomplices, or at least bystanders during the *Shoah,* but also by the centuries of Christian theological negation of Judaism and the Jewish people. Consequently, I saw *Yom HaShoah* observances as needing to create a reservoir of memory, contrition, and resolve that can sustain the Church community in its determination to resist any similar attacks on Jews, and that can reinforce the more positive Christian teachings about Jews and Judaism that have recently been coming from a number of Christian churches.[23] I also insisted that Christian services of remembrance must not attempt to "Christianize" Holocaust suffering, nor strip the *Shoah* of its terrifying character. I noted that, strange as it may seem, such services can and often do deepen and enrich the life of a congregation by making the faithful more aware of the impact of language on actions and by sensitizing them to the need to examine theological claims and moral decisions very carefully.[24]

But much more than congregational observance of the *Shoah* is necessary if we in the churches are to experience conversion of heart toward Jews and Judaism. The needed liturgical reform and renewal will require an upheaval throughout the church year. Traditionally, anti-Jewish teachings have accompanied central Christian theological claims, and these have been expressed in liturgies and sermons during all seasons of the church calendar. Now that many churches have produced documents denouncing anti-Judaism and antisemitism and have, instead, begun to promote a positive appreciation of Jews and Judaism, it is time to have these changes reflected in liturgies throughout the year.

Conclusion

For more than half a century now I have been challenging many traditional Christian teachings. To say that mine is a "faith transformed" by "encounters with Jews and Judaism" is to put it mildly! My faith is replete with as many doubts as convictions. One of my convictions, gained through decades of Christian-Jewish encounters, is that we must dare to doubt, to remain committed to questioning and to rethinking our faith. I am convinced that "we must never cease to question our own faith and to ask what God means to us," as Rabbi Abraham Joshua Heschel claims. "For faith is not the clinging to a shrine but an endless pilgrimage of the heart. . . . To rely on our faith would be idol-worship. We have only the right to rely on God. Faith is not an insurance, but a constant effort, constant listening to the eternal voice."[25] Indeed! For I believe there is yet "more light and truth to break forth from God's Holy Word."[26] So openness to new understanding that may seem radical at first is part of the unending task of interpreting the never finished revelation of God. "No word is God's last word, no word is God's ultimate word."[27] Therefore, "history under God," as one Church document asserts, requires "a continuing reclaiming of the truth and power of God *in every generation*."[28]

Notes

[1] While these are James Parkes' words, I was already convinced of this insight before ever reading them.

[2] I don't recall being aware of the murders of Blacks in our own South during those same years. Although the KKK had burned a cross on the front lawn of a Black family who lived not far from us and whose children rode on the same school bus, I had not been told about it. Had I known of it I am certain my reaction would have been the same shocked anger as was my later feeling about the Nazis' treatment of Jews.

[3] My late husband, A. Roy Eckardt, who grew up in another Methodist Church, also had no recollection of anti-Judaism from the pulpit.

[4] Because of this experience, I understand how other Christians can be unaware of Christian anti-Judaism, though much more information is in the public realm now.

[5] A. Roy Eckardt, *Christianity and the Children of Israel* (New York: King's Crown Press, 1948). Most of the book focuses on different types of theology with a closing section on Roy's own theological position. Since I typed much of the manuscript, I was very familiar with its content.

[6] The result of the sabbatical was Roy's book, *Elder and Younger Brothers: The Encounter of Jews and Christians* (New York: Charles Scribner's Sons, 1967; Schocken paperback reprint, 1973).

[7] *The Four Lives of Elsbeth Rosenfeld,* with a foreword by James Parkes (London: Victor Gollancz, 1964).

[8] Alice L. Eckardt and A. Roy Eckardt, "Again, Silence in the Churches," *The Christian Century* (July 26, 1967) 970–72, and *The Christian Century* (August 2, 1967) 992–95. With this publication I was breaking another kind of silence, since this was my first publication.

[9] Quoted in Alice L. Eckardt and A. Roy Eckardt, *Encounter with Israel: A Challenge to Conscience* (New York: Association Press, 1970) 268.

[10] Quotations in this paragraph are from Alice L. Eckardt, "The Enigma of Christian Hostility to Israel," *World Outlook* (Spring 1972) 6–7. Even some Christians who rejected traditional negative teachings about Jews questioned the need for the State of Israel.

[11] Alice L. Eckardt, "An Unnecessary Christian Predicament," *CCI Notebook* (June 1973) 1, citing Philip Scharper and Alan Davies.

[12] Alice L. Eckardt, "Post-Holocaust Theology: A Journey Out of the Kingdom of Night," *Holocaust and Genocide Studies* (1986) 238–39.

[13] Alice L. Eckardt, "The *Shoah* Road to a Revised/Revived Christianity," *From the Unthinkable to the Unavoidable,* eds. Carol Rittner and John K. Roth (Westport, Conn.: Greenwood Press, 1997) 145.

[14] Quotations in this paragraph are from Alice L. Eckardt, "The Holocaust: Christian and Jewish Responses," *Journal of the American Academy of Religion* (September 1974) 454; reprinted in *Essential Papers in Jewish-Christian Relations in the United States,* ed. Naomi W. Cohen (New York: New York University Press, 1990) 210–11.

[15] The Evangelical Church's position would change in time, especially in the statement of the Rhineland Synod in 1980, though other statements would continue to insist on the required mission to the Jewish people. For a more detailed rendering of our thoughts on German responses to the *Shoah* (including those cited in the last three paragraphs) based

on our sabbatical research in Germany, see Alice and Roy Eckardt, "How German Thinkers View the Holocaust," *The Christian Century* (March 17, 1976) 249–52. I have done considerable work analyzing Church statements since the mid-1980s. See n. 23 for details.

¹⁶ Quotations in this paragraph are from A. Roy Eckardt with Alice L. Eckardt, *Long Night's Journey Into Day: Life and Faith After the Holocaust* (Detroit: Wayne State University Press, 1982) 62, 61, 65, 148; an enlarged edition of this book was published in 1988 with the subtitle *A Revised Retrospective on the Holocaust.*

¹⁷ Quotations in this paragraph are from Hans Jonas, "The Concept of God After Auschwitz," *Out of the Whirlwind: A Reader of Holocaust Literature,* ed. Albert H. Friedlander (New York: Union of American Hebrew Congregations, 1968; New York: Schocken Books, 1976) 473, 468, 469.

¹⁸ Quotations in this paragraph are from Ibid., 470–72.

¹⁹ Ibid., 476.

²⁰ Alice L. Eckardt, "Suffering, Theology, and the *Shoah,*" *Contemporary Christian Religious Responses to the Shoah,* ed. Steven L. Jacobs (Lanham, Md.: University Press of America, 1993) 33–57.

²¹ This section on forgiveness, as thus far developed, includes parts of my essay, "The Dilemma of Forgiveness," *The Holocaust and the Christian World: Reflections on the Past, Challenges for the Future,* eds. Carol Rittner, Stephen D. Smith, Irena Steinfeldt (London: Kuperard, 2000; NewYork: Continuum International Publishing Group, 2000) 228–30.

²² Alice L. Eckardt, "Forgiveness and Repentance: Some Contemporary Considerations and Questions," *Remembering for the Future,* eds. Yehuda Bauer, Alice L. Eckardt, and others (Oxford: Pergamon Press, 1989) 571–83.

²³ Over the last several decades, a fairly large number of Protestant and Roman Catholic documents have been issued that confront Christian anti-Judaism and antisemitism in Christian history and promote a more positive attitude toward Jews and Judaism. Most, if not all, of these statements through 1983 are in *Stepping Stones to Further Jewish-Christian Relations: An Unabridged Collection of Christian Documents,* compiled by Helga Croner (New York: Paulist Press, 1977) and *More Stepping Stones to Jewish-Christian Relations: An Unabridged Collection of Christian Documents 1975–1983,* compiled by Helga Croner (New York: Paulist Press, 1985). Eugene Fisher and Franklin Sherman are compiling a forthcoming, updated collection of Church documents on Christian-Jewish relations (also to be published by Paulist Press). *More Stepping Stones* contains an introductory essay by me in which I consider how Protestant statements deal with seven major topics bearing on Christian-Jewish relations. The forthcoming volume will include another essay of mine dealing with Protestant documents. In addition, my article "How Are the Protestant Churches Responding 50+ Years After?" has been published in *Remembering for the Future: The Holocaust in an Age of Genocide,* eds. John Roth and Elizabeth Maxwell (Basingstoke, England, and New York: Palgrave, 2001). I am pleased to note that both Protestant and Catholic statements reveal significant progress in Christian-Jewish relations in the post-World War II years. Yet I am convinced that most of these documents do not go far enough, since they continue to suggest that Christianity, while not replacing Judaism (as the tradition had it) nevertheless surpasses Judaism.

²⁴ Alice L. Eckardt, "In Consideration of Christian *Yom HaShoah* Liturgies," *Shoah: A Review of Holocaust Studies and Commemorations* (1979) 1–4; reprinted as "Christian

Observance of Holocaust Day," *Christian Attitudes on Jews and Judaism* (December 1979) 7–11; under original title in *Christians Confront the Holocaust,* ed. Donald McEvoy (New York: NCCJ, 1980) 7–11; as "Creating Christian *Yom HaShoah* Liturgies," *Liturgies on the Holocaust,* ed. Marcia Sachs Littell (Lewiston, Maine: Edwin Mellen Press, 1986) 6–12, and in a revised edition of the latter, eds. Marcia Sachs Littell and Sharon Weissman Gutman (Valley Forge: Trinity Press International, 1996) 6–12.

[25] Abraham Joshua Heschel, *Man Is Not Alone: A Philosophy of Religion* (New York: Farrar, Straus, and Young, 1951) 160, 174.

[26] John Robinson, one of the Pilgrims' pastors in England and Holland.

[27] Abraham Joshua Heschel, "No Religion Is an Island," *Union Seminary Quarterly Review* (January 1966) 128.

[28] Statement by the Christian Church (Disciples of Christ), 1988–1993, *The Church and the Jewish People: A Study Guide for the Christian Church (Disciples of Christ),* ed. Clark Williamson (St. Louis: Christian Board of Publications, 1994).

three

EVA FLEISCHNER

Encountering Anew the Living God
—in a Living People

My Early Years

I spent the first thirteen years of my life in Vienna, the child of a Catholic mother and a Jewish father. I was aware of the Jewish dimension of my life only through the closeness I felt to my father and his relatives, but like so many middle class Jews in Vienna, they were assimilated Jews, with little knowledge of Judaism. The Catholic dimension, on the other hand, was alive and vivid, reinforced by my attending a Dominican school *(Gymnasium),* beginning at age ten, where I received the then-customary instruction in the Catholic faith.

My childhood came to an end in 1938, soon after Hitler's annexation of Austria, when my parents were able to send me out of harm's way to a convent school in England. I was thirteen years old and spent my most impressionable teenage years in the pious environment of a Catholic girls' convent school, steeped in the religious atmosphere traditional at that time. My milieu and experience during the nearly six years there were entirely Catholic.

At age eighteen I was able to join my parents in the United States and soon thereafter entered Radcliffe College. Although I now found myself in a secular atmosphere, this did nothing to diminish my Catholic fervor. I attended Mass daily throughout my years at Radcliffe and beyond. During the three years I worked as an editorial assistant for Houghton Mifflin in Boston.

My acquaintance with Judaism as a living faith remained non-existent. While we had Jewish relatives dear to us and many Jewish friends—

fellow refugees—they were all secular Jews. The religious world that nourished me remained exclusively Catholic.

This cocoon began to crack open in 1949–1950, when I was on a Fulbright fellowship at the University of Paris. During that year I came into contact with one of France's leading theologians, the Jesuit Jean Daniélou. He invited me to join a study group of university students he was directing.

Daniélou, whose little book *The Salvation of the Nations* had already been published in English, was one of the first Catholic theologians to take seriously Christianity's encounter with other world religions, and to begin asking questions arising from that encounter. Under his guidance we—members of the *Cercle S. Jean Baptiste*—engaged in serious study of Hinduism, Buddhism, and Islam, as well as the Jewish roots of Christianity. A seed had been sown, one that was to take many years before coming to fruition.

Over the next fifteen years that seed was nourished by my involvement with the Grail, an international ecumenical women's movement, Catholic in origin, and by an intense Christian formation program at its United States headquarters in Loveland, Ohio.[1] The heart of this program was Scripture and liturgy, enriched and deepened by some of the finest Catholic scholars from both sides of the Atlantic. It was here that I discovered the Hebrew Scriptures and came to love them, especially the psalms and the prophets.

I knew of course that these writings were Jewish. But had I been asked in those days what their enduring value was, I would no doubt have replied: "They are the foundation of my Christian faith, and find their fulfillment in Jesus Christ." To use today's terminology, I must reluctantly admit that I was a typical Christian "supersessionist," believing that the Hebrew Scriptures derived their value exclusively from their pointing to Christ.

Yet, despite this inadequate understanding, the psalms in particular profoundly and permanently changed my prayer life and my relationship to God, and, I believe, they predisposed me to eventually appreciate Judaism. Let me, then, before continuing the account of my journey, speak about the impact of the psalms on my life.

The Impact of the Psalms on My Life

The psalms are one of the greatest treasures I have been given, and I have carried them with me wherever I have gone for more than half a century. They have been and remain an unfailing source of strength and faith in

my life, and here I wish to indicate this by reflecting briefly on what seem
to me their main characteristics.

The psalms bespeak *longing and thirst for God.* Here is the early
biblical expression of St. Augustine's marvelous sentence in the *Confessions:* "You have made us for yourself, O God, and our hearts can find no
rest until they rest in you!" What could more vividly express our longing
for God than the first verse of Psalm 42, "As the deer longs for living
streams, so my soul longs for you, O my God," or the opening of Psalm 63,
"O God, my God, for you I long at break of day. My soul thirsts for you,
my body longs for you, as desert, parched land"? These psalms both call
forth and give voice to my longing for God.

While expressing deep longing for God, the psalms also convey a
profound sense of intimacy with God. I had been taught that such intimacy is experienced only by Christians, thanks to Jesus Christ. Now I discovered that nearly a thousand years before, Jews had known and lived
such an experience with the living God. "You have hold of my right hand,"
sang the psalmist. "My flesh and my heart may fail, but God is the strength
of my heart and my portion forever" (Ps 73:23, 26). This intimacy has endured within Judaism down through the centuries and finds expression in
the writings of many contemporary Jews, especially, for me, in the poetic
prose of Abraham Joshua Heschel.

While conveying both longing for God and intimacy with God, the
psalms give expression to the *full range of human experience.* There is no
situation of danger, terror, love, etc. which is not mirrored somewhere in the
psalms; there is no emotion, from ecstatic joy to the depths of near despair,
that cannot be found in them. I say *near* despair because even Psalm 88,
the darkest of the psalms, is addressed *to God,* showing that there is hope.

Included in the range of emotions expressed in the psalms are rage,
hatred, and the desire for revenge. This is a stumbling block for many
Christians, leading some to dismiss the psalms as unfit for Christian prayer.
I disagree, as this implies that we Christians have no enemies, never hate
others, and are always forgiving. We should remember, however, that some
of the most terrible atrocities in human history have been carried out by
Christians. Dare we suggest that hatred and revenge are unknown to us?
For me, expressions of these emotions in the psalms mirror my own hostile feelings and reactions, which come much more readily than "turning
the other cheek." There is no pretense in the psalms that we are perfect,

that we are beyond anger and hatred. We may wish we were such creatures, but we are not, at least not yet, at least not most of us. Moreover, as
Walter Brueggeman points out, however fierce the violence in the psalms,
it is verbal, not physical.[2] No one is actually hurt or killed. In that sense,
such texts can be therapeutic, since giving vent to rage may diffuse it.

It is true that Jesus, in the Sermon on the Mount, warns us against
thinking or speaking evil, since this may lead to murder (Matt 5:21-22).
But it is also true that to articulate the rage we feel can purge us of it. This
is, or can be, I believe, one of the great benefits we can gain from praying
the psalms. Moreover, we not only confront our rage here, but offer it to
God. As we face our hatred and desire for vengeance, we bring these feelings to God and pray: "May you heal what you see!"

Another characteristic of the psalms is that they *dare to confront
God,* to call God to account, to challenge God. "Why do you hold back your
hand?" cries the psalmist. "Why do you keep your hand idle in your bosom?"
(Ps 74:11). This confrontational element I had not found anywhere in Christian prayer or liturgy. It is the same spirit of arguing with God that we
find in the story of Jacob wrestling with God, in the prophet Jeremiah calling God to task, or, today, in Elie Wiesel confronting God for allowing so
much suffering here on earth. Discovering this spirit of confrontation in
the psalms has freed me to express in prayer emotions that I otherwise
may have felt obliged to repress.

Breakthrough at Marquette

To return to my journey: Despite my love for the psalms, and for much of
the Old Testament, I still saw no connection between these texts and a
contemporary living Judaism. There was only one full and complete truth,
and that was contained in and taught by my Church.

The breakthrough came during my doctoral studies at Marquette
University. Already in my forties, I went to Marquette in the late 1960s to
pursue a Ph.D. in Christian historical theology and I emerged, four years
later, deeply involved with Judaism and the *Shoah* (the Holocaust). Two
doctoral seminars and a book started me on the road that eventually led to
my life's work. One seminar was on the church fathers, the other on *Luther's
Commentary on the Psalms.* Although Luther lived a thousand years later
than the Fathers of the Church, one theme kept cropping up in both semi-

nars and profoundly shocked me: the theme of anti-Judaism. It recurred repeatedly both in patristic writings and in the work of Luther. What was going on here? Why this persistent animosity on the part of Christians—many of them canonized saints in my Church—toward the people to whom they owed the origins of their faith?[3]

I was being confronted here for the first time with the dark and ugly legacy of Christian anti-Judaism, with what French historian Jules Isaac called the Church's "teaching of contempt" for Jews and Judaism, and which he described as "the Christian roots of antisemitism."[4] I was deeply troubled that the Church I loved so much had contributed to the antisemitism that led to the Nazism from which my own family had fled and to the *Shoah* in which so many Jews were murdered. True, Christian anti-Judaism, as the centuries-old denigration of the Jewish people and their religious tradition, is not identical with modern antisemitism, which is prejudice against Jews as a "race" (a misnomer, since the Jews are not a race but a people of many ethnicities). Nonetheless, besides preparing the ground for anti-semitism, the Church's anti-Judaism has so often and so easily gone hand-in-hand with antisemitism, that the distinction between the two is slight.[5]

About the same time that I was becoming aware of the Church's anti-Judaism, a friend who was in graduate school with me handed me a book with the words, "You *must* read this!" The book was *Treblinka* by Jean-François Steiner. It was my first real encounter with the *Shoah,* and I was profoundly shaken. I was also profoundly inspired. The word "life," which recurs throughout the book, gives expression to the deepest meaning of what Jews strove to achieve in that world of death. Whether it is the young girl Lydia who worked with the ss in order to learn their plans; or the old woman who, upon arriving at Treblinka, says to a fellow-inmate whom she is seeing for the first and last time, "Swear to me that you will stay alive"; or Chocken who, having escaped, returns mortally wounded in order to call the camp to revolt: they all act as they do in order that the people may live. This life of the people, this faith in the people, sustains and animates their actions.

In reading this book the familiar words "people" and "life" took on new meaning for me. I was reminded of passages from Deuteronomy, "You shall be My people," and "Choose life, then, that you may live." What a costly witness it took to show the world that these words of Scripture had not been spoken in vain—these words which, thirty centuries later, restored to members of this people the power to come back to life from the pit of death.[6]

I went on to read Elie Wiesel's *Night,* and then the other seven books Wiesel had written by that point. I was overwhelmed by the world that was now opening before me, in particular through Wiesel's writings. I was encountering for the first time the ancient yet ever new history of the Jewish people, who in my lifetime had suffered—and also survived—one of the most terrible catastrophes in all of human history. I became haunted by the *Shoah* and by the question: What has enabled this people to survive persecution for thousands of years, even the unparalleled catastrophe of the *Shoah?* For survive they did, and not only physically, as I also discovered during my years at Marquette.

It was at this crucial moment in my journey that, blessedly, I came into contact for the first time with a living Judaism; with Jews—modern American Jews—whose faith deeply informed their lives. I became friends with a young Jewish couple who invited me into their home to share the joys of *Shabbat,* the high point of their week. I clearly remember a conversation with my new Jewish friend. In response to my question, "How would you explain Judaism to a Christian?" her answer was immediate and simple: "I would invite her to my home for *Shabbat.*" Then she asked me how I would explain Christianity to a Jew. I fumbled around, and finally answered that I would try to explain some of our key doctrines, such as the incarnation. I was painfully aware of the inequality in our "contest," and felt greatly impoverished vis-à-vis my friend: on one side there was life, concrete and rich; on the other, doctrine, sounding—at least in my version and in that situation—quite disembodied.

I met other Jews in Milwaukee to whom their tradition was important and who also inspired my newfound love of Judaism. And I began to pursue the study of Judaism wherever I could, beginning with Rabbi Dudley Weinberg's course at Marquette. Summer institutes for Catholics were being offered at that time at Seton Hall University's Institute for Judaeo-Christian Studies and elsewhere, and I enrolled in as many of these as I could. After all these years—years of having a Jewish father and Jewish relatives, years of praying the psalms that are so much a part of Jewish liturgy—I was only now discovering Judaism. It was all so new to me: the beautiful observance of the Sabbath, the concrete ways in which some Jews I met lived their faith, the wealth of stories and traditions, and, yes, the ancient yet ever new history of the Jewish people.

No longer could I consider Christians the exclusive witnesses to God in the world. In fact, in those days, the Jews, far more than Christians, were for me God's principal witnesses in this world—not only the six million murdered in the *Shoah,* so many of whom died bearing witness to God, but the Jewish people who had survived centuries, millennia, of persecution and still maintained their faith in God. I knew quite well that not all Jews live according to their tradition—it is difficult to do so in the modern world—but I was deeply impressed and inspired by the phenomenon of Jewish survival, after so many centuries of suffering, culminating in the *Shoah.* Again, I asked: What has enabled the Jewish people to survive? It seemed to me then, as it seems to me now, that there is but one answer, although I am aware that many, including some Jewish friends, may disagree with me: the deep sense of Jewish identity, forged over thousands of years and still alive even in secular Jews, a sense of identity that I trace back to Sinai and the Jewish covenant with God.

Research and Discovery

As a teaching assistant at Marquette, I had the opportunity to offer a course in the department of continuing education. I chose as the topic the relationship between Jews and Christians through the centuries. I focused on the first four centuries, particularly the origins of the split and hostility between the two communities, deepening my understanding of Christian anti-Judaism, a subject that has remained a life-long central concern of mine.

When it came time for the choice of a dissertation topic, I knew it had to relate to the *Shoah* in some way. Through the kindness of Rabbi Weinberg I was able to meet prominent Jewish intellectuals, including Irving Greenberg, Michael Wyschogrod, Zalman Schachter, and Abraham Joshua Heschel. All were sympathetic to my research and gave generously of their time. A conversation with Rabbi Heschel made me realize that my original idea, to study the meaning of the *Shoah* for Christians, was a dead end. "My dear Eva," he said gently but emphatically, as we talked in his study at the Jewish Theological Seminary, "there is no meaning to be found in that event." This was part of an important learning process I underwent in those years.[7]

I decided to focus on the impact that the *Shoah* had on post-war German Christian theologians. I spent the spring of 1970 in Germany, mainly at the *Institutem Judaicum Delitzschianum* in Münster, and I interviewed Christian theologians who had an interest in Judaism. With the help of Krister Stendahl, then dean of Harvard Divinity School, I eventually narrowed down my focus to *Judenmission,* the effort to convert Jews to Christianity through active missionary work involving special organizations and trained personnel, and the attitude of German Christian theologians toward this missionary effort. Tracing the development of *Judenmission* from its nineteenth-century beginnings to the post-*Shoah* era proved to be an unexpectedly fascinating study, with repercussions for my own theological development.[8]

I discovered that there were three main approaches to the question of *Judenmission.* According to traditional *Judenmission,* which was still alive and being strongly advocated by some theologians in post-*Shoah* Germany, Christians should work to convert Jews to Christianity because the Church is the sole organ of salvation in the world. All non-Christians, including Jews, are considered potential Christians, and the Church must actively work for their conversion. There can be only one true people of God, and that is the Church. The Jewish people, the *old* people of God, has outlived its role and purpose—to prepare the world for the coming of the Messiah—and has been replaced by the Church, the *new* people of God.

The ecumenical movement within Christianity introduced a new dimension into the discussion of *Judenmission.* Once theologians acknowledged that various Christian groups other than their own denominations were *also* a part of the people of God, it made it easier for them to then recognize the Jews as *also* a part of this people. While claiming that there is only one people of God, a number of German Christian theologians influenced by the ecumenical movement suggested that this people has existed in a state of division or schism ever since the break between Christianity and Judaism. They considered the Church as the true people of God and the Jews as estranged members of this people. Someday the Jewish people will recognize Jesus as the Messiah, and then the schism between Christians and Jews will be healed. But this conversion will be the work of God alone; hence *Judenmission,* active missionary work directed toward Jews, should be abandoned.

In a further step there were some German Christian theologians who perceived the Jews as the people of God and the Church, thanks to its Jewish origins, as *also* a part of the people of God. The Church can claim to be the people of God only by assuming, not by excluding, all that it has received from those first chosen as God's people, and who still remain the people of God. As early as 1952, Karl Barth put it this way: "The Jews are without any doubt at all the chosen People of God down to this day, in the same sense as they were from the beginning, according to the Old and New Testaments. They have God's promise, and if we Christians from among the gentiles also have this promise, then we have it as those chosen along with them, as guests come into their homes, as branches grafted on to their tree."[9]

The influence of Romans 9–11, a text too long neglected, is clearly evident in this view. It is not the Jews who are *also* people in covenant with God, but rather it is we Christians who have become incorporated into God's covenant with the Jewish people. As the original people of God, through whom God's promises to Abraham and the revelation of Sinai have come to the Church, the Jewish people must not be the object of Christian mission.

Many German Christian theologians who rejected *Judenmission* advocated interfaith dialogue with Jews in its place. The majority of them hoped that such dialogue would eventually lead Jews to the acceptance of Christ. While they recognized Judaism's continuing validity, they nevertheless saw it as inferior to Christianity. Consequently, they hoped that Judaism would in time give way to the full truth of Christianity. A small minority of those theologians who advocated dialogue with Jews did so in a spirit of radical openness, willing to let the dialogue lead where it may, for example to the reformulation of some traditional teachings about Christ. A few theologians pointed out that conversion should not be seen as converting the other to one's own religion but, in the biblical sense of *teshuvah* or *metanoia,* as the reorientation of one's whole being to God. The call to conversion, which is of the essence of the Hebrew Bible's prophetic message, is reiterated in the New Testament by Jesus himself. However, Jesus' call to conversion was not about conversion to himself but to the One he called "Father." Therefore, Christians should not attempt to convert Jews to Christianity but should, along with Jews, strive for ongoing conversion in their covenant with God.[10]

My New Perspective on Christianity's Relationship to Judaism and Other Religions

I have recounted the various approaches of German Christian theologians to *Judenmission* in some detail because of the impact my research in this area had on my own view of the Church's relationship to Judaism and, ultimately, to other faiths.

The Church's relationship to Judaism is different than its relationship to any other religion. Christian faith *in* Jesus connects us to the Jewish faith *of* Jesus. Having been born within Judaism, Christianity must remain related to Judaism. Though now distinct from Judaism, Christianity must never be alien to Judaism. This means, at the very least, that the Church must continue to repudiate its anti-Jewish past and must purge itself of any remaining anti-Judaism and antisemitism. More positively, while the Church may allow itself to be influenced by various religions, it should especially be open to learning what it can from the Jewish tradition.

Among other things, we Christians can learn much from Jewish ways of longing for God, wrestling with God, and being intimate with God; from Jewish ways of acknowledging the terrible incompleteness of redemption and the need to assist God in redeeming the world; and from Jewish ways of keeping holy the Sabbath. We can also learn some important lessons from how Jews pray. For example, I am struck by the difference between Judaism and Christianity with regard to blessing—a difference that becomes clear in the traditional Catholic grace before meals. Generations of Catholics have prayed, and still pray, "Bless us, O Lord, and these your gifts, which we are about to receive from your bounty." Not so in the Jewish tradition. Instead of asking God to bless them, Jews bless God and in the process become blessed themselves. I prefer the Jewish way here; it seems to me much more God-centered and unselfish.

Having been spiritually enriched by my encounter with Jews and Judaism, I am convinced that we Christians should renounce attempts to convert Jews to Christianity and, instead, pray that Judaism continues to flourish and to bear fruit not only for Jews but for others as well. Abraham Heschel's recounting of a conversation he had with Catholic theologian Gustav Weigel the night before Weigel's death drove this point home to me.

> We opened our hearts to one another in prayer and contrition and spoke of our own deficiencies, failures and hopes. At one moment I posed the question: Is it really the will of God that there be no more Judaism in the world? Would it really be the triumph of God if the scrolls of the Torah would no more be taken out of the Ark and the Torah no more be read in the Synagogue, our ancient Hebrew prayers in which Jesus himself worshiped no

more recited, the Passover Seder no more celebrated in our lives, the Law of Moses no more observed in our homes? Would it really be *ad majorem Dei gloriam* to have a world without Jews?[11]

As I reflected on this more than a decade after Heschel himself had died, I began to wonder what Weigel had said in reply. Heschel does not tell us. I thought that perhaps Heschel's widow, Sylvia, would know, so I went to see her. She remembered Heschel coming home late that night very moved by his conversation with Weigel, but did not recall his speaking of the Jesuit's response. So the two of us sat there wondering and talking, and soon we were joined by the Heschels' daughter, Susannah, and a friend, who were visiting that Sunday. We read the whole passage aloud, slowly. And suddenly the answer emerged, quite clearly. "We opened our hearts to one another in prayer and contrition and spoke of our deficiencies, failures, and hopes." That was how their discussion began: in prayer and contrition. How could Fr. Weigel's response to what followed have been anything but a profound affirmation of Judaism as a living religion worthy of continuation? The four of us, as we sat in the Heschels' living room that sunny Sunday afternoon, felt in agreement, reassured, and at peace.[12]

Regardless of how Father Weigel answered Heschel's questions, I know how I would have responded to them: the survival of Judaism and the Jewish people is *ad majorem Dei gloriam,* to the greater glory of God! I believe more and more Christians nowadays share this view. Those of us who do must rethink how we understand our Christian faith in relation to Judaism. This necessarily requires our reformulating traditional christological doctrines. Our efforts to reinterpret the meaning of Christ are in continuity with a process that engaged the early Church. The New Testament gives us no dogmatic christological formulations; these are the outgrowth of prolonged theological speculation, frequently aimed at combating heresies. Instead, the New Testament expresses in various ways the conviction that "God was in Christ." Thus, for example, in the Acts of the Apostles, Peter speaks of the coming of the Messiah as being still in the future, and that this Messiah will be Jesus (Acts 3:19-21). We have here an expression of the early Christians' faith in the Parousia, the Second Coming of Christ, as well as of their struggle to understand who Jesus was.

Many contemporary Christian theologians continue this struggle of the early Church. Some of us have been profoundly influenced by the deep-seated Jewish awareness of history as precarious and of redemption as still a dream. Our assertions of what Christ has wrought for humankind have, therefore, become more modest, less dogmatic. This does not mean we think less of Christ; we simply believe we are more realistic about what has been accomplished in and through him. God has been revealed to us through Jesus, and we approach God in his name. This makes us Christians, not Jews, and we are grateful for life in Christ. But we recognize that the very same God is present to Jews who approach God not in the name of Christ but in ways similar to those of Jesus the Jew. We therefore recognize Judaism as a way of truth, a way to God, valid in its own right. Christianity is *our* way; it is not the *only* way to the Living God.

In this age of interfaith dialogue, questions raised for the Church by its encounter with Judaism inevitably lead to questions about its encounter with other religions as well. Largely because of the work I did for my doctoral dissertation, and even more because of my ongoing encounters with Jews and Judaism, I have become convinced that religious pluralism is not some inevitable but passing phenomenon, to be endured temporarily in a time of theological turmoil, but rather a positive development, part of the very stuff of salvation. I believe Heschel had it right when, in an interview shortly before his death, he said: "God is to be found in many hearts all over the world—not limited to one nation or to one people, to one religion. . . . Yes, I think it is the will of God that there should be religious pluralism."[12] Nevertheless, Heschel firmly believed in the distinctiveness or uniqueness of each religion willed by God. With regard to his own tradition, Heschel asserted: "Judaism has allies but no substitutes."[14] I believe the same about Christianity. It is unique, but we need not consider it superior to Judaism and all other faiths. No one tradition holds the key to all of revealed truth, or can claim to be the only and full revelation. Again, in Heschel's words: "The voice of God reaches the [human] spirit . . . in a multiplicity of languages. One truth comes to expression in many ways of understanding."[15]

I have come to believe that the Church's relationship to the Jewish people is in some way a test, a touchstone, for its relationship to other world religions. Its encounter with Jews and Judaism presents a direct challenge to any absolutist claim to truth. It suggests the possibility that the depth and richness of humanity's quest for God are revealed in the differences among peoples, at least as much as through what they hold in common.

Conclusion

My spiritual life has been immensely enriched by my encounter with Jews and Judaism. Among other treasures, I have gained a deeper appreciation of the Living God and a more passionate relationship with that God, particularly through the psalms; a deeper appreciation of keeping holy the Sabbath and of the role of blessing in the life of prayer; a new openness to and respect for other world religions and, consequently, a humbler, more realistic image of my Church.

My love of the Church has been, and continues to be, tested, but has not been destroyed. I am willing to live with an image of the Church that is a good deal less glorious than my earlier image of it. I have come to realize that "the bride without spot or wrinkle" of the book of Revelation is a far-off eschatological reality and that, meanwhile, we live in a Church where Jesus' message of love has been, and still is, all too often disfigured almost beyond recognition. And yet, this is the faith community to which I feel called, of which I remain a member, and which I love.

Notes

[1] Founded in the Netherlands in the 1920s, the Grail came to the United States in 1940. The Grail website is www.grail-us.org.

[2] Walter Brueggeman, *Praying the Psalms* (Winona, Minn.: St. Mary's Press, 1982) 70.

[3] See Eva Fleischner, "A Door that Opened and Never Closed: Teaching the *Shoah*," *From the Unthinkable to the Unimaginable: American Christian and Jewish Scholars Encounter the Holocaust,* eds. Carol Rittner and John K. Roth (Westport, Conn.: Greenwood Press, 1997) 19–20.

[4] Jules Isaac, *The Teaching of Contempt: The Christian Roots of Anti-Semitism* (New York: Holt, Rinehart & Winston, 1964). See also Eva Fleischner, "The Teaching of Contempt: The Christian Origins of Anti-Judaism," *New Conversations* (Autumn 1993) 3–8.

[5] The history of anti-Judaism and its connection to antisemitism has been brilliantly told by James Carroll in his book *Constantine's Sword: The Church and the Jews—A History* (Boston and New York: Houghton Mifflin Co., 2001).

[6] See Eva Fleischner, "Response to Emil Fackenheim," *Auschwitz: Beginning of a New Era? Reflections on the Holocaust,* ed. Eva Fleischner (New York: KTAV, 1977) 230.

[7] See Eva Fleischner, "A Door that Opened," 20.

[8] Completed in 1971, my doctoral dissertation was published in 1975. See Eva Fleischner, *Judaism in German Christian Theology Since 1945: Christianity and Israel Considered in Terms of Mission* (Metuchen, N.J.: Scarecrow Press, 1975). *Judenmission* is a German term that, strictly speaking, designates the specific form of missionary work carried out among Jews by German Lutherans in the nineteenth and twentieth centuries. In my dissertation it

is used both in this strict sense and also in the broader sense of any Christian missionary activity directed toward Jews. Ch. 1 deals with *Judenmission* in the nineteenth and early twentieth centuries; ch. 2 discusses the presence of "Jewish Christians" in the Church; chs 3–6 focus on the views of Judaism and missionary activity toward Jews since 1945, the end of World War II and the Holocaust, which marked the beginning of a new era in the Church's attitude toward Jews and Judaism.

[9] Karl Barth, "Die Judenfrage und ihre christliche Beantwortung," *Judaica,* vol. 6 (1952) 72.

[10] I am struck by how relevant this topic remains, some thirty-five years after I examined it in my dissertation. That the issue of Christian mission to the Jews is no mere academic issue is evident from the at times passionate controversy sparked by a document published in August 2002, *Reflections on Covenant and Mission,* Consultation of the National Council of Synogogues and the Bishops' Committee for Ecumenical and Interreligious Affairs, U.S.C.C.B., August 12, 2002. See also, among others, the critique of this document by Cardinal Avery Dulles. S.J., and the response by Mary C. Boys, Philip A. Cunningham, and John T. Pawlikowski, in *America,* October 21, 2002, 8–16.

[11] Abraham Joshua Heschel, "No Religion is an Island," *Union Seminary Quarterly Review* (January 1966) 355.

[12] See Eva Fleischner, "Heschel's Significance for Jewish-Christian Relations," *Abraham Joshua Heschel: Exploring His Life and Thought,* ed. John C. Merkle (New York: Macmillan, 1985) 149.

[13] Abraham Joshua Heschel, "A Conversation with Dr. Abraham Joshua Heschel," interviewed by Carl Stern, transcript of "The Eternal Light" program (National Broadcasting Company, February 4, 1973) 4, 13.

[14] Heschel, "No Religion is an Island," 129.

[15] Ibid., 127.

four

FRANKLIN SHERMAN

Steps Along the Way

Early Experiences

The story of my involvement in Christian-Jewish dialogue and my indebtedness to Jews and Judaism begins with my childhood and youth, growing up in Allentown, a small city in eastern Pennsylvania. Small but diverse—if you count as diversity all sorts of European groups: German, Italian, Polish, Ukrainian. Many were attracted by the silk mills and steel mills in the area. There were very few Blacks and practically no Hispanics, though the latter meanwhile have become the dominant minority in the area. And there was a substantial population of Jews, several thousand, I'm sure, in a city population of about a hundred thousand.

Insofar as there was prejudice openly expressed in my presence, it was prejudice against Jews. There were not enough Blacks to worry about, and no Hispanics. The Jews were the ones who were different, who were prominent, who "always stuck together." I didn't know the term anti-semitism, and I hadn't heard of Jules Isaac's phrase "the teaching of contempt," but I knew how the word "Jew" was spoken.

Later I came to realize that the still dominant Germanic culture of the region may have had something to do with this. This was the area of the so-called Pennsylvania Dutch—not the picturesque Amish, who resided further to the south towards Lancaster, but more mainstream Protestant, and largely Lutheran, immigrants who settled the area between Reading on the one side and the tri-city complex of Allentown/Bethlehem/Easton on the other. "Dutch" was of course a misnomer, a mistake by the English-speaking residents when the newcomers identified themselves as Deutsch (i.e., German). There weren't any tulips growing around Allentown, only potatoes!

Growing up in this context, what was my reaction? Fortunately, it was a reaction in the direction of tolerance and understanding, not an acceptance or furtherance of such prejudice. This was due, I think, partly to the inherent idealism of youth, and partly to my Christian faith, especially as interpreted by the very inspiring pastor by whom I was confirmed. I became involved in an interfaith youth movement, which of course in those days meant Protestant/Catholic/Jew (no others were as yet on the scene). I am immensely grateful to the farsighted adult leaders who brought such a movement into being in our area. The net result was that discussing things with young Jewish counterparts and being inside the Jewish Community Center for various events became something natural to me.

Let me add just one other point about those early years. The Allentown public school system had a pronounced "streaming" system in those days, i.e., the grouping of students according to their perceived ability. Falling into the upper group, I found that many of my fellow students were Jewish. This was true from the fifth grade onward, and though I may not have realized it at the time, I believe that this was the earliest source of my profound respect for the sheer intelligence and range of talents of so many Jews. Later, I was to learn of the immense Jewish contributions to so many realms of Western culture, and in my doctoral studies at the University of Chicago, I was privileged to study with some of the great European Jewish émigré scholars who so enriched the life of American universities from the 1930s onward, such as, in my case, Hans Morgenthau and Leo Strauss.

My reason for noting this is that I think I have always been motivated, in my approach to Christian-Jewish relations, as much or more by a positive appreciation of Jews and Judaism as by a dismay at their tribulations down through the centuries—though the latter has by no means been absent from my concerns. This explains, I think, why I didn't become a Holocaust scholar, but rather, in my later years, the director of something called the "Institute for Jewish-Christian Understanding."

Encounter with Heschel

The next great turning point in this story was my encounter, first through his writings and then face to face, with someone who came to represent, not only for me but for many, the very embodiment of what it means to be Jewish. This was the famous Jewish philosopher, theologian, historian, mystic, and prophetic voice in American society, Abraham Joshua Heschel.

Heschel became known to the general public in the 1960s chiefly through his participation in the civil rights and anti-war movements. The picture of the bearded Heschel, looking the very image of a Hebrew prophet, marching arm in arm with Martin Luther King in Selma, Alabama, is a classic of American social and religious history. With Michael Novak and Robert McAfee Brown, he founded Clergy Concerned about Vietnam (later changed to Clergy and Laity Concerned), and added his powerful voice of protest. He also made his voice heard on a wide range of other social issues.

But it was in another capacity that I first encountered him. It was in the early 1950s, as I was browsing in Woodworth's bookstore near the University of Chicago, that I came across a yellow-covered volume—later inscribed to me by Heschel and still a treasured possession—titled *Man Is Not Alone: A Philosophy of Religion.*[1] Fascinated both by the line of thought and by the beauty of the prose in which it was expressed, I stood there for a long time reading the book.

"There are three aspects of nature which command man's attention: power, loveliness, grandeur," Heschel writes in the opening sentence. "Power he exploits, loveliness he enjoys, grandeur fills him with awe."[2] Starting from that theme, "the awareness of grandeur," he proceeds to evoke what he calls "the sense of the ineffable," that is, of the indescribable, of that which lies beyond our power to comprehend or to express, or to manipulate, and yet which we encounter in the immediacy of our experience—or, more precisely, which we *can* encounter, if we but open ourselves to it.

As I read on, I realized that what Heschel was describing was *the reality of God,* and doing so in a way that was more persuasive than any I had known before. I don't know if at that point I was acquainted with Rudolph Otto's concept of the *mysterium tremendum,* but later I came to see that this was Heschel's equivalent of it (and indeed, he had probably been influenced by Otto). Rudolph Otto, however, spoke in the analytical and measured tones of the philosopher or phenomenologist of religion. Abraham Heschel spoke in the language of poetry, the language of the heart.

So here was I, someone reared in the Christian faith, trained for the Christian ministry—for I was already a seminary graduate, and beginning doctoral studies—finding myself being "ministered to" (to use a Christian phrase) by a Jewish philosopher/theologian, and that at the most basic level, that of my sense of the reality of God.

How appropriate, I thought, for is not the Christian faith built upon Jewish foundations? Does not the New Testament presuppose the Old (I may not have learned as yet to call it anything but that)? Is it not in the majestic cadences of the creation story, or in the thunderings of the prophets, or in the praises of the psalmists, that our most basic sense of God is evoked? And those are Jewish sources! But the new realization, for me, was that these sources were not just in the past, but were still alive today, not only through the Scriptures but through the life and witness of the Jewish people, whose continuity with those ancient sources had never been broken, and who had a powerful witness to make through their own prayer and proclamation and application of the wisdom of Scripture and tradition to the circumstances of the present day.

My personal acquaintance with Heschel began at the University of Iowa, where I was a young instructor and where he came as a visiting professor in 1960–1961. I let him know of my interest in his thought, and he responded warmly. Later, I wrote an article about him that he seemed to like.[3] I had the opportunity to have *Shabbat* dinner in his home in New York City, to meet his charming wife Sylvia and his gifted daughter Susannah—now herself a prominent figure in Jewish studies—and to see him on many of his visits to Chicago for speaking engagements. It was typical of his generosity that he often took the initiative in suggesting that we meet; I hesitated to impose on his time. He encouraged me in my own work, and always inquired about it.

In 1970 Martin E. Marty invited me to contribute to a series of books that he was editing called "The Promise of Theology," for each of which he invited someone to write a book about a recent or contemporary figure whose thought, in the writer's judgment, had not been as fully appreciated or appropriated as it deserved to be. I chose to write about Abraham Heschel, and the resultant *The Promise of Heschel* was published in 1970.[4] I was gratified to learn, again, that Heschel liked it and seemed to consider it a reasonably faithful rendering of his views.

Most sadly, Heschel died just two years after the book was published, at the distressingly young age of sixty-five. So our dialogue *viva voce* was cut off. But I continued to learn from and be inspired by his writings, and continue to do so to this day.

Two further themes are examples of what I have learned from Heschel. The first is *the inextricable interrelation of the mystical and prophetic dimensions of faith and life.* These are often contrasted with one another: the mystic deals with the wordless immediacy of the divine, and is transported into a world beyond the realm of normal experience, while the prophet speaks a word from God on high, a word spoken precisely into the midst of normal human experience—spoken both in judgment and in hope. The mystic, as typically understood, leads one away from the mundane; the prophet shoves one more deeply and more critically into it.

What Heschel showed—both in his writings and in his life—was that the prophetic pathos, in the sense of a fierce devotion to justice and to the cause of the poor, is rooted in the prophet's experience of God's pathos. Heschel points out that in the Greek tradition, the most common symbol for justice is the scales; this implies an impartial weighing of evidence, which in itself is of course admirable. He then contrasts with this the Hebraic image of justice as a mighty, creative-destructive force at work in history: "Let justice roll down like waters, and righteousness as a mighty stream" (Amos 5:24).[5] God is not neutral. In Martin Luther's words, God is "a burning fire of love." If the God with whom the mystic communes is the same God to whom the prophets testify, then the consequences will be transformative.

The other theme is the one embodied in Heschel's classic phrase, "It is a joy to be a Jew." Dietrich Bonhoeffer wrote a book called *The Cost of Discipleship.* Abraham Heschel could have written one called *The Joy of Discipleship*—though without minimizing in any way the cost of "discipleship," i.e., of covenant faithfulness, for Jews over the centuries.

This motif of joy is set forth most eloquently in the earliest of Heschel's publications after his arrival in the United States, the beautiful volume titled *The Earth is the Lord's: The Inner World of the Jew in East Europe.*[6] Handsomely illustrated with wood engravings by Ilya Schor, it is devoted to recovering and re-presenting to the contemporary reader the very tradition out of which Heschel himself had emerged, a tradition which had been so cruelly destroyed. It is a masterly evocation of that lost world of Eastern European Jewry. "For these people," Heschel writes, "Jewishness was more than a set of beliefs and rituals, more than what was compressed into tenets and rules. Jewishness was not in the fruit but in the sap that stirred through the tissues of the tree. Bred in the silence of the soil, it ascended to the leaves to become eloquent in the fruit. Jewishness was not only truth; it was vitality, joy; to some, the only joy. The intellectual majesty of the Shema Israel, when translated into the language of their hearts, signified: 'It is a joy to be a Jew.'"[7]

The form of piety that Heschel depicts here, as well as in his closely related work *The Sabbath: Its Meaning for Modern Man,*[8] can be called, in the best sense, a "this-worldly" spirituality. Attend to the life you have, and you then may be prepared for the life to come. Recognize the preciousness of every moment that you are granted by the Creator, and live it to the full. Heschel depicts in inimitable fashion what this meant for daily life in the communities he is describing: "The dishes to be served on certain days, the manner of putting on or removing one's shoes, the stance of one's head when walking in the street—everything was keyed to a certain style. Every part of the liturgy, every prayer, every hymn, had its own tune; every detail its own physiognomy, each object its individual stamp. Even the landscape became Jewish."[9]

It was the French Catholic philosopher Jacques Maritain, I believe, who once remarked that "humanism" can be defined either in terms of what it denies or of what it affirms. If it is interpreted to mean *the denial of the transcendent,* then humanism is incompatible with the Christian faith. But if it is interpreted to mean *an affirmation of the human*—that is, of the nobility and preciousness of human life—then, said Maritain, it is most certainly compatible with the Christian faith. I believe the same could be said about Judaism; indeed all the more assuredly than about Christianity.

Speaking still of that world of Eastern European Jews, Heschel underscores this point: "They were taught to care for the most distant in the most immediate, knowing that the passing is a reflection of the lasting, that tables in their humble homes may become consecrated altars. . . . Characteristic of their piety was the unheroic sacrifice: unassuming, inconspicuous devotion rather than extravagance, mortification, asceticism. The purpose was to ennoble the common, to endow worldly things with hieratic beauty."[10] There could be no finer expression also of the Christian's highest aspirations for the meaningful expression of faith in daily life.

A Teaching Partnership

I want to touch now on another relationship that became deeply meaningful to me over the years, my friendship and joint teaching experiences with Rabbi Hayim Goren Perelmuter in Chicago.

Our paths crossed shortly after the Lutheran School of Theology at Chicago opened at its new campus in Hyde Park in 1967. I had been appointed to teach Christian ethics there, and later became director of graduate studies and then dean. But from the beginning, I also found ways to express my continuing interest in Judaism and Christian-Jewish relations.

Just down the street from the new seminary was an imposing synagogue, K.A.M. Isaiah Israel Temple. I soon became acquainted with one of the rabbis there, the gracious and scholarly Hayim Perelmuter, who served also as lecturer in Jewish Studies at the nearby Catholic Theological Union. It was not long before we decided to offer a course together. We called it "Current Issues in Christian-Jewish Dialogue," deliberately choosing that general title so that we could offer it repeatedly and fill it with whatever content seemed best at the time. We offered it every two or three years until I left Chicago in 1989.

To me, a highlight of that series was the one on "Christology and Messianism," in which the Christian claims and categories regarding Jesus of Nazareth could be tested against the background of the whole panoply of Jewish messianic claimants and movements down through the centuries. A key book for me in preparing for the course was Gershom Scholem's magisterial study, *The Messianic Idea in Judaism*. How remarkable it was to have as my teaching partner someone who had himself studied with the great Scholem and had served as his aide for his first lectures in America in 1938.

Hayim Perelmuter had a distinctive way of contrasting early Christianity and rabbinic Judaism, those two "sibling" faiths, as he loved to call them, both sprung from loins of ancient Israel.[11] Christianity, he suggested, adopted a "short-range messianism," while rabbinic Judaism espoused a "long-range messianism." Both looked to the fulfillment of the prayer, "Thy will be done on earth as it is in heaven." Early Christianity, however, caught up in apocalyptic fervor, looked to an imminent consummation, whereas rabbinic Judaism, sobered by the Jewish defeat at the hands of the Romans, forswore any expectation of immediate redemption and settled down for the long haul of history.

I found this very illuminating, although I came to feel that the scheme needed significant modification. With the so-called "delay of the Parousia," Christianity also found that it had to reckon with the long haul of history. In so doing, it fortified itself with the structures of canon, creed, and episcopacy, and eventually settled into the Constantinian accommodation to the world. Rabbinic Judaism, on the other hand (if this term is used for the whole sweep of Judaism during the past two thousand years), has experienced repeated outbreaks of messianic fervor, an undercurrent that was always there underneath the seemingly placid surface. Thus both faiths have experienced both types of messianism.

Perelmuter's distinction between short-range and long-range messianism implies a similarity of goals, with only a difference of timetable. But I wondered if the pivotal difference did not lie, rather, in a *redefinition* of messianism, and hence a redefinition of redemption. The Christian Messiah is not a world-transforming hero; he is a mediator between God and humanity. He functions, frankly, more like a Hasidic *zaddik* (righteous one) than as a messiah traditionally conceived in Judaism. Like the *zaddik,* he serves as a teacher of living Torah, an intercessor for the needs of the faithful, and an exemplar of the holy life. The *zaddik,* in Hasidism, functions both as a representative of God to the people and of the people to God. Redemption, in this perspective, consists in restoration to a right relationship to God, not in world-improvement—although the works of love and justice, *tzedekah,* do follow from it.[12]

Thus Jesus functions for Christians, one can say, more as a "mystical messiah," to use the term applied by Scholem to the seventeenth-century messianic claimant Sabbati Zevi, than as a messiah in the eschatological mode, if the latter be taken to imply a visible transformation of the world order, whether achieved slowly or suddenly.

In addition to these more advanced seminars, Rabbi Perelmuter and I also created an entry-level program for Lutheran seminary students that we called "Introduction to Judaism: The Sabbath Experience." On my part at least, this was inspired by Abraham Heschel's book *The Sabbath,* which conveyed so beautifully the spiritual meaning of traditional Jewish sabbath observance.

Late Friday afternoon, I would take the Lutheran students, usually numbering a dozen or so, down the street to K.A.M. Isaiah Israel Temple for an orientation session with Rabbi Perelmuter. Then we would sit down at a *Shabbat* meal, served in the social hall and conducted with all the customary prayers and ceremonies. A lay couple from the congregation would preside. Discussions about the meaning of it all would occur both during and after dinner.

We then took a narrated tour of the synagogue, while waiting for the congregants to gather for Friday evening worship. Taking our seats when the service began and trying to be inconspicuous, we followed along as best we could, marveling at the resonance of the cantor's voice and the combination of familiarity and strangeness of the liturgy. Afterward, more lively conversation with the congregants over refreshments during the Oneg Shabbat (the socializing following the Friday night service).

The following morning, we would return for a special session on Jewish music with the cantor, who at that time was Max Janowski, a noted composer of Jewish liturgical music. Following the noon meal, a study session with the rabbi on the Torah portion of the week, and finally the Havdalah service, which takes leave of the Sabbath with wine, candles, and sweet spices, reminding one to take the holiness and sweetness of this day into the week to come.

What did the students and I learn from such an experience? So much! We gained a profound respect for the integrity and meaningfulness of Jewish prayer and worship; an understanding of the significance of the family for Jews, and of the family table as an altar; a deeper awareness of how the Hebrew Scriptures give us a common foundation and a common vocabulary; an appreciation of what the "the Lord's Day" as a time set apart can mean, something well known to the Puritans but long since lost in American culture; an acquaintance with both joyous and melancholy tunes from the Jewish tradition; an appreciation of the teaching role of the rabbi, so important for future pastors to note; an experience of the liveliness of conversation on common themes by persons of different faiths.

These are the sorts of things for which I remain indebted to my dear friend, the late Rabbi Hayim Goren Perelmuter.

The Star of Redemption

The third Jewish figure to whom I feel especially indebted, in addition to Heschel and Perelmuter, is one whom I could not have known personally, since he preceded me by a full generation, but who nevertheless stands large on my horizon, as he does on that of any history of modern Jewish thought. I am speaking of the great Franz Rosenzweig (1886–1929).

I don't know when I first became acquainted with Rosenzweig's thought. My copy of his magnum opus *The Star of Redemption*[13] bears the purchase date of 1973, but I believe I learned of him well before that through the work of Nahum Glatzer. As Glatzer states, "The story of Franz Rosenzweig is the story of a rediscovery of Judaism."[14] Born into an assimilated German Jewish family, he became part of a circle of brilliant young intellectuals of Jewish origin, several of whom were considering or had already undergone conversion to Christianity. This they saw as the logical culmination of the process of emancipation and identification with Western civilization in which Jews had been engaged since the Enlightenment.

Indeed, in 1913 Rosenzweig himself decided to take this step. But before doing so, he decided to attend High Holy Day services, for he wanted to enter Christianity, he declared, "as a Jew, not as a pagan." It was during the *Yom Kippur* (Day of Atonement) services, which begin in the evening with the *Kol Nidre* and continue all the following day, that Franz Rosenzweig experienced the depth and power of Jewish prayer and the reality of repentance and forgiveness. He felt irresistibly called back into solidarity with his people. A few days later, he announced to his friends that he had reversed his decision. Later he discussed this in a letter to his friend and cousin Rudolf Ehrenberg, who had already converted, and who had apparently cast up to him the saying of the Johannine Jesus, "No one comes to the Father except through me" (John 14:6).

"We are wholly agreed," Rosenzweig states, no doubt to Ehrenberg's surprise, "as to what Christ and his Church mean to the world: no one can reach the Father save through him." But he continues: "No one can reach the Father! But the situation is quite different for one who does not have to reach the Father because he is already with him."[15] Somehow, this simple thought has served for me, ever since I first encountered it, as the best way of understanding the basic relationship between Judaism and Christianity, Jews and Christians. Jews have been granted the blessings of the covenant, and we, through Jesus Christ, have been adopted into it.

This does not explain all the similarities and differences or continuities and discontinuities between the two faiths, nor could any simple formulation do so. Judaism in the time of Jesus was already a complex phenomenon; some have used the plural, speaking of the "Judaisms" of the time. I would prefer to speak of a plurality of interpretations and realizations of Judaism. The new messianism—Christianity—embodied in itself a particular set of such interpretations and realizations, while excluding others. And those that it did adopt, it considerably transformed over the years and centuries, while borrowing yet other features from the surrounding cultures. So Christianity today is not simply a Judaism ("Judaism for the Gentiles," as it has sometimes been called.) It has its own unique configuration and intentionality. Yet it still is, fundamentally, a shoot grafted onto a Jewish root, as Paul declared in Romans 11. "Remember," he reminds the Gentile Christians, "that it is not you that support the root, but the root that supports you" (Rom 11:18).

Though this thought about being "already with the Father" was first expressed by Rosenzweig in the letter to Rudolph Ehrenberg, it is explicated more fully in his correspondence with his close friend Eugen Rosenstock-Huessy, who had converted to Christianity at age sixteen. In a very frank exchange of views, Rosenzweig attacks the notion that a Jew needs an intermediary to approach God: "For to the Jew it is incomprehensible that one should need a teacher, be he who he may, to learn what is obvious and matter of course for him, namely to call God our Father. Why should a third person have to be between me and my Father in heaven?"[16] Later in the same letter, he puts it even more succinctly: "Shall I become converted, I who was born 'chosen'?"[17]

Franz Rosenzweig went on to become one of the most significant interpreters of Jewish thought in modern times. He began his massive work *The Star of Redemption* as a soldier at the front in World War I, writing out the text on army postcards and sending them home one by one. In 1920 he became head of an institute for Jewish studies in Frankfurt, and in 1925 began a collaboration with Martin Buber on a new German translation of the Hebrew Scriptures. But meanwhile, he fell seriously ill, and was diagnosed as suffering from amyotrophic lateral sclerosis (ALS). He gradually lost his ability to move, then to write, then to speak. During his last years, his writing was done by pointing at letters one by one, or making a slight sound when his wife pointed at the correct one. In this manner he completed scholarly articles and carried on a lively correspondence until just days before his death in 1929.

Why do I tell this tale? Because I find it inspiring, and others may as well. Because, as with Bonhoeffer's *Letters and Papers from Prison,* the circumstances of a work's composition may add gravity to its words. Because we have here once again a vivid testimony to the power of the fidelity of the Jewish people to their ancient covenant and to their contemporary calling, a fidelity that is exemplary for us Christians.

The Star of Redemption sets forth an understanding of Judaism, of Christianity, and of religious phenomenology in general that is of vast scope and subtlety, and cannot be summarized here. Let me allude only to the basic image of the "star" that underlies the work. It is formed by a triangle representing the three basic elements of reality—God, the world, and humanity—over which is superimposed another triangle (hence a six-pointed star) representing creation, revelation, and redemption. The star consists of two things: the core and the rays. At the core is a burning fire; this is Judaism and the Jews, ever living in God's presence and ever faithful to the covenant. The rays extending from the core are Christianity, with its mission to carry the word of revelation and redemption "to the ends of the earth."

Thus the final three chapters of Rosenzweig's book are titled: "The Fire, or The Eternal Life"; "The Rays, or the Eternal Way"; and "The Star, or the Eternal Truth." Only the fire and the rays together constitute the star. Only Judaism and Christianity together represent the fullness of God's purpose. That is Rosenzweig's formulation. One can argue with his specific interpretation of Christianity, or for that matter of Judaism, but this kind of generosity of spirit towards "the other" and this kind of deeply theological effort to express the relationship between the two traditions is surely a model for anyone concerned with Christian-Jewish dialogue.

On Repentance and Reconciliation: Luther and the Jews

The final theme that I want to cover is not a pleasant one. It concerns the topic "Luther and the Jews."

My involvement with this difficult subject has been chiefly at two points. The first was the decision to include a translation of Luther's treatise *Von den Juden und ihre Lügen (On the Jews and Their Lies),* first published in 1543, in the massive fifty-five volume set of Luther's works in English translation known as the "American Edition." The second main aspect of my involvement, forming a counterpoint to the foregoing, was in the issuance by the Evangelical Lutheran Church in America of an official statement forcefully repudiating Luther's anti-Jewish views.

Let me take as my starting point a book published in 1994 with the intriguing title *Tainted Greatness: Antisemitism and Cultural Heroes.*[18] Containing lectures given at a conference at Boston University, it presents an exposé of the covert or overt antisemitism of some of the most prominent intellectuals in modern culture. Included are, in the literary realm, T. S. Eliot, Ezra Pound, H. L. Mencken, Joseph Campbell, Paul de Man. In the field of psychology, Carl Jung. In philosophy, Martin Heidegger, and in theology or religious studies, Gerhard Kittel, Mircea Eliade—and Martin Luther. In fact, Luther (the only pre-twentieth-century figure to be included) is dealt with in the very first chapter, in an essay by the Reformation historian Carter Lindberg. I would like to set forth my own view of this matter in conversation with his.

Unlike the authors of most of the other chapters, Lindberg does not feel that an exposé, in the strict sense, of Luther's views is really necessary, since his anti-Jewishness is so well known. Rather, he reviews the diverse responses to Luther's views in subsequent generations. He divides these into three types: what he calls "denial by explanation"; "moral rejection"; and "theological efforts to overcome Luther by Luther."

One example of "denial by explanation" is the tendency to write off Luther's views as the product of ill health and old age. Over against this, Lindberg cites the judgment of the Luther scholar Mark Edwards that, in fact, Luther's "vulgarity and violence was by choice."[19] Lindberg seems more sympathetic to another common "explanation," the contention that Luther was no worse than others in his time. To me, however, the fact that a contemporary (and opponent) of Luther like Johannes Eck could also write viciously about Jews in no way excuses Luther. Not all were so cruel; Luther's colleague Philip Melanchthon, for example, was a conspicuous exception.

Lindberg is also somewhat sympathetic to another such denial by explanation: the contention that since Luther's antipathy toward the Jews was religious rather than racial in nature, his anti-Judaism cannot be compared to modern antisemitism. It would of course be an anachronism to apply the *term* "antisemitism" to Luther, since it was only invented in the nineteenth century. But neither can it be maintained that Luther's writings against the Jews are merely a set of cool, calm, and collected theological judgments. His writings are full of rage, and indeed hatred, against *an identifiable human group,* not just against a religious point of view; it is against that group that his action proposals are directed.

Luther cannot be distanced completely from modern antisemites. Regarding Luther's treatise *On the Jews and Their Lies,* Karl Jaspers was close to the mark when he exclaimed, *"Da steht das ganze Programm der Nazi Zeit schon"* ("There you already have the whole Nazi program").[20] I would qualify this only by saying: the Nazi program down to and including *Kristallnacht;* but not the decision for genocide. Luther warned, even in his severest recommendations, "You must not harm their persons."

In considering whether to include *On the Jews and Their Lies* together with several related treatises in the new translation, one thing that had to be recognized was that the worst parts were already in print, in the form of pamphlets published over the decades by anti-Jewish groups such as the Ku Klux Klan. So Luther's writings were already being used for nefarious purposes. To publish them now in a prestigious scholarly edition, however, would surely give them greater currency and, possibly, greater legitimacy. Nevertheless, the decision was made by the co-editors of the edition, Jaroslav Pelikan and Helmut Lehmann, that this must be done, for the sake of scholarly integrity and completeness; and they asked me to edit the volume. How to do this in such a way as to mitigate the possible effects of these hateful writings?

The answer was, first, in the introductory and explanatory material, to place these later writings in the total context of Luther's life, including his very different earlier treatise, *That Jesus Christ Was Born a Jew,* first published in 1523. It is ironic to reflect that if this were Luther's only extant treatise on the Jews, he would rank as one of the pioneers of Christian-Jewish dialogue. How potent is his evocation here of the family relationship between the Jews and Jesus. "We are but Gentiles, while the Jews are of the lineage of Christ," he writes. "We are aliens and in-laws; they are blood relatives, cousins, and brothers of our Lord."[21] He recommends that they be treated kindly:

> If we really want to help them, we must be guided in our dealings with them not by papal law but by the law of Christian love. We must receive them cordially, and permit them to trade and work with us, that they may have occasion and opportunity to associate with us, hear our Christian teaching, and witness our Christian life. If some of them should prove stiff-necked, what of it? After all, we ourselves are not all good Christians either.[22]

There has been much debate about why Luther's views changed so drastically between 1523 and 1543, and in my introduction to the treatise as eventually published in volume 47 of *Luther's Works,* I review some of the factors that evidently played a part. These included his anxiety about re-Judaizing tendencies among some Christians, such as the "Sabbatarians"; his unhappy encounters with certain rabbis; and above all, his disappointment at their refusal to convert, despite the new preaching of the Gospel, as he saw it, in all its winsomeness.

What dawned on me as I studied Luther's context and became more and more aware of the depth and pervasiveness of *Judenhass* (hatred of the Jews) in late medieval culture, was that what needs to be explained was not why Luther became anti-Jewish in his later years, but why he was so affirmative towards them earlier. How did he rise, at least temporarily, above the anti-Judaism of his culture? This question becomes all the more salient if we take into account the fact that, as scholarly research has demonstrated, practically the whole burden of Luther's later polemic against the Jews, at least in its theological dimensions, was already present in his earliest works dating from 1513–1516.

The picture is three-fold rather than two-fold. We have (a) an early Luther deeply immersed in the animus towards Jews and Judaism that had been characteristic of Christian preaching and teaching practically throughout its history, and that had been greatly exacerbated by economic tensions and other factors in the late Middle Ages. Then, (b) a middle Luther, who is lifted out of that medieval morass by the power of the Gospel or, otherwise stated, by the idealistic zeal of a reformatory movement, (c) only to fall back into it once again in his late writings.

If this is the case, then there is some hope of "overcoming Luther by Luther," as Carter Lindberg hopes, by appealing from his baser moments to his finer ones. What happened in Luther's thought is that he failed to follow his own "theology of the cross," and instead embraced what he had denounced as a "theology of glory" (but what might better be called a "theology of triumph") vis-à-vis the Jews. Contrary to his doctrine of the *deus absconditus,* he felt that history itself had vindicated the Gospel, and that the Jews' suffering was only what they deserved. This is the taint in Luther's greatness, the taint of Christian triumphalism.

Already in the Introduction to the volume as a whole, I cited the judgment of the great Luther scholar Roland H. Bainton, "One could wish that

Luther had died before ever this tract was written."[23] And I persuaded the publisher, Fortress Press, to come out from behind the veil of anonymity and join me in making a statement that would repudiate the treatise, as it were, in the very act of publishing it. Here is how it was put:

> The fact that Luther, during the last years of his life, wrote treatises harshly condemnatory of the Jews and Judaism is rather widely known. The treatises themselves, however, have not previously been available in English. The publication here of the longest and most infamous of them, *On the Jews and Their Lies*, will no doubt prove dismaying to many readers, not only because it shows Luther at his least attractive, but also because of the potential misuse of this material. The risk to Luther's reputation is gladly borne, since the exposure of a broader range of his writings to modern critical judgment is an inherent purpose of this American Edition. However, the thought of possible misuse of this material, to the detriment either of the Jewish people or of Jewish-Christian relations today, has occasioned great misgivings. Both editor and publisher, therefore, wish to make clear at the very outset that publication of this treatise is being undertaken only to make available the necessary documents for scholarly study of this aspect of Luther's thought, which has played so fateful a role in the development of anti-Semitism in Western culture. Such publication is in no way intended as an endorsement of the distorted views of Jewish faith and practice or the defamation of the Jewish people which this treatise contains.[24]

In the subsequent years, I have not heard of any specific misuse of the treatise as published in this edition. Fortunately, bigots are not usually scholars, and are unaccustomed to look on the dusty shelves of libraries for their material.

Let's fast-forward about twenty years, to the early 1990s. Tens of thousands of copies of *Luther's Works,* including volume 47, had been sold, but it is doubtful that many purchasers had penetrated very far into the set. Even most Lutheran clergy were unaware, or only vaguely aware, of the existence of this material. But toward the beginning of the 1990s, it began to become evident that even if Lutherans didn't know about these writings, other people did. For example, in 1992, a series of television programs on antisemitism, titled "The Longest Hatred," gained widespread attention. Produced by the BBC and shown on America public television, it featured Luther very prominently. At about that same time, the Harvard scholar Alan Dershowitz published a book in which he recounted his own experiences with antisemitism, and cited Luther as a chief source of such prejudice. Quoting Luther at length, he asked how contemporary Protestants could still honor as a hero a man who could write such things.[25]

In April 1993 the United States Holocaust Memorial Museum opened in Washington, D.C., and it soon became clear that it would have a major impact on the American consciousness, with visitors numbering in the millions. Toward the beginning of the exhibits, there is a small theater in which the visitor can pause to see a brief film on the history of antisemitism— a film in which, again, Martin Luther figures prominently. As his visage appears on the screen, some of the most hateful passages from his writings are read out, and demonic images of the Jews from woodcuts of the time are shown.

It was not long before Lutheran leaders began to realize that although our own members, and even our clergy, had been almost entirely unaware of this dimension of Luther's life and thought, Americans generally were very rapidly becoming aware of it. I am proud of the fact that we never protested against Luther being included in that film or asked that any part of the story be suppressed. How could we? The citations were completely accurate. Rather, we determined that we had to take decisive steps to dissociate ourselves, as contemporary Lutherans, from Luther's views. The statement that resulted, which I was privileged to have a hand in drafting, was titled "Declaration of the Evangelical Lutheran Church in America to the Jewish Community." Issued on April 18, 1994, it is just four paragraphs long, and I believe deserves citation here, representing as it does the culmination of several decades of concern on my own part with this matter:

> In the long history of Christianity there exists no more tragic development than the treatment accorded the Jewish people on the part of Christian believers. Very few Christian communities of faith were able to escape the contagion of anti-Judaism and its modern successor, anti-Semitism. Lutherans belonging to the Lutheran World Federation and the Evangelical Lutheran Church in America feel a special burden in this regard because of certain elements in the legacy of the reformer Martin Luther and the catastrophes, including the Holocaust of the twentieth century, suffered by Jews in places where the Lutheran churches were strongly represented.
>
> The Lutheran communion of faith is linked by name and heritage to the memory of Martin Luther, teacher and reformer. Honoring his name in

our own, we recall his bold stand for truth, his earthy and sublime words of wisdom, and above all his witness to God's saving Word. Luther proclaimed a gospel for people as we really are, bidding us to trust a grace sufficient to reach our deepest shames and address the most tragic truths.

In the spirit of that truth-telling, we who bear his name and heritage must with pain acknowledge also Luther's anti-Judaic diatribes and violent recommendations of his later writings against the Jews. As did many of Luther's own companions in the sixteenth century, we reject this violent invective, and yet more do we express our deep and abiding sorrow over its tragic effects on subsequent generations. In concert with the Lutheran World Federation, we particularly deplore the appropriation of Luther's words by modern anti-Semites for the teaching of hatred toward Judaism or toward the Jewish people in our day.

Grieving the complicity of our own tradition within this history of hatred, moreover, we express our urgent desire to live out our faith in Jesus Christ with love and respect for the Jewish people. We recognize in anti-Semitism a contradiction and an affront to the Gospel, a violation of our hope and calling, and we pledge this church to oppose the deadly working of such bigotry, both within our own circles and in the society around us. Finally, we pray for the continued blessing of the Blessed One upon the increasing cooperation and understanding between Lutheran Christians and the Jewish community.[26]

In 1998 the Evangelical Lutheran Church in America issued a further document, which I was also pleased to help author. Titled "Guidelines for Lutheran-Jewish Relations,"[27] it is designed to foster interfaith cooperation at the local level and the removal of any remaining aspects of prejudice toward Jews and Judaism from Lutheran preaching and teaching.

The third major step in this development came with the publication in 2002 of "Talking Points: Topics in Christian-Jewish Relations."[28] This is a set of eight leaflets dealing with basic theological questions arising out of the Christian-Jewish dialogue. Some of the issues, such as what to make of the biblical promise/fulfillment schema, are pertinent to Christians generally, while other topics, such as how the Jewish understanding of Torah relates to the traditional categories of "Law and Gospel," touch on matters that have been especially problematic for Lutherans. The hope is to foster a widespread discussion throughout the Church that could lead to a possible formal statement on these issues.

These, then, are some aspects of my involvement with Jews and Judaism over the years, and some of the reactions and reconsiderations it has called for on my own part. There are so many other persons who could be mentioned, other themes that could be explored, and other authors cited. The agenda remains open, and the task goes on.[29]

Notes

[1] Abraham Joshua Heschel, *Man Is Not Alone: A Philosophy of Religion* (New York: Farrar, Straus and Young, 1951).

[2] Ibid., 3. Heschel wrote before the rise of the concern for inclusive language. In a later time, he would no doubt have expressed himself differently, perhaps writing here: "which command *our* attention" and "Power *we* exploit," etc. The book itself might have been titled *We Are Not Alone* or *Humanity Is Not Alone.*

[3] Franklin Sherman, "Abraham Joshua Heschel: Spokesman for Jewish Faith," *Lutheran World: Publication of the Lutheran World Federation* (October 1963) 400–08.

[4] Franklin Sherman, *The Promise of Heschel* (Philadelphia and New York: J.B. Lippincott, 1970).

[5] Abraham Joshua Heschel, *The Prophets* (New York: Harper & Row, and Philadelphia, The Jewish Publication Society of America, 1962) 212.

[6] Abraham Joshua Heschel, *The Earth Is the Lord's: The Inner World of the Jew in East Europe* (New York: Henry Schuman, 1950).

[7] Ibid., 21.

[8] Abraham Joshua Heschel, *The Sabbath: Its Meaning for Modern Man* (New York: Farrar, Straus and Young, 1951).

[9] Ibid., 19.

[10] Ibid., 20.

[11] Perelmuter later wrote a book dwelling on this theme: Hayim Goren Perelmuter, *Siblings: Rabbinic Judaism and Early Christianity at Their Beginnings* (New York: Paulist Press, 1989).

[12] The most useful guide to these matters has been, for me, Aryeh Rubinstein, ed., *Hasidism* (Jerusalem: Keter, 1975).

[13] Franz Rosenzweig, *The Star of Redemption,* trans. William W. Hallo (New York: Holt, Rinehart and Winston, 1971); originally published in 1921, this is a translation of the 2nd German ed. of *Stern der Erlösung,* 1930.

[14] Nahum N. Glatzer, *Franz Rosenzweig: His Life and Thought* (New York: Schocken Books, 1953; rev. ed. 1961) x.

[15] Ibid., 341.

[16] Ibid., 347.

[17] Ibid. For the whole correspondence, see Eugen Rosenstock-Huessy, ed., *Judaism Despite Christianity: The "Letters on Christianity and Judaism" between Eugen Rosenstock-Huessy and Franz Rosenzweig* (Tuscaloosa, Ala.: University of Alabama Press, 1969). The volume contains an epilogue written some sixty years later by Rosenstock-Huessy, who meanwhile had become an American university professor.

[18] Nancy A. Harrowitz, ed., *Tainted Greatness: Antisemitism and Cultural Heroes* (Philadelphia: Temple University Press, 1994).

[19] Mark U. Edwards, Jr., *Luther's Last Battles: Politics and Polemics 1531–46* (Ithaca: Cornell University, 1986) 19.

[20] Cited by Carter Lindberg, "Tainted Greatness: Luther's Attitudes toward Judaism and Their Historical Reception," *Tainted Greatness,* ed. Harrowitz, 30.

[21] Martin Luther, *Luther's Works,* American Edition, vol. 45 (Philadelphia: Fortress Press, 1962) 201.

[22] Ibid., 229.

[23] Roland H. Bainton, *Here I Stand: A Biography of Martin Luther* (New York: Abingdon, 1950) 379.

[24] *Luther's Works,* vol. 47 (Philadelphia: Fortress Press, 1971) 123.

[25] Alan M. Dershowitz, *Chutzpah* (New York: Touchstone, 1992).

[26] *www.elca.org/ea/interfaith/jewish/declaration.html.*

[27] *www.elca.org/ea/interfaith/jewish/guidelines.html.*

[28] *www.elca.org/ea/interfaith/jewish/talkingpoints.html.*

[29] For other aspects of my work on related themes, see the following articles: "Speaking of God after Auschwitz," *Speaking of God Today: Jews and Lutherans in Conversation,* eds. Paul D. Opsahl and Marc H. Tanenbaum (Philadelphia: Fortress Press, 1974) 144–59; "Messianism, Mysticism, and the Mitzvot: Some Reflections on Jewish Ethics in Relation to Christian Ethics," *American Society of Christian Ethics: Selected Papers from the 20th Annual Meeting, 1979,* 167–77; "The Search for the Jewish Jesus," *Reconciliation: Essays in Honour of Michael Hurley,* ed. Oliver Rafferty, S.J. (Dublin: Columba, 1993) 201–14; "Is the Passion Play Anti-Jewish?" *The Lutheran* (June 2000) 23–25; "Oberammergau 2000," *The Christian Century* (August 16–23, 2000) 822–23.

five

NORMAN A. BECK

Replacing Barriers with Bridges

My Parochial Beginnings

During the first forty-two years of my life, I lived in a sheltered, parochial, exclusively Christian world. I had no relationships with Jews, or with Muslims, Hindus, or Buddhists. There were no Jews in the rural and small town northwestern Ohio area where I grew up, nor any in my elementary or high school. Some of you who are reading this may have come from backgrounds that are similar to my own. Although many American communities are becoming increasingly pluralistic, perhaps some of you also have lived most or all of your lives with no personal friendships with Jews, or with people in other religions.

I was born during the depths of the Depression, the year the banks failed and the price of hogs and grain was so low that the total income of my parents, who both worked full-time on the eighty-acre farm that belonged to my mother's parents, was $400. I was in elementary school during World War II. I read *The Toledo Blade* each day after school, especially the reports of the war, the comics, and the sports pages. We heard stories about the atrocities committed by the Japanese. Some members of our congregation and others in our county were in the National Guard Tank Corps of the 37th Division of the U.S. Army that was forced to surrender in the Philippines and to endure the Bataan death march.

Because of Pearl Harbor and the Japanese, we were also at war against Germany. For our nation to be fighting against Germany for the second time within a few decades caused mixed feelings in my home congregation. We were Americans, of course, but almost everyone in the congregation was of German background and knew that their distant cousins were in that country and probably in the German military. During World War II and for nearly two decades after it, we heard and read almost nothing about the Holocaust. If we did, it was of no more than passing interest to us. During the first few years after the end of World War II, we helped a few families of "displaced persons" from Germany settle in our town, but only because they were Lutheran Christians, who to our disappointment in most instances were not particularly interested in active participation in the life of our congregation.

While farming with my parents for three years after my graduation from high school and becoming increasingly active in Luther League activities on the local congregational, conference, and district level, and teaching a seventh-grade Sunday School class, I felt increasingly called to the Lutheran Christian ministry. As a student at Capital University and in our seminary in Columbus, now Trinity Lutheran Seminary, I was aware that there were Jews living in North Bexley near the campus and that there was a Jewish Community Center in the area. There was virtually nothing about Jews as such in the curriculum of that time, however, and, for me, among my most important new experiences in an extra-curricular way were occasional visits to Presbyterian, Methodist, Baptist, and Congregationalist churches in Columbus on Sunday mornings, something that I could not have done in my home town.

The one memorable exception to the paucity of interest in Jewish subjects in my environment during those years was Ron Hals' Yiddish jokes at the beginning of his Old Testament Studies seminary classes. As the first non-Jew to earn a Ph.D. at the Hebrew Union College—Jewish Institute of Religion in Cincinnati, he had picked up on many Jewish tales, and being a master storyteller, he shared them with us. That was a positive, though indirect, exposure to Jewish life for me. My Danish Lutheran heritage wife, Esther, for now more than forty years has also brought to my life a positive attitude with regard to Jews and Jewish tradition. For Esther, the word "Jew" has always been a noun, whereas in my own German and German-Swiss family tradition it had been a verb.

One might expect that during my four years of earning a Ph.D. in biblical studies at Princeton Theological Seminary in the mid-1960s, I would have been exposed in a positive way to Jewish life and to Jewish interpretations of Scripture, especially the Old Testament. In that Calvinist environment at that time, I recall a much-heralded visit of the elderly Karl Barth and a variety of visiting professors and guest speakers from many segments of Christianity, but no rabbis or other Jewish scholars, nor interest in Jewish perspectives.

During my eight and one-half years as a parish pastor in southern Michigan, at the height of the Civil Rights Movement, it was thrilling for me to work for the first time with Roman Catholics on social justice issues, but I had no involvement with Jews, even on such issues. A small Episcopal parish a few blocks away began to share its worship and study facilities with a small Reform Jewish congregation. That seemed to me to be a wise and practical arrangement, and gracious of the Episcopalians.

My Entry Into Christian-Jewish Dialogue

My first direct relationships with Jews began in 1975 as I was beginning my teaching responsibilities in biblical theology and classical languages at Texas Lutheran University. I was interested in developing a specialty for research and publication. After participating in a Jewish-Lutheran Concerns Consultation co-sponsored by the American Lutheran Church and the Anti-Defamation League at Luther Seminary in St. Paul, Minnesota, in fall 1975, I was invited to prepare a paper on anti-Jewish material in the New Testament for presentation and discussion at the next meeting of the same group in Madison, Wisconsin, the following year. In addition to searching through the secondary literature on this subject, I read the New Testament itself again, specifically looking for anti-Jewish material. Although I had read the entire Bible while I was a seventh and eighth grader being prepared for confirmation, and again while I was a student at Capital University, I had read it with no particular interest in Jews or in how they were portrayed in the New Testament. The Bible was the story of salvation through Jesus Christ our Lord. The Israelites were the earlier people of God, but the Jews, who according to the New Testament story did not accept Jesus as the Christ, were minor characters in that story. I wonder now how I depicted Jews in the sermons I provided during those years. I suspect that I said very little about them.

Now, however, with the new assignment in mind, and having met Rabbi Solomon S. Bernards, who was at that time the director of

Jewish/Christian Relations for the Anti-Defamation League of B'nai B'rith, and other Jews, I read the New Testament with my new Jewish friends in mind. The condemnation of the Jews in 1 Thessalonians 2:14-16, as the people who had killed both the Lord Jesus and the prophets and upon whom at last the wrath of God has come, demanded my attention. I wondered why this text was so blatantly a contradiction of the concern for the Jews that Paul expressed in Romans 9–11 and his conclusion that "all Israel will be saved." I wondered why the Pharisees, whom I had learned from listening to presentations by Sol Bernards and others at the previous Jewish-Lutheran Concerns Consultation were the Jews whose efforts, far more than those of any other group, had produced the Jewish religion that has evolved over the centuries, should be castigated so viciously in the Synoptic Gospels, especially in Matthew. I wondered why "the Jews" should be depicted as having the devil as their father in John 8:44. I wondered why in the major speeches of Peter and of Stephen in the Acts of the Apostles the Jews are addressed with the accusatory language, "You crucified Jesus!" I shared my amazement over these texts at the consultation in Madison.

During the discussion that followed my presentation of these and other texts, Dr. Fredrik A. Schiotz, who at that time had recently retired from the top leadership position of the American Lutheran Church, stated that he had read and used the New Testament his entire life and had not realized that such hateful texts were included in it. He was speaking, actually, for most of us who were the Lutheran pastors and church leaders at the consultation. One of the most insightful Lutheran participants at the consultation was Trudy Rogness Jensen, who was among the key Lutheran leaders whose efforts made these Jewish-Lutheran consultations possible. Trudy and Sol Bernards urged me to continue my work on the texts and to develop it into a book, which I eventually produced as *Mature Christianity: The Recognition and Repudiation of the Anti-Jewish Polemic of the New Testament* in 1985, and as an expanded and revised edition, *Mature Christianity in the 21st Century* in 1994.[1]

Further Opportunities to Participate in Productive Christian-Jewish Dialogue

Five days of active involvement in the Institute on Judaism at Vanderbilt University in June 1977 served as a "crash course" on Jewish life and thought for me. Rabbi Sol Bernards, whom I mentioned above, provided for about a dozen of us the excellent interactions with Jewish scholars that we had not experienced in our parochial, exclusively Christian world. This was followed for me by the development of a most meaningful friendship with Rabbi Samuel M. Stahl, the now-retired senior rabbi of Temple Beth-El in San Antonio, who has been our guest lecturer in the annual Jewish Chautauqua Society Lectures at Texas Lutheran University each fall term for the past quarter century. Also, during the spring term of most of those years, I have had the opportunity to interact in positive ways with the rabbis who have taught a course on Jewish life and thought in our department of theology and philosophy curriculum. And three times each year during the past quarter century I have taken large groups of Texas Lutheran University students to the Friday evening *Shabbat* services at Temple Beth-El.

During my participation in the Tenth National Workshop on Christian-Jewish Relations in Minneapolis in November 1987, I met key leaders among the group of Christians and Jews who had planned the Ninth National Workshop held in Baltimore two years earlier and had expanded their efforts by forming the Institute for Christian and Jewish Studies (ICJS). With them I was able to participate in the Maryland Interfaith Israel Study Project in spring 1989, highlights of which were study and discussion sessions at the Shalom Hartman Institute in Jerusalem with Rabbi David Hartman.

My understanding of Jewish life and Jewish interpretations of our shared Scriptures has been expanded through my involvement in several ICJS projects and through my membership for fourteen years now in the Christian Scholars Group on Christian-Jewish Relations. Finally, one of my most significant experiences was the opportunity to team-teach with Rabbi Stahl a five-day course which we titled "Bridges and Barriers in the Jewish-Christian Encounter" at the Chautauqua Institution in New York State in summer 1998.

The two principal barriers that I discussed with more than one thousand participants were (1) the supersessionist and defamatory anti-Jewish polemics of the New Testament and (2) the way in which the Christ concept has been used within our Christian tradition. Later in this chapter I shall say more about these barriers and suggest ways in which we can replace them with bridges that Christians and Jews can cross whenever we wish to learn from each other, increase our respect for each other, and work together to repair the world. First, however, I shall share briefly with you something of what I have learned about how Christians use the scriptures we share with Jews and a few things I have learned about Jewish interpretations of those same scriptures.

Christian Approaches to Scriptures We Share with Jews

My understanding of what some of us now call "our shared Scriptures," what we as Christians know as the Old Testament, has been greatly enhanced by my active participation in Christian-Jewish dialogue. What Jews call "the Hebrew Bible" or "the Tanakh"—a word formed by connecting the consonants of the first letter of the Hebrew words *Torah, Nevi'im* (Prophets), and *Ketuvim* (Writings) with the "a" vowel—is basically what we as Christians call "the Old Testament" (but might also call the "older" or "earlier" Testament). Since the Old Testament is so much larger than the New Testament (or might also call the "newer" or "later" Testament), approximately 77 percent of our Bible is Sacred Scripture also for Jews.

We Christians, however, have a few more Jewish documents in our Old Testament than appear in the Hebrew Bible and we arrange the documents of the Israelite-Jewish Scriptures into a sequence that differs from the Jewish sequence. I began to realize, more importantly, that Jews and Christians *use* and *interpret* these Scriptures quite differently. For Jews, the Torah (Genesis, Exodus, Leviticus, Numbers, and Deuteronomy) is the most precious, basic, and heavily studied and used of all the Scriptures. For Christians, our New Testament is the most precious, basic, heavily studied and used. For Christians, the first five documents (the Torah) are not the most precious documents in the Hebrew Bible. The favorite documents in our Old Testament for most Christians are Genesis and the first half of Exodus from the Torah, Isaiah from the Prophets, and Psalms from the Writings. I began to understand that we interpret the Old Testament with and from a Christian perspective, as preparation for the New, as background for the coming of Jesus as the Christ, as a prediction of that coming—all vastly different from the Jewish perspective.

The Torah, the Prophets, and the Psalms were Sacred Scripture for the earliest Christians. During the middle decades of the second century of the common era, specifically Christian documents, most notably the seven basic letters of Paul (that are largely interpretations of the Old Testament) and the Gospel According to Luke (that utilizes the literary style of the earlier narrative portions of the Old Testament) replaced the Old Testament as Sacred Scripture for many Christians. When the Old Testament was "brought back" as Sacred Scripture for Christians later in the second century, it was brought back in a level of importance and usage secondary to the developing New Testament canon. The manner in which texts from the Old Testament are selected in the three-year lectionary that we use, as "promises" fulfilled in the Gospel selections, or as complements to the Gospel selections, amply illustrates our continuing use of Old Testament texts as of secondary importance.

As a result of my participation in productive interreligious dialogue with Jews, I became much more aware that the Jewish use and interpretation of the Scriptures we have in common with them is much different from our Christian use. We define ourselves as Christians primarily in terms of what we believe and only secondarily in terms of how we live. Jews define themselves primarily in terms of how they live and secondarily in terms of what they believe. Consequently, for Jews, all 613 commandments included in the Torah are items of great importance and subjects of continuing and intense discussion and reflection. Therefore, second in importance, following the Torah itself, are the extensive, voluminous Talmudic collections of rabbinic literature, with the remainder of the Hebrew Bible, the Prophets and the Writings, third and fourth in importance. Most of us as Christians, however, are not aware that there are 613 commandments in the Torah, and we consider only ten of the 613 to be significant for us—and we often refer to them as *our* Ten Commandments!

For Christians, the prophetic traditions foretell the birth of the Christ in Bethlehem, his entry into Jerusalem, and his role as the "Suffering Servant." For Jews, the people of Israel are the "Suffering Servant" of the LORD. Far more important for Jews than for Christians, however, is the text of Zechariah 14:9 that expresses the hope that on the great day of the LORD, a day that is obviously still in the future, "the LORD will become king over all the earth; . . . the LORD will be one, and his name one."

Jewish Interpretations of Scripture

My understanding of Jewish methods of interpreting Sacred Scripture has also been greatly enhanced through participation in Christian-Jewish dialogue—and this has proven beneficial to me in my own approach to Scripture. I have learned that Jewish interpretations of Scripture are characterized principally by three methods: (1) the juristic, (2) the midrashic, and (3) the mystical.

The juristic method was developed and refined by the rabbis who lived during the first six centuries of the common era. The "Oral Torah" that they developed and eventually put into written form in the Talmud provided detailed discussions of the 613 commandments and of other portions of the Torah. These teachers, many of them Pharisees, were well aware that the commandments of the Torah were, for the most part, designed to be civil and moral guidelines for Israel as a nation, as a free and independent nation, even though the times when Israel had been free and independent as a nation were brief. These rabbis knew that at the time of the Babylonian captivity centuries earlier the emphasis had shifted to individual accountability to God, to individual judgments and responsibilities. They developed detailed schools of interpretation, the best known being the schools of Hillel and Shammai.

Each Jew was, in a sense, expected to be the "jury" of one member, deciding from a school of interpretation how to live in response to God. It was not a matter of "Do whatever you wish!" The choices were to be made from within the parameters, the range of options suggested by the learned rabbis. When that choice had been made by an individual Jew, that person was expected to live in accordance with those commandments as interpreted by the rabbis. Self-judgment and judgment by God was to be on the basis of that interpretation. There was to be no judgment of others. Although the self-judgment was continuous, provisions were made for an annual period of *teshuvah* (self-examination, repentance, and restitution to the persons whom one had harmed during that year), culminating in the annual Day of Atonement *(Yom Kippur)*. This tried and tested method of interpretation continues to be used effectively within the Jewish tradition today, updated and complemented by the *responsa,* answers to questions on Jewish law and observances given by scholars on topics addressed to them.

The midrashic method (from *midrash:* interpretation through story) is older than the juristic, although components of the juristic method obviously were also used in the Israelite tradition prior to its development by the Pharisees and later rabbis. In the midrashic method, one interprets a commandment or develops specific concepts by telling a story. The story-teller and the hearers become intimately involved in the story, and, by means of their involvement in the story, they interpret the commandment, respond to specific concepts, and make applications in their own lives. The rabbis were famous for telling stories to interpret Scripture. They realized, of course, as we also now realize, that many, if not most, of the biblical stories are midrashic. Nathan's parable told to King David, the story of Ruth, the story of Jonah, the story of Adam and Eve, the flood story, and the call stories of Moses, Isaiah, Jeremiah, Ezekiel, to cite merely a few examples, are midrashic. As in the juristic method, the *midrashim* (plural for *midrash*) are intended to result in self-judgment, not in the judgment or condemnation of other people.

The mystical method may be the oldest method of all. Used both individually and communally, it characteristically takes a multiplicity of forms. The goal to attain mystical union with God, other people, and nature may be sought within the full range of human experience, from silently listening for God to speak, to actively, even playfully applying numerical values to Hebrew consonants in a search for new messages and interpretations. I have learned that the mystical interpretive method has been employed in some instances in the context of the intense suffering caused by illness, misfortune, or persecution. One's emotions, as well as one's intellect and will, are engaged, resulting in certain instances in what might be called holy joy and ecstasy. Like the other two methods, the mystical is intended to result in self-judgment, not in the judgment of other people.

I find all three of these Jewish methods of interpretation admirable and I recommend that we Christians develop our counterparts to them. For example, it is clear that we have a Christian counterpart to the midrashic method of Jewish interpreters. Truth be told, many of the stories in our New Testament are as midrashic as those in the Hebrew Bible. The parables and many other stories in the Gospel According to Luke and in the Acts of the Apostles were recorded by the early Christian writer who most explicitly followed the method of the midrashic accounts in the Hebrew Bible. All four of our canonical Gospels, of course, use this midrashic method extensively. Our story sermons are contemporary examples of the popularity and effectiveness of this interpretative technique—a technique that is so preferable to the polemical method of interpretation to which we now turn.

The First Major Barrier:
The Christian Teaching of Contempt for Jews

As mentioned earlier, the first of the two major barriers between Christians and Jews is the supersessionist and defamatory anti-Jewish polemic of the New Testament. This is radically different from the three methods of interpretation described above. Unlike those methods promoting self-judgment, the supersessionist and defamatory anti-Jewish polemic stands in judgment of others—in this instance, in judgment of some or all Jews. In this section I examine the structure of this first major barrier and explore reasons why it was constructed by early Christians.[2]

I must point out that although there is anti-Jewish polemic throughout the New Testament, most of it is not supersessionist and defamatory, but rather *christological.* The christological polemic is founded on the claim that Jesus is the Messiah (the Christ) of Jewish expectations and the Word of God made flesh. It is anti-Jewish inasmuch as it suggests that the Jews have been wrong to reject Jesus as the Christ and as God's incarnate Word. This christological polemic becomes defamatory and supersessionist when it also involves the claim that, in rejecting Jesus as the Christ and as God incarnate, the Jews have rejected God and have been replaced in God's favor by Christians. But the christological claim can be made, and at times has been made, without defamatory and supersessionist charges. Somewhat similar to the way Jews understand God through Torah, early Christians began to understand God through Jesus as Lord, and this has been normative for Christians ever since. This christological essence of Christianity should be expressed by each generation of Christians in new and dynamic ways, but should never be repudiated.

We must, however, repudiate the supersessionist and defamatory anti-Jewish polemic of the New Testament that has contributed so much to the suffering of Jews, especially during the Christian Crusades, the Christian Inquisition, and the Holocaust. The supersessionist polemic is expressed in the claim that the "new covenant" in Christ "has made the first one obsolete" (Heb 8:13), giving rise to the long-standing teachings that Christians have replaced Jews as "the people of God" and Christianity has replaced Judaism as the one true religion. The defamatory anti-Jewish polemic goes even further. It is expressed in accusatory language that charges the Jews with killing Christ (Acts 2:36; 4:10; 7:52; 1 Thess 2:14-15) and being children of the devil! (John 8:44), and that claims "the wrath of God has come upon them at last!" (1 Thess 2:16). These and other defamatory anti-Jewish texts constitute what the Jewish historian Jules Isaac labeled "the Christian teaching of contempt for Jews."[3]

Why would some early Christians whose writings became the inspired "Word of God" for us in the New Testament have expressed such contempt for Jews? After many years of reading and reflecting about this question, I have attempted an answer by identifying seven interrelated factors.

The first and most basic factor was human perversity—yielding to the evil impulse. Even inspired people sometimes do this. If we can choose to follow the evil impulse, we can choose also to reject it and to follow the good. Today we are being inspired to recognize and repudiate the supersessionist and defamatory anti-Jewish polemic in the New Testament.

The second factor is the arrogance of those who think that they alone have possession of the "truth" and access to God. This position is most prevalent in the portions of our New Testament in which there is the most defamatory anti-Jewish polemic: the Gospels of Matthew and John and the Acts of the Apostles. Fortunately, this is not a position taken by most of the writers of the New Testament. Unfortunately, it became and has remained the position of many Christians throughout history. Due to increased exposure to religious diversity and interfaith dialogue today, this exclusivist position is increasingly being seen as untenable.

The third factor was the frustrations of exclusivist Christians because of their inability to convert Jews to their own Christian beliefs and practices and this remained a factor throughout Christian history. But during the past half-century a growing number of Christians have begun to realize that Jews have a viable and valid religious tradition and do not need to convert to Christianity in order to be close to God.

The fourth factor, closely related to the third, was the jealousy among Christian leaders caused by the mature ethical monotheism of the Jewish people, by the tenacity of Jews in maintaining their traditions even when subjected to persecution, and by the consequent fear that Christians may want to become Jews. But a Christianity that overcomes its exclusivism while being similar to yet distinct from the Jewish religion is not one that Christian leaders will have to fear will be less attractive to Christians than the Jewish faith.

The fifth factor was the failure of exclusivist Christians to understand that both Jews and Christians perceive God in similar (though not identical) ways: as transcendent, as active in human history, and as pervasive in all aspects of life. As more Jews and Christians share their perceptions of God with each other, this excuse for the Christian teaching of contempt is evaporating.

The sixth factor was the attempt to protect Christian lives during the persecution of Christians by zealous advocates of Roman civil religion. Already within the four Gospels and with much literary skill in the Acts of the Apostles, Christian writers attempted to exonerate Pontius Pilate and other Romans of guilt for the crucifixion of Jesus and to place the blame for Jesus' death on "the Jews." What is most repugnant about this scapegoating of Jews is that Christian lives were considered valuable, while Jewish lives were deemed expendable. This dehumanization process, together with the distortion of history, may have reduced Roman oppression of Christians during the reign of Domitian and during the second and third centuries, but at a horrific long-term cost![4] I am confident that Christians will increasingly understand and accept this and, therefore, that Christian antisemitism will continue to decrease in the coming years.

The seventh factor was the immaturity of some early Christians whose writings were later included within the New Testament. These writings were produced during the adolescence of the Christian movement. Some of the New Testament documents clearly reflect the adolescent tendency to look with contempt upon one's parents. If we had documents from the childhood stage of the Christian movement we would likely find a more loving relationship with the parental Jewish tradition. I am confident that as we Christians mature through open and honest interfaith contacts with Jews, we will find the adult strength to repudiate the supersessionist and defamatory teachings formulated in our tradition's adolescence.

The Second Major Barrier:
The Exclusivist Christ Concept

At the outset of the previous section I noted that most of the anti-Jewish polemic of the New Testament is not supersessionist and defamatory, but rather christological. I suggested that the christological polemic can be made without being accompanied by contempt for Jews, but I also acknowledged that the christological polemic can become supersessionist and defamatory. In fact, this has too often been the case, and that is why I identify the exclusivist use of the Christ concept as the second major barrier erected by Christians between themselves and Jews.

The Christian Christ concept is, of course, an appropriation of the Jewish concept of the Messiah, which throughout Jewish history has been a dynamic and complex concept, bound up with the idea of a "messianic age." Simply put, the Jewish expectation is that when the Messiah comes, suffering, sin, and death will be overcome and there will be peace on earth. In fact, the concept of the messianic age is more important to many Jews than the concept of the Messiah. For them, referring to the coming of the Messiah is a way of speaking about hope for a world transformed into the reign of God.

Unfortunately, in appropriating the concept of the Messiah, Christians have taken a broadly conceived Jewish concept and narrowed it into an exclusivist Christian concept used to accuse and condemn Jews. How often we have heard the judgmental question, "Why can't you Jews accept Christ?" We have failed to listen to the Jewish response: "We believe that the coming of the Messiah will be marked by peace on earth." Most Jews have been too considerate, or, in light of the suffering inflicted upon Jews in the name of Jesus, too reluctant to respond, "Why can't you Christians continue to accept Adonai as the one and only LORD?"

We have work to do on our Christ concept during this twenty-first century, and our constructive interreligious dialogue with Jews will help us as we do this. Besides being untenable for an increasing number of Christians, an *exclusivist* Christ concept is a major barrier between Christians and Jews. But a *Christ concept* as such need not be a barrier to fruitful Christian-Jewish relations. In fact, I am convinced that we Christians can formulate a Christ concept that, while being distinctively Christian, may serve as a bridge of understanding and respect between Christians and Jews.

Replacing Barriers with Bridges

Let us begin by considering the supersessionist and defamatory anti-Jewish polemic. The first step that we must take before we can remove this barrier is to recognize that it exists. As indicated above, I lived two-thirds of my life before I became aware of this barrier. It is likely that many of you also have not been aware of it, and that when you are made aware, it is very painful and traumatic. The Bible is holy, "the inspired Word of God" for us, "the authoritative source and norm" of our "proclamation, faith, and life," a most important means by which the grace of God comes to us. How can there be anything in it that is harmful?

When we hear about harmful elements in the Bible, we feel a deep sense of grief. Something very precious has been taken from us. Our defensive emotions spring up quickly: denial that this exists and anger against the messenger who brought this news to us. "No, there is nothing like this in 'my' Bible!" This period of denial may continue, understandably, for some time. It may take many forms. One form is to insist that the problem, if it exists, is not in the Bible itself, but in the interpretation of it. Maybe this material was inserted into the Bible during the process of making translations of it. We look again at the biblical texts. It is, in fact, there. We learn that the defamatory polemic is just as prevalent in the earliest hand-written copies of the Greek manuscripts available to us as it is in those made centuries later. There is no discernible increase or decrease in the defamatory anti-Jewish polemic throughout the long period of handwritten transmission of the texts.

We look at the intentions. Perhaps it was not intended to be anti-Jewish when it was first written. Maybe it had its origin in what many scholars today call a Jewish "family feud." These scholars point to the vast diversity within Jewish life and practice of the period in which the documents that later became our New Testament were written. They suggest that the early Christians were still Jews at that time. They say that Jews like to "argue" among themselves, and that which some consider to be anti-Jewish is actually intra-Jewish. This view has become widespread in the scholarly community.

Nevertheless, the "family feud" explanation is actually a form of denial, a carefully-constructed scholarly form of denial. Yes, there was much diversity within Jewish life and practice of that time, and there was much tolerance of diversity in that culture. Because of the juristic method of interpretation used by the Pharisees, it is true that Jews articulated a variety of ways in which Torah texts could be understood. Indeed, the earliest followers of Jesus were Jewish. The Messiah concepts were varied, and many Jews at that time did put their faith and trust in Jewish Messiah figures. And yes, the transition from being Jewish to becoming Christian was a gradual process for the early followers of Jesus.

We must ask, however, whether a Jew would say "Jesus and the Father are one" (John 10:30); "Jesus is the way, and the truth, and the life [and] no one comes to the Father except through" Jesus (John 14:6); "There is salvation in no one else, for there is no other name under heaven given among mortals by which we must be saved" (Acts 4:12); "Go, therefore, and make disciples of all nations, baptizing them in the name of the Father, and of the Son, and of the Holy Spirit" (Matt 28:20), etc. If the charge that "the Jews" killed Christ (Acts 2:36; 4:10; 7:52; 1 Thess 2:14-15) and the statement that the Jews are "children of the devil" (John 8:44) are evidence of a "family feud," why are the documents that include these statements in our Scriptures but not in rabbinic writings? Scholarly denial is still denial. If we deny that we have a problem, we shall never be able to do anything about it. Even worse, the Jewish "family feud" explanation unwittingly becomes a rationalization that blames the victim, the Jews, for a problem that Christians have caused.

If we recognize that the supersessionist and defamatory anti-Jewish elements in the New Testament are a problem, what are we called to do in response? I suggest three actions, and all three are being taken by an increasing number of sensitive and mature Christians.

The first action, the least intrusive of the three, is to avoid using the most hateful elements in the New Testament for private devotion and public worship. In terms of public worship, this means careful selection of texts and revision of our lectionaries. The three-year lectionary that the Roman Catholic Church commissioned during Vatican II (1962–1965), and that Lutherans have been using with some variations for the past three decades, avoids the texts in the New Testament in which women are relegated to an inferior status and denied leadership roles in the Church. Unfortunately, it does not avoid the supersessionist and defamatory anti-Jewish texts.

Among the most blatant of these texts in the lectionary are those that we read from Sunday through Friday of Holy Week and some from the Acts of the Apostles that we read in place of Old Testament texts during the Easter cycle. Even a three-year lectionary includes only a small percentage of the Bible. There are plenty of inspiring texts that we can use in community worship. We need a revision of the lectionary that does not use the supersessionist and defamatory texts. Perhaps we should adopt a new lectionary, possibly a four-year lectionary in which there is a year of readings from Mark and a year of readings from John and not the mixture of the two that we have now, and in which there is not use of the super-sessionist and defamatory texts. I have written a four-year lectionary that has these characteristics. It is included as an appendix in my recently published *The New Testament: A New Translation and Redaction.*[5]

The second action that we must take involves the education and sensitizing of all Christians regarding this problem. It is a mammoth task, to educate and to sensitize nearly two billion Christians in hundreds of languages and dialects, especially when the majority of Christians do not want to hear that there are hateful and harmful elements in our Bible. It is an educational task that will take decades, perhaps centuries, to accomplish. It begins in colleges and universities, especially in our church-sponsored institutions. Our cherished Lutheran tradition began in a small German university. The most significant educational work regarding anti-Jewish polemic in the New Testament has begun in colleges and universities of the Evangelical Lutheran Church in America. It is a task to which I have dedicated much of my life.

The third action that we must take is to produce and use translations of the New Testament that in a variety of ways repudiate the teaching of contempt for Jews. The revisions of the *Good News Bible* and the publication of the *Contemporary English Version* are important steps already taken in that direction. If we do not want our children and grandchildren to look with disgust at our Christian tradition because of the hateful and harmful elements in it, we must take further steps in our repudiation of those elements in our foundational texts. In my own translation of the New Testament I place the most problematic texts—both the viciously anti-Jewish and the blatantly sexist—into small-type print. I include prefaces and explanatory footnotes to explain the reasons for this.

While this demoting of some biblical texts may seem radical to some people, the truth is that in practice we Christians have stood in judgment over our scriptural traditions throughout history. The early Church boldly reinterpreted sections of the Hebrew Scriptures to meet its needs, pressing them into service as messianic prophecies and typologies of Jesus' life. Allegorical interpretations were commonly employed. Moreover, large portions of the Hebrew Bible were ignored in practice; for example, the requirements of circumcision and dietary regulations were dropped at an early date. Even segments of the New Testament have been largely ignored in practice by most Christians; for example, the suggestion to remain unmarried (1 Corinthians 7) and the stipulations concerning hairstyles and head coverings (1 Cor 11:4-16; 1 Tim 2:9; Acts 18:18). In our own time there are attempts to repudiate some New Testament perspectives on the role of women in the Church.

To be sure, acknowledging the significant authority of scriptural traditions is imperative in order that there may be proper accountability within the Christian community. But imputing ultimate authority to them is idolatrous. We are accountable to God to be responsible for our own scriptural traditions. A relationship of mutual authority is desirable: we must acknowledge that our Scriptures have significant authority over us and that we have significant authority over them as well. A basic presupposition of my work has been and remains the conviction that it is idolatrous to suppose that any entity except God is ultimate, inerrant, or infallible, and since in practice we are responsible for our own scriptural traditions and have stood in judgment over them throughout our history, *we can carefully and deliberately repudiate portions of our scriptural traditions that have proved to be deleterious to persons either within or outside of the Christian community.*[6]

The above-mentioned actions are being taken to dismantle the first of the two major barriers that stand between Christians and Jews and, in its place, to build a bridge of interfaith dialogue and respect. In addressing how to replace the second major barrier that stands between Christians and Jews, the Christ concept, it is important to note that although the *exclusivist* Christ concept is problematic, it is possible to imagine a Christ concept that actually facilitates fruitful Christian-Jewish relations instead of impeding them. What would be some of the characteristics of such a Christ concept?

First, a Christ concept that would constitute a bridge between Christians and Jews would go back to the Jesus of history, the Jesus who lived and died as a faithful Jew. We would have to reject the docetic view that is so pervasive in the Christian tradition, the view that Jesus just seemed to be human, a view that does not take the Jesus of history seriously—and thus does not take seriously his Jewishness. Of all Christians today, perhaps we who are Lutheran are in the best position to take the humanness of Jesus seriously, because of our Pauline belief that it was when God raised Jesus from the dead that Jesus became the Christ, the Son of God, our Savior. Then, having taken the humanness of Jesus seriously, we can begin to reconstruct a Christ concept on that base. One of the ways in which I have taken the Jesus of history seriously is to write a movie script, "Jesus, the Man," which I am using in my classes at Texas Lutheran University and sharing with others. Only when we take the Jesus of history seriously can we begin to construct a credible Christ concept and one that might serve as a bridge for interfaith dialogue with Jews.

Second, a Christ concept that would constitute such a bridge would be one whereby we acclaim Jesus as Christ because, through him, we who are not Jews have been brought to the God of Jewish faith and now share the Jewish hope in the fulfillment of God's reign on earth. Relationships and dialogue with Jews are improved and Christianity becomes more credible when emphasis in Christian theology is placed upon Jesus as anticipating the fulfillment of the messianic age rather than having already fulfilled it. Instead of undermining Christian faith, this emphasis makes clear why we express hope in "the Second Coming of Christ."

Third, a Christ concept that would constitute a bridge would recognize that God is, has been, and will continue to be active in history in a multiplicity of ways and in a multiplicity of people. As Christians, our Christ concept must be accompanied by the acknowledgment of the multiplicity of God's actions. Our Christ concept should not rule out of order God's actions among the ancient Israelites and among Jews and other peoples. Relationships with Jews and others are enhanced and Christianity becomes more credible when we Christians acknowledge that, although the way to God through Jesus as the Christ of Christian faith may be the only way to God for us from our standpoint, ultimately God cannot be limited nor access to God restricted by any of us. As Christians, we have access to God by clinging to Jesus' coattails, or I should say clinging to Jesus' cross, but there has been access to God also in other times and in other cultures. A mature Christianity in the twenty-first century can recognize this without repudiating its own christological essence—that Jesus is for us the Word of God incarnate, the one through whom we have come to know God, and therefore he is our Christ. That other people know God apart from his name does not diminish our faith in Christ, and our acknowledgment that others know God will be an important part of the bridge that we help to build.[7]

Some of this bridge building we must do by ourselves. Some of it we must do together with others, in productive interreligious dialogue in which we appreciate and seek to understand them and give them our respect. It is this bridge building that will strengthen Christianity during the twenty-first century, as it will help to answer questions that have troubled Christians for centuries. It is this bridge building that will make our Christianity much more attractive to those who are not Christians as well as to those who are. This bridge building will be good for us as Christians and will be good for Jews, as we continue to relate to one another, under God.

Notes

[1] Norman A. Beck, *Mature Christianity: The Recognition and Repudiation of the Anti-Jewish Polemic in the New Testament* (Selinsgrove, Pa.: Susquehanna University Press, 1985); *Mature Christianity in the 21st Century: The Recognition and Repudiation of the Anti-Jewish Polemic in the New Testament,* rev. ed. (New York: Crossroad, and Philadelphia: The American Interfaith Institute/World Alliance, 1994).

[2] This analysis of the structure of and reasons for the anti-Jewish polemic in the New Testament is an adaptation of *Mature Christianity in the 21st Century,* 321–28.

[3] Jules Isaac, *The Teaching of Contempt: The Christian Roots of Anti-Semitism* (New York: Holt, Rinehart & Winston, 1964).

[4] For more about this, see Norman A. Beck, *Anti-Roman Cryptograms in the New Testament: Symbolic Messages of Hope and Liberation* (New York: Peter Lang, 1997).

[5] Norman A. Beck, *The New Testament: A New Translation and Redaction* (Lima, Ohio: Fairway Press, 2001).

[6] The argument in the last two paragraphs is an adaptation of *Mature Christianity in the 21st Century,* 70–72.

[7] Parts of the last two paragraphs are drawn from *Mature Christianity in the 21st Century,* 322.

CLARK M. WILLIAMSON

Blessed *Chutzpah*, Blessed Questions, Blessed *Chaverim*

The story that I am asked to tell about my interfaith involvement with Jews and Judaism and its effect on my understanding and practice of Christian faith is one that I tell with some hesitation. I am not prone to talk about myself when thinking theologically, having grown up in and been shaped by a Church that treasured telling "the story of Jesus and his love." That is the story that I have been trying for a long time to learn how to tell and to tell faithfully. My involvement with Jews and Judaism long ago convinced me that for the most part we Christians have great difficulty telling the story of Jesus appropriately. How I came to this understanding and what the steps have been in my changing view of how to tell it is what follows.

Early Influences

This account must begin with the congregation in which I grew up as a child and from which I received my early formation in Christian faith. I was born in 1935 in Memphis, Tennessee; the congregation was Hollywood Christian Church, a Disciples of Christ church. The most important influences on my life there were my grandfather (who was also the pastor, the Rev. J. Murray Taylor whom I called Pops), Mrs. Martin, our childhood Sunday School teacher who taught us to read and love the stories of the Bible (I was particularly taken by the dramatic stories of biblical Israel), and such Sunday school teachers and elders as Mr. Mayo, who taught us to think seriously about matters of life and ethics in relation to our faith.

My grandfather was a liberal evangelical, by which I mean that his understanding and articulation of the Christian faith were ruled by three principles. First, the Gospel, the "evangel," was central and spoke of God's all-embracing love disclosed in Jesus Christ (but not only in Jesus Christ, for he found this same good news throughout the Scriptures). Second, no one was beyond God's reach or outside the realm of Christian moral obligation. Third, faith required commitment to the social gospel, the understanding that the transformation that God seeks and that faith represents (when it is real and not sham) is not limited to individuals but extends as well to all the arrangements that people make for how they shall live together. According to the third principle the structures of society, government, economics, and law, to name some, all result from human decisions. If and when they are unjust, human beings are responsible for changing them.

Hence, my grandfather was an evangelical, although it can be misleading to say that since the word has been purloined to refer to those who affirm scriptural inerrancy. He did not affirm scriptural inerrancy for two reasons. One was the centrality of the gospel, which governs our conversations with Scripture. The second was the "liberal" part of his makeup. He thought that we should bring to the study of Scripture all the critical tools that liberal scholarship could devise. Both of these reasons he had picked up and with many others of his generation developed further from the Disciples of Christ tradition.

In the American South of the 1940s and 1950s, the time when I was growing up in the Church and in frequent contact with my grandfather, there were several critical social-economic arrangements that were badly in need of being changed, of which racial segregation was the most obvious. At this time when African-Americans and Caucasian-Americans were rigorously separated from each other, African-Americans would be invited to preach in our congregation. Reform rabbis as well visited our congregation on occasion and spoke in our services of worship. During World War II when propaganda signs depicted Japanese as inhuman figures with blood dripping from their fangs, the narthex of our congregation featured a picture of Kagawa, the Japanese Christian highly regarded for his service to the poor, and a poster of Jesus Christ as the Prince of Peace. This silent witness contradicted the message posted on lampposts along the street.

In short, I grew up a liberal who was taught to think, to trust in the loving grace of God disclosed in Jesus Christ, to question the social arrangements of the time, to promote peace instead of war, to be open to African-Americans and Jews and work against segregation (I later went on my first civil rights-era sit-in in 1960 in Lexington, Kentucky). Never did I have a crisis of faith for intellectual reasons. Only when I discovered the persistence of anti-Judaism in the Church's history did I face such a crisis. I still face that crisis, although now I call it the dialectical tension between trust and radical questioning. I trust that this is acceptable to God.

College and Graduate Studies

In undergraduate school at Transylvania University, I majored in philosophy and benefited greatly from the kind, questioning mind of Professor B. F. Lewis.[1] We read and discussed the major works of important philosophers and theologians from the Greeks to Tillich, Whitehead and Wittgenstein. Religion courses were oriented to historical-critical modes of inquiry. All this was in the larger context of a strong liberal arts education in many fields and was solid preparation for the University of Chicago Divinity School where after my professional education for the ministry I took the Ph.D. in theology. My professors included Paul Tillich, Bernard Meland, Bernard Loomer, Joe Sittler, Jaroslav Pelikan and Coert Rylaarsdam. Of them, Rylaarsdam directly addressed issues of Jewish-Christian relations.[2] What I learned from him, mainly, was that the "Old Testament" is a Jewish book and that if we cannot read it as Jews read it, we cannot understand it. I put quotation marks around "Old Testament" because in the anti-Jewish tradition of the Church, "old" has a pejorative connotation. It means "displaced, cancelled, no longer valid."[3] The Letter to the Hebrews uses the term precisely in that way: "In speaking of a 'new covenant,' he has made the first one obsolete. And what is obsolete and growing old will soon disappear" (Heb 8:13). The "Old Testament" first got its name from Marcion and others who wanted to get rid of it. Attempts to find an alternative name, including my own, are less than successful.[4] "Hebrew Bible" is not accurate for two reasons: not all of it, in the Roman Catholic canon, is in Hebrew and the order of the books is not that of the *Tanakh*, the Jewish Scriptures. Lately I have settled for referring to it as "the Scriptures," a term that has the advantage that it itself is scriptural; it is what the Scriptures call themselves.

This is a digression, but one cannot mention Rylaarsdam without being tossed into a discussion of matters pertaining to Jewish-Christian relations. Yet even at the end of my Ph.D. program at the Divinity School, I had not tumbled to the fact that the anti-Jewish, supersessionist tradition of the Church is a problem.[5] When I try to understand why I had not tumbled to an awareness of the problem, what took me so long, I come up with only a few answers. First, I never encountered anti-Judaism (in these years) in any way that was obvious, offensive, or blatant. Since then, I came to realize that anti-Judaism is most effective when it is not blatant. Second, whenever it was mentioned (as by Rylaarsdam), it was for the purpose of criticizing and rejecting it. Third, theologians like Tillich argued that each religion, when it is authentic, points to its own ultimate unimportance in pointing beyond itself to what is genuinely ultimate, as Tillich would put it, or to the One who alone is ultimate, as I would prefer to put it.[6] I wrote my Ph.D. dissertation on the theology of Ernst Troeltsch (1865–1923) and the problem posed for any effort at theological affirmation by the recognition of the thoroughgoing historicity of all our thinking. The question for Troeltsch became whether it was possible to make any affirmations of ultimacy whatsoever, given the fact that claims to absoluteness on the part of various religions were just so many relative claims.[7] Troeltsch's work radically undercut any attempt to make the claim that one religion (always "ours") displaces another in God's providence and favor.

Another reason why I did not encounter anti-Judaism as a problem no doubt lies in the fact that most of the theologians by whom I was intrigued in those days were theologians of the ontological-existential type of theology. This would include Paul Tillich and Schubert Ogden. In later life, re-reading Ogden's early work again, particularly his *Christ Without Myth,* I noticed that not only was it completely free of supersessionism, but that it implicitly denied the very possibility of it. Ogden's program of consistent demythologizing and his claim that the possibility for human existence presented to us in Christ is new in the sense of being the decisive re-presentation of a possibility previously re-presented cuts the ground out from under any supersessionist claim.[8] But Ogden does not make this point explicit in relation to supersessionism. Only later did I notice its principled absence from his theology. Consequently, with all this theological education, with four degrees in hand, and having taught at Christian Theological Seminary for six years, I still did not "get it."

A Life-changing Semester in Switzerland

Then, everything changed. In 1972–1973 I was invited to be a visiting faculty member at the Graduate School of the World Council of Churches' Ecumenical Institute at the Château de Bossey, Switzerland. The school annually gathers an ecumenical student body from around the world for an intense immersion in theological education. The theme for the semester was "dialogue on salvation among persons of living faiths and ideologies." There were weekly seminars on dialogue between Christians and Buddhists, Christians and Jews, Christians and Marxists, Christians and Hindus, and so forth. Nikos Nissiotis, a Greek Orthodox theologian, directed the Graduate School. Professor Bitika Mukerji of Benares University and I were the visiting faculty members; she directed the seminar in Hindu-Christian dialogue and I the one in Marxist-Christian dialogue. Alain Blancy chaired the seminar on Jewish-Christian relations. Jewish scholars who participated in that seminar—Uriel Tal and Marc Tanenbaum—came in from Israel and the United States. The whole faculty and student body met regularly in plenary sessions in which the presentations for each seminar and all lectures took place. This approach to theological education created a community of conversation—or yelling—at the same time that it provided opportunity to explore one topic more deeply.

It was here at the heart of Protestant ecumenism and in the Ecumenical Institute that I awakened to the problem of Christian anti-Judaism, the history of the teaching and practice of contempt for Jews and Judaism.[9] It happened like this. First, various Christian proponents of "dialogue" visited Bossey to lecture at the Graduate School. Often the smugness of their assumptions about the superiority of Christianity was almost unbearable. Sitting next to Professor Mukerji, one could feel her pain as stories of the conversion of the dialogue partner were told. To many ecumenical Christians, dialogue and mission were in tension if not utter conflict. How can one converse as an equal with those whom one is inviting to convert to a superior way? This was a general problem, one that affected every aspect of the discussion of the Graduate School's theme for that semester.

Second, the work of the Jewish-Christian seminar landed in the Graduate School in the context of the Middle East conflict, which seemed as intractable then as it seems now. Passions ran high, especially and understandably among some Arab and third-world Christians who readily identified with those whom they saw as "oppressed." Yet often this concern was itself expressed in rhetoric derived from the Christian teaching of contempt for Jews and Judaism. The fact that such contempt entered into these conversations between Christians and Jews astounded me. While I quite agreed that all nation-states are ambiguous and criticizable (to think otherwise is idolatrous), the view expressed by some at that seminar that, theologically, Jews ought not to have a state was a different matter. Also, the idea that salvation is somehow limited to those within the Church seemed to be accepted by far too many people. Most remarkably, Christian relations with Hindus and Buddhists, for example, could be discussed calmly (if nonetheless smugly), while relations between Christians and Jews brought out stronger reactions and counter-reactions.

The views and attitudes that I found appalling and astonishing were by no means expressed by all members of the Bossey community, many of whom were as depressed by such views as I was. Nonetheless, they were and are shocking. I should add that although my experience at Bossey was upsetting (to put it mildly), even so Bossey provided a transformative involvement in theological education, as it has continued to do for many people across the decades.

A Paradigm Shift

All the time this was going on, I still knew nothing about the Christian tradition of the teaching and practice of contempt for Jews and Judaism to which I have referred several times in these pages. I was ignorant of the history of the Church in relation to the people Israel. Shortly after I returned to Indianapolis, I expressed my distress and confusion to two good rabbinical friends—the late Sidney Steiman (may his name be remembered) and Murray Saltzman. They responded helpfully and handed me some books to read. Most of these were by Roy Eckardt, like *Your People, My People* and *Elder and Younger Brothers.* Also Rosemary Ruether's *Faith and Fratricide* shortly became available.[10] Within a year, Rabbi Steiman and I began team-teaching a course on dialogue between Jews and Christians, a course that I have continued to team-teach with Rabbis Saltzman, Jonathan Stein, and Dennis Sasso ever since. They are "my" rabbis, and experiencing the warmth and intelligence in evidence at their synagogues, the Indianapolis Hebrew Congregation and Congregation Beth-El Zedeck, has greatly enriched my understanding of Judaism and my life. Students regularly report that this is the most transformative course they have ever taken.

Reading these and other books that Rabbis Steiman and Saltzman suggested was theologically (as well as emotionally and psychologically) wrenching. Almost immediately my theology, by which I mean simply my understanding of the Christian faith, underwent a paradigm shift. My theological work had previously concentrated mostly, but not exclusively, on the question of the intelligibility or credibility of theology. My published papers had in their titles the names of Tillich, Hegel, Whitehead, Fichte, and Marx and responded to questions raised by controversies such as the "death of God" debate. My focus was largely on matters of philosophical theology. Now, my theological work began moving more in the direction of doctrinal and ethical concerns.

New Realizations

This happened because several points now stood out in my mind with considerable clarity, particularly as I continued to dig around in the history of the Church.

First, anti-Judaism is an ideology (a distortion of truth in the interest of power) that controls Christian thinking unless and until we become conscious and clear about it and reject it. I now made it a goal to try to liberate Christian theology from its inherited ideology, particularly its anti-Jewish ideology. Much later I would become familiar with and affirm Christopher Morse's contention that authentic Christian theology must be a theology of "disbelief." Morse quotes Tolstoy's reflections at the time in Russia when "in the name of Christian love Russians were killing their brothers." Said Tolstoy: "I have no doubt that there is truth in the doctrine; but there can be no doubt that it harbors a lie; and I must find the truth and the lie so I can tell them apart."[11] The truth of what Christians want to affirm only becomes clear when we know what that truth requires us to reject. Post-*Shoah* theologians, not unlike feminist, womanist, and liberation theologians of various stripes, say "No" because they "have experienced an intolerable contradiction between the life to which the gospel calls them and what they see in specific instances being done in the name of Christianity."[12]

Second, anti-Judaism is precisely such a lie. It is not merely an unfortunate mistake. Karl Barth was on the mark in claiming that lying is "the specifically Christian form of sin."[13] We can only lie if we know the truth. The truth of the Gospel, that God graciously justifies the ungodly, cannot be true for some of us unless it is true for all of us. Hence, Christians and Jews face one another standing on the ground, and only on the ground, of God's gracious and unmerited love. Doctrines identifying Jews as the displaced people and Christians as the replacement people are, therefore, not simply mistakes. They are lies.

Third, anti-Judaism is not found in Church history only in the explicitly anti-Jewish tracts of presbyters, bishops, and the Reformers. (Often titled *Adversus Judaeos,* it is fair to call such documents "anti-Jewish." That, after all, is what their authors often called them.) Nor is it just one theme that can be picked up from time to time and, just as readily, dropped. Rather, it is found in writings having to do with God, Christ, the Church, the sacraments, eschatology, in short, all over the place. Two things began to come clear to me in those years: one was the structure and character of anti-Judaism itself, as a Christian ideology, and the second was the fact that anti-Judaism is not simply an occasional theme of Christian writers but, instead, a systematic way of interpreting and distorting every Christian teaching.

Fourth, anti-Judaism is the claim that the Church replaces the people Israel in the covenant with and favor of God. It may, or may not, appear in concert with negative and pejorative language about Jews or in connection with the language of vilification. The absence of nasty language does not mean that a document is not anti-Jewish. That it is supersessionist is enough. Supersessionism implies that Jews should no longer exist *as Jews,* and this implication became explicit in Christian history. The Letter to the Hebrews is supersessionist, but free of more overtly "anti-Jewish" language. Nonetheless, it is deeply anti-Jewish in its claim that the original covenant between God and the Jewish people has been canceled. In its simplest form, anti-Judaism plays out on two themes—the displacement/replacement theme and the superior/inferior religion theme.[14]

The displacement/replacement theme holds that Jews lost their place in the covenant with God because they said "no" to Jesus Christ. We Christians gained their lost place because we said "yes" to Jesus Christ. We who once sat in darkness have seen the light, whereas they who had all the advantages of sitting in the light refused to see the light when it appeared among them and, in consequence, now are in the dark. The outsiders became insiders and evicted the previous residents of God's house. As Jews had always "killed the prophets," so they killed Jesus; they whose history was a "trail of crimes" added calamitously to it by committing the greatest crime of all, deicide, literally "killing God."

Melito of Sardis was the earliest to issue the deicide charge, having done so in the second century. He talks about Israel and the Church as the old and the new, respectively, and regards the old as the shadowy type of which the Church is the new, clear reality. When the new arrives, it replaces the type that preceded it. Here is Melito in his own words:

> But when the church arose,
>   and the gospel was shed abroad,
> the type was rendered useless,
>   yielding its power to the reality;
> and the law came to its end,
>   yielding its power to the gospel.
> Just as a pattern is left empty
>   when its image is surrendered to reality,
> and a parable is made useless
>   when its interpretation is made known,
> so also the law was finished
>   when the gospel was revealed,
> and the people was abandoned,
>   when the church was established,
> and the type was abolished
>   when the Lord had appeared.[15]

Melito spells out what is now worthless: Jewish teaching, worship, ethics, biblical interpretation, the Scriptures of Israel, the synagogue, rabbis, the works. Yet the main focus of his sermon is on the suffering of Jesus, in which Melito clearly states the charge of deicide:

> He who hung the earth was hung;
> He who affixed the heavens was affixed;
> He who sustained all was suspended on the tree;
> the master has been outraged;
> God has been murdered;
> the king of Israel slain by an Israelite hand.[16]

The displacement/replacement theme stresses Israel's fault and the Church's innocence. It is a form of works-righteousness: we earn a place in God's favor by doing the good work of believing in Jesus Christ while Jews lose that same place by failing to do this same good work. Strikingly, in this first theme we already see systematic theological ideas taking shape. For example, the Church is now talked about as the "replacement" people—this is how Melito encourages his listeners in Sardis to understand themselves. Most importantly, the Church is us. We benefit from the Jews' loss. Mustn't we conclude, then, that according to this theological perspective, God is the kind of God whose promises of covenant faithfulness cannot be trusted, the Scriptures are the backing and warrant for an ideological claim, and Jesus becomes the kind of mediator who cuts a displacement deal with God—the very kind of deal that Moses refused to cut after the sin of the golden calf (Exod 32:30-32). Moses is the superior mediator of the two, the one whom I would want making my case with God.

The other theme of the Church's anti-Jewish ideology is the superior/inferior religion theme. According to this theme, we Christians are the new, universal, spiritual people of God, "Israel according to the spirit," who are everything good that the old, carnal, ethnocentric, particular Israel, "Israel according to the flesh," can never be. Ours is the religion of faith, grace, love, and spirituality. Theirs is the religion of works, legalism, dour fulfilling of duties, and works-righteous drudgery. Ours is the religion of the spirit, theirs of the letter. We know the truth that we are justified by grace; their religion epitomizes the sin of self-justification. Indeed Jews and Judaism in their stubbornness typify nothing so much as sin.[17] It is always fair game to criticize people in any religious community for any or all of the sins of which Jews and Judaism are here accused. What is not fair game, and this characterizes Christian anti-Judaism, is to assume that such traits as self-righteousness, legalism, literalism, and dour works-righteousness on the one hand and attitudes of grace, warmth, love, faith, and spirituality on the other are ways to distinguish one religion from another. Those of us who grew up in the Church have our hands full with all the narrow-mindedness, literalism, works-righteousness, and legalism that we can handle. We do not need to be pointed to Jews and Judaism to see such things.

Fifth, all this is not just "theory," if anything is ever "just" theory. It is what Christian leaders have taught their congregations, and teaching is a practice. How we talk is probably our most important behavioral question. Language cannot be separated from the people who use it. Anti-Judaism is first and foremost a way of forming Christian identity, of telling Christians who they are; it forms communal social identity. We Christians, it says, are other-than-Jewish, not-Jewish, and better-than-Jewish. It is also a way of talking about how we ought to do things. How should we do things? Not as Jews do them. We should not read the Bible, pray, eat, worship, act morally in ways in which Jews do. We do all of these in better, more "spiritual" ways.

This process of identity formation and behavioral advice has gone on unnoticed (for the most part) in Christian preaching and teaching until today. Much of the rhetoric of anti-Judaism is no longer what Christians are aware of as they talk and think about matters of faith and life. Rather, it is often the way we think and talk, the lens through which we perceive who we are and what we ought to do. Sadly, this lens distorts rather than corrects our sense of who we are and who Jews are, not to mention who God and Christ are.

The repetition of this anti-Jewish perspective in Christian teaching and preaching has had a profound effect on Christian language, and on our minds and psyches. We relegate Jews to several roles in Christian rhetoric: they are allowed to disappear as if they had vanished from history and become *invisible;* they are the *scapegoats* who are, for example, responsible for the crucifixion of Jesus; they are the *negative counterexamples* of what the life of faith essentially is and ought to be.[18] The numerous negative roles played by identifiably Jewish groups in the gospels exemplify particularly this last function. The gospels contain no "parable of the good Jew." The endless repetition of this outlook from pulpit and lectern has resulted in the fact that, as Pamela Payne puts it, anti-Judaism is the default position of the Christian mind.[19]

Anti-Judaism has been a practice in two other senses: it has been used to shape actual relations between Christians and Jews, and it has been used to define the role and place of Jews in every aspect of the social, cultural, economic, and political life of Christian societies. For example, a council of Spanish bishops meeting in the town of Elvira early in the fourth century, about 304–305, passed four canons (church rules/laws) governing relations between Christians and Jews. These laws forbade (a) marriage between daughters of Christians and Jewish men, (b) landholders from having their crops blessed by Jews, (c) Christians from eating with Jews, and (d) Christian men from committing adultery with Jewish (and pagan) women.[20] Church councils would continue publishing and re-publishing laws governing relations between Jews and Christians well into the Middle Ages. Some such laws sought to ban Christians from eating Passover meals with Jews, from entering synagogues, from participating in Jewish feasts, from patronizing Jewish doctors, from living in Jewish homes. Conversely church laws also banned Jews from appearing in public during Holy Week, from conversing with nuns, from being judges or tax collectors, from working on Sunday, from holding public office, from owning slaves, from building new synagogues, and from obtaining academic degrees.[21] Notably, the Fourth Lateran Council in 1215 (an ecumenical council of the Church) required all Jews in Christendom to wear distinctive dress.

Two points are worth noting about all this legislative practice. First, every one of Hitler's Aryan laws concerning Jews took its precedent from a canon law passed by a council of bishops. The law requiring Jews to wear the Star of David, for example, took the 1215 decision of the Fourth Lateran Council as its precedent. Laws to "protect German blood and honor" or to ban Jews from dining cars on trains found their precedents at Elvira. Second, if laws are passed to stop behavior regarded as unacceptable, then this spate of lawmaking argues that Jewish and Christian laypeople were getting along with one another quite well. They were eating together, celebrating together, sleeping together, marrying, conversing, and so forth. The leadership of the Church found this unacceptable and sought to stop it. It saw separating the two communities from each other as in its interest. Ecumenism is incompatible with authoritarianism. Insistence on this separation clearly follows lines of power and authority in the Church.[22]

We see the other aspect of Christian legislative practice in the numerous laws passed by the state (first the Roman Empire and later the medieval states) at the behest of the Church. The Christian state functioned as the secular arm of the Church. Emperor Constantine in 315 made it a capital crime for a Jew to bring back to the faith another Jew who had been converted to Christianity; he also made it a crime for a Jew to convert a Christian to Judaism. His son Constantius in 339 made intermarriage between a Jewish man and a Christian woman a capital crime. Constantius also made it illegal for Jews to own Christian slaves, but not for Christians to own any kind of slaves they pleased. The purpose was partly to prevent conversions of slaves and partly to subject Jews to economic disadvantages. Jews were later barred from holding any office in the government, or any position in the economy or military that would put them over a Christian. Most ways of earning a living were closed to Jews, who increasingly became relegated to dealing in old clothes, to making minor repairs, and to money-lending (barred to Christians by church laws against lending money at interest). Eventually, Jews would be forced by papal decree or state law to live in ghettoes. The ghettoes in France were not ended until the French Revolution in 1791.

New Approaches to Theology

How have these new realizations about anti-Judaism in Christian history and theology affected my understanding and practice of Christian faith? As I have wrestled over the years with the question of how to do Christian theology, I have come or been led to the following new emphases, each of which is as much a matter of the life of faith as of theology. I will discuss them as briefly as possible.

First, these new realizations make me *tell the story of the Christian teaching and practice of contempt for Jews and Judaism.* I have done that in this paper. The story is the context that gives post-*Shoah* theology its pertinence. So I do not launch into post-*Shoah* theology in class without first acquainting students with the Church's anti-Judaism. This history remains largely unknown to Christian people. It is not safe to make any assumptions in this regard. My first book on Jewish-Christian relations was essentially an attempt to do nothing more than tell the story of the interaction of Christians and Jews with an admitted emphasis on the Church's teaching and practice of contempt.[23] I wrote it because I learned from lecturing on several college and seminary campuses that we need to continue to tell this story.

My second new approach is that *I practice a hermeneutic of suspicion or an ideology critique on the Christian tradition and on the Scriptures.* Feminist, womanist, and African-American theologians do the same. My more basic instinct is to trust and appreciate Scripture and tradition as the only final grounds of our faith (I do not know how to ground faith in anything other, in the last analysis, than the ongoing creative, transformative, and self-critical process known as tra-ditio, "passing on" from one generation to the next). The point is not to erode the proper authority of Scripture and tradition by suspicion. Rather, the point is to put Scripture and tradition into the service of life and well-being. It is simply the act of questioning. As Johann-Baptist Metz put it: "Ask yourselves if the theology you are learning is such that it could remain unchanged before and after Auschwitz. If this is the case, be on your guard."[24]

My third new emphasis is to *teach respect for Jews and Judaism*. It is not possible to replace something with nothing. We cannot simply quit making negative comments about Jews or supersessionist remarks about Judaism. That would be to subject Jews and Judaism to benign neglect. Instead, we should replace the teaching of contempt with the teaching of respect for Jews and Judaism.[25] This means taking the time and effort to understand and appreciate Jews and Judaism and making these matters clear to congregations and theological students. It is a question of learning to appreciate and value difference, of being excited by it rather than threatened. It means learning to love strangers as we are, after all, commanded to do: "You shall love the alien as yourself, for you were aliens in the land of Egypt" (Lev 20:34).

The fourth difference in my theology is to *make clear that all forms of oppression, to which we can refer as systemic evils or structural sins, are interlinked.*[26] For example, the Gnostics, the most extreme representatives of anti-Judaism in the early centuries of Church history, spurned this world of God's good creation, the human body, women, the Torah of Israel, and the God of Israel who created this world. For them, salvation was to be found in the rejection of the created world, Israel, and Israel's God. Also, only the elite, those who were assumed to be by nature spiritual, could be saved. The more material human beings, especially the lower classes and women, could not be saved. "What contemporary ideology criticism has uncovered," says Sandra Schneiders, "is the intrinsic connection among all forms of systemic domination."[27] What this means practically is that we cannot play off the concern for the liberation of one group of people from oppression against a similar concern for another group. The good news of the Gospel requires us to reject any attempt to say that because we are committed to the liberation of African-Americans, for example, we cannot then be concerned with the liberation of the environment from the travail into which we have placed it. Nor, with regard to the conflict in the Middle East, can we pit our concern for the well being of Israelis against that of the well-being of Palestinians and vice-versa. An impoverished African-American single mother living in the ghetto of the urban under-class does not suffer only from racism. She also suffers from sexism, including sexism in the African-American community, and classism, the unequal distribution of goods and services, as well as environmental racism. Jewish women are oppressed both by sexism and anti-Judaism and, ironically, sometimes by the anti-Judaism of Christian feminist theologians.[28] Christian theology is called to make clear its rejection of all systemic evils—to say an unmistakable "no" to racism, sexism, classism, militarism, terracide (the assault on the environment), as well as anti-Judaism. We cannot coherently oppose one form of systemic evil while condoning the rest.

The fifth change is that *I have become convinced that we need to find more adequate ways to tell the Christian story.* The typical way of telling this story focuses on redemption. God created the world and placed Adam and Eve in the garden, they sinned and fell, and Jesus came (admittedly somewhat later) to redeem them and the rest of us who, in some mysterious fashion are trapped in the dilemma brought about by the sin of the first human beings. The proviso on this story, usually, is that whereas the consequences of Adam's sin are universally given to all of us, the benefits of Christ's redeeming work are available only to those who do the good work of believing in him and affixing themselves to the Church that can then broker this mercy to us. It is paradoxical in the extreme that, in this version, Adam seems more influential than Christ. This way of telling the story not only relegates the history of the Israel of God with the God of Israel to irrelevance, but it supports what R. Kendall Soulen calls a "Gnosticism of history," according to which God's redeeming action in Jesus Christ liberates Jesus' followers from the history of the God of Israel with the Israel of God. Without so much as breathing a word about it, the typical way of telling the story "fosters and supports a triumphalist posture toward the Jewish people." As a result, theology loses its biblical orientation and the need to engage "the hard edges of human history."[29] Equally worth noting is the fact that we can tell this story by using from Scripture only the first three chapters of Genesis and one of Paul's letters.

My across-the-hall conversation partner since 1968, Gerry Janzen, long ago helped me to see, as he put it in his commentary on Genesis, that "the divinely intended governing principle is the power of blessing." Genesis 1 and 2 display the world and people "as a place of blessing and fruitfulness" and describe a garden "as a picture of the total blessedness of creation." Indeed, the entire biblical story, beginning with Abraham and Sarah, "is a journey in blessing from a single person to all the families of the earth." Blessing is well-being, and "Abraham and his descendants are called to serve the well-being of all human communities, by becoming the kind of community they would all like to become (cf. Deut 4:5-8)."[30] On this reading, the purpose of God's redemptive activity, of God's acting salvifically in history, "is to counteract the workings of evil in the world and to restore the world to its divinely intended blessedness."[31]

Blessing is well-being, "inclusive well-being" as Marjorie Suchocki puts it, and it now becomes the norm for what human life essentially is and ought to be and the standard against which sin is assessed; sin is whatever is opposed to well-being.[32] The modifier "inclusive" points out that well-being cannot be for me and not you, for us and not them, for some at the expense of others. Relational thinkers (of whom I have been one for longer than I have been a post-*Shoah* theologian) hold that all things are related to all other things, that God is the One who interacts with all others (we cannot think of another who does that), that our moral, spiritual, psychological, emotional, intellectual and physical being finds its basis and nurture in interdependence. Children are nourished by smiles and hugs as well as by food, clothing and shelter; and all children should have all of these. Well-being is *shalom,* peace, justice, economic sufficiency for all, homelessness for none; "steadfast love and faithfulness will meet; righteousness and peace will kiss each other" (Ps 85:10).

What has this to do with the people Israel and the Church, and with our relationship to each other? This "more basic story," as both Janzen and Soulen refer to it, holds that blessing, well-being, is offered to us in our relationships of mutuality with and difference from one another. It was offered to Adam and Eve in their relationship of difference from and mutuality with one another; it was offered to them in their relationship of mutuality with and difference from "all the living things." It was offered to Abraham and Sarah in their relationship of mutuality with and difference from one another; it was offered to them and all their descendants in their relationship with and difference from "all the families of the earth," all the Gentiles. It is offered to us in our relationship of mutuality with and difference from the people Israel, the Israel of God. Notice: blessing is offered to the Church in its relationship of mutuality with and difference from the Jewish people. Difference is not to be annihilated, swamped, or overwhelmed,

but valued and appreciated. The Church cannot be faithful to the God of
Israel if it is not a friend of the Israel of God.

This is not a sentimentality, another version of mainline blandness.
The point that genuine well-being is available on the condition and only
on the condition that it be received in relationships of difference and mutuality is a point with bite to it. As soon as we think of any particular
issue, that this point has bite becomes clear. Race relations in the United
States will finally be dealt with when both black people and white people
can deal with each other in relationships of mutuality and difference. Peace
will come to the Middle East when and only when both Palestinians and
Israelis can affirm each other's justified demand for well-being in relationships of mutuality and respected difference.

Sixth, *Christian theology must become hospitable to Judaism, must
welcome it as a friend and coworker in the theological enterprise.* Since we
cannot understand Christianity except in relation to Jews and Judaism
(pre-*Shoah* theology is a huge example of how not to do this), we should
do our theological thinking now in conversation with Jews. In *Pirke Aboth
(The Sayings of the Sages),* Joshua ben Perahyah says: "Provide thyself
with a teacher and get thee a fellow-disciple [student]."[33] Jewish feminist
theologian Rachel Adler argues that a distinctively Jewish kind of intimacy, the study-companion relationship, that of the *chaverim,* developed
from this beginning.[34] *Chaverim* are friends who experience each other as
wholes, not as fragmented beings and certainly not as caricatures and
stereotypes. *Chaverim* study together by *questioning* each other. They question lovingly and they love questions. The root of *chaver* means to join together at the boundaries. Boundaries are essential to the identity and
integrity of a person, an entity, or a faith-tradition. Boundaries keep us
from "dribbling out into everything else." Being "joined together at the
boundaries," as Adler suggests the *chaverim* are, is a wonderful model for
relations between Jews and Christians and between Jewish and Christian
theologians. God's gracious love is far too abundant to be kept within any
boundaries. God's love frees us to transcend boundaries without destroying them, as *chaverim* love each other without destroying each other's distinctiveness.

Doing theology with Jews as *chaverim* opens us to seeing ourselves
through their eyes. Theology is supposed to be critical and self-critical
thinking about matters of ultimate importance. Nothing can move Chris-

tians to make this actual, however, more than doing their thinking with Jews. For example, reading the New Testament with a knowledgeable Jewish friend can be a rivetingly transformative experience. Seeing ourselves as others see us, which is what self-transcendence is all about, is easier if we will actually listen to those others. Openness to questions from our friends, indeed regarding friendly questions and questioning friends as blessed, as the way in which God loosens us up to a self-transcending openness to the future, is a blessing.

"Different models of faith," as Darrell Fasching rightly points out, "have different ethical consequences."[35] The biblical and Jewish understanding of faith locates faith in the covenant between the God of Israel and the Israel of God. Covenantal faith involves a conversation between faithful people and God, a conversation in which we are expected "not only to trust and obey God but . . . also [to be] allowed to question (and even to call into question) the behavior of God." Profoundly basic trust not only permits but requires questioning. Radical trust evokes an audacious faith. Abraham, the first model of biblical faith, epitomizes both a radical trust in God and *chutzpah,* the audacity to question even God. Abraham, Jacob, Job, Jesus, all question God.

Conscious of the *Shoah,* Rabbi Irving Greenberg made this a standard for contemporary theology: "Nothing dare evoke our absolute, unquestioning loyalty, not even our God, for this leads to the possibility of SS loyalties."[36] In the covenant with the God of Israel, faith is a dialectical tension between trust and *chutzpah,* obedience and questioning. Unquestioning obedience is morally offensive. No one should demand it of us and we should give it to no one. We may now define idolatry as the refusal to question. The God of Abraham, Sarah, and Jesus, by contrast, invites questioning.

Post-*Shoah,* we Christians have a lot of questions to ask of ourselves and our tradition. But we have many friends, among whom we may thankfully count all those *chaverim* among Jewish scholars and theologians who will gladly think, pray, and study with us. And both Jews and Christians have access to the One who is the Friend of All and who will graciously continue to put questions to us to keep us open to the transforming future to which we are now called out of our long wilderness wandering.

Notes

[1] Founded in Lexington, Kentucky, in 1780 and endowed initially by such folks as George Washington and Thomas Jefferson, Transylvania became a liberal arts college of the Christian Church (Disciples of Christ) after the Civil War.

[2] Although I worked for Tillich as his teaching assistant and what he called the "Englisher" of the third volume of his *Systematic Theology,* and in spite of all our conversations together, I never heard or read anything from him about the Holocaust or Jewish-Christian relations. Years later I discovered Albert H. Friedlander's "A Final Conversation with Paul Tillich," in *Out of the Whirlwind: A Reader of Holocaust Literature,* revised and expanded edition, edited by Albert H. Friedlander (New York: UAHC Press, 1999), 515–21. This conversation took place in the last summer of Tillich's life, in 1965.

[3] See, e.g., David Patrick Efroymson's "Tertullian's Anti-Judaism and Its Role in His Theology," Ph.D. dissertation, Temple University, 1976.

[4] Clark M. Williamson, *When Jews and Christians Meet* (St. Louis: CBP Press, 1989) 12–15.

[5] "Supersessionism" is derived from two Latin words, *super* (on or upon) and *sedere* (to sit). It is the claim in the context of Jewish-Christian relations that Christians now sit on the seat formerly occupied by Jews in the covenant with God. We displace and replace them.

[6] For Tillich, the only adequate symbol (religious symbol, that is) is a broken symbol, one that cannot be confused with the Ultimate to which it points; this is Luther's theology of the cross, the claim that God always reveals Godself under a contrariety, that the glory of God is hidden in the agony of Jesus; see Tillich, *Systematic Theology,* I (Chicago: University of Chicago Press, 1951) 133.

[7] See, e.g., Troeltsch's *Die Absolutheit des Christentums und die Religionsgeschichte,* 3rd ed. (Tübingen: J. C. B. Mohr, 1929).

[8] Shubert Ogden, *Christ Without Myth* (New York: Harper & Row, 1961).

[9] See Jules Isaac, *The Teaching of Contempt: Christian Roots of Anti-Semitism* (New York: Holt, Rinehart & Winston, 1964), who coined the term "teaching of contempt." I often amend it to "teaching and practice of contempt," partly because teaching is a practice and also because teaching reflects and reinforces other practices of contempt.

[10] A. Roy Eckardt, *Elder and Younger Brothers: The Encounter of Jews and Christians* (New York: Charles Scribner's Sons, 1967); *Your People, My People: The Meeting of Jews and Christians* (New York: Quadrangle, 1974); Rosemary Ruether, *Faith and Fratricide: The Theological Roots of Anti-Semitism* (New York: Seabury Press, 1974).

[11] Christopher Morse, *Not Every Spirit: A Dogmatics of Christian Disbelief* (Valley Forge: Trinity Press International, 1994) 12.

[12] Ibid.

[13] Karl Barth, *Church Dogmatics* IV, 3, 1, trans. G. W. Bromiley (Edinburgh: T. & T. Clark, 1961) 374.

[14] It was the merit of Ruether's *Faith and Fratricide* to make clear this dual structure of anti-Judaism.

[15] Melito of Sardis, *Sermon "On the Passover,"* trans., intro., and commentary by Richard C. White (Lexington, Ky.: Lexington Theological Seminary, 1976) 28–29.

[16] Ibid., 47.

[17] On this point, unfortunately, Karl Barth for most of his career fell afoul of his understanding articulated above of the lie as the specifically Christian form of sin. See his *Church Dogmatics,* 2/2, 206–07. See also David E. Demson, "Israel as the Paradigm of Divine Judgment: An Examination of a Theme in the Theology of Karl Barth," *Journal of Ecumenical Studies* (Fall 1989) 611–27.

[18] See Michel Foucault's analysis of the use of language to oppress, in *The Archaeology of Knowledge,* trans. A. M. Sheridan Smith (London: Tavistock, 1972).

[19] Pamela K. Payne is a Ph.D. candidate in systematic theology at Vanderbilt Divinity School where she is writing a dissertation on post-*Shoah* feminist theology; her remark was made in conversation.

[20] See Jacob R. Marcus, *The Jew in the Medieval World, A Source Book: 315–1791* (New York: Atheneum, 1974) 101–02.

[21] An extensive list of Church legislation against Jews can be found in James Parkes, *The Conflict of the Church and the Synagogue* (New York: Atheneum, 1977) 379–91; first published in London by the Soncino Press, 1934.

[22] As ably argued by John Gager, *The Origins of Anti-Semitism* (New York: Oxford University Press, 1983).

[23] Clark M. Williamson, *Has God Rejected His People? Anti-Judaism in the Christian Church* (Nashville: Abingdon, 1982).

[24] Johann-Baptist Metz, *The Emergent Church* (New York: Crossroad, 1981) 29.

[25] I first suggested the "teaching of respect" extensively in my *When Jews and Christians Meet: A Guide for Christian Preaching and Teaching* (St. Louis: CBP Press, 1989) ch. 2.

[26] A. Roy Eckardt was getting at this in his *Black—Woman—Jew: Three Wars for Human Liberation* (Bloomington, Ind.: Indiana University Press, 1989).

[27] Sandra Schneiders, "Does the Bible Have a Postmodern Message?" in *Postmodern Theology,* ed. Frederic B. Burnham (San Francisco: Harper & Row, 1989) 67.

[28] See Katharina von Kellenbach, *Anti-Judaism in Feminist Religious Writings* (Atlanta: Scholars Press, 1994).

[29] R. Kendall Soulen, *The God of Israel and Christian Theology* (Minneapolis: Fortress Press, 1996) 19.

[30] J. Gerald Janzen, *Abraham and All the Families of the Earth: Genesis 12–50* (Grand Rapids, Mich.: Eerdmans, 1993) 5, 15, 17.

[31] Ibid., 4.

[32] Marjorie Suchocki, *The Fall to Violence: Original Sin in Relational Theology* (New York: Continuum, 1995) 66.

[33] *Pirke Aboth* 1:6, *The Mishnah,* trans. Herbert Danby (London: Oxford University Press, 1933).

[34] Rachel Adler, "Breaking Boundaries," *Tikkun,* (May/June 1991) 43–46, 87.

[35] Darrell J. Fasching, *Narrative Theology After Auschwitz* (Minneapolis: Fortress Press, 1992) 50.

[36] Irving Greenberg, "Cloud of Smoke, Pillar of Fire: Judaism, Christianity, and Modernity after the Holocaust," *Auschwitz: Beginning of a New Era?,* ed. Eva Fleischner (New York: KTAV, 1977) 38.

s e v e n

JOHN T. PAWLIKOWSKI, o.s.m.

Drawing from Jewish Wellsprings

Boyhood Experiences

I grew up in a religiously and ethnically diverse neighborhood in Chicago. Among the significant groups present in our community were Orthodox Jews. When people ask me how I became involved in Christian-Jewish dialogue, I sometimes respond "through my stomach," for most of the shops in the area, including the popular bakery and deli, were Jewish-owned. In a sense, then, food was my first introduction to Judaism.

There was another Jewish encounter in my boyhood, one that I could not fully comprehend until much later in life when I studied Judaism and Jewish experience as an academic. Quite often I would meet up in the corner grocery store with a young Orthodox Jewish lad (the only Jews in our neighborhood were Orthodox) who was my age. While in the store we would exchange friendly greetings and smiles and chit-chat while waiting to make our purchases. We seemed to hit it off as boyhood friends. Yet, once we stepped outside the store, my Orthodox friend's demeanor completely changed. Suddenly he would become cold and distant. For a long time I was haunted by the question of why this lad, so apparently my friend inside the store, was so distant on the sidewalk outside?

In a sense, my puzzlement was similar to what the late pioneer in Christian-Jewish relations Fr. Edward Flannery experienced as he walked down Park Avenue in New York with a Jewish friend who told him of her shivers looking at the cross emblazoned in the lights on the Grand Central building at Christmastime. Like Father Flannery, I had little contact with the inner world of Jews and their reactions to Christians that influenced both my boyhood friend and Father Flannery's colleague. I now realize that my Jewish friend was afraid to be seen on the street in a friendly pose towards me lest he be reported to his family. Controlled interchange with Christians was tolerable in the grocery, deli, or bakery. But, beyond that, social relations were taboo. The Jewish collective experience of Christian antisemitism had created a climate of deep reserve, even outright fear, of social contact with Christians.

There was one exception to the social distancing between Christians and Jews in the neighborhood of my youth. My grandmother would sit for hours on the parkway benches near our home socially interacting with Jewish women her own age from Poland and Czechoslovakia—despite the fact that her operative theology was anti-Judaic. She used to always tell us that it rained heavily during September because that was the month of the Jewish holidays and "God was crying, over the Jews." I would not term this antisemitic because it was never associated with hatred of Jews. On the contrary, my grandmother always urged tolerance and respect towards people of other faiths in our diverse community of Christians and Jews, as did my parents and the teachers in my parochial school. In fact, my teachers always invited the residents of the Jewish retirement home on the same square as our parish church to view the annual May crowning procession in honor of the Virgin Mary. So I learned early on that theological anti-Judaism need not be automatically associated with hostility towards Jews.

On the whole, then, I came out of my boyhood with a generally positive, though limited, experience of Jews. While questions remained about the reluctance of my Jewish friend to transfer his "store friendship" to the street outside, my overall feeling for Jews was positive. The only negative comments I heard occasionally (other than my grandmother's September theology, which I did not take seriously since neither my parents nor teachers endorsed it) came from my mother and some of her friends who would sometimes complain that they had to work both outside and in their homes, while the Jewish women could afford maids to do their housework. But this was a class complaint rooted in economic inequality more than a religious complaint. I cannot recall that this complaint was ever tied by my mother and her friends to Christian antisemitism, nor did it stop them from enthusiastically shopping at the Jewish stores in the area, where on Sunday morning after Mass the waiting line at the Jewish bakery stretched for nearly a block outside.

Theological Studies

My understanding of Judaism and the Jewish community, including appreciation for the predicament faced by my Orthodox Jewish boyhood friend, came only towards the end of my seminary studies at Stonebridge Priory, the theological house of studies for my religious order, the Servites, in Lake Bluff, Illinois. This was the time the Second Vatican Council (1962–1965) was concluding its groundbreaking work, including finalizing its historic statement on the Church and the Jewish people in article four of *Nostra Aetate,* which dealt with the Church's relationship with other religions.

While in the seminary I was asked to write a weekly reflection on the Hebrew Scriptures for a publication called *Novena Notes* published by my order, which then had the largest circulation of any Catholic publication in the United States. My reflections often took up the theme of Christian-Jewish relations. They caught the attention of Hans Adler, a Holocaust survivor who worked at the Anti-Defamation League office in Chicago, and he called me in for a discussion. It was through this contact that I first entered the world of the more formal Christian-Jewish dialogue.

One faculty person at Stonebridge Priory who influenced me most profoundly on the issue of Christian-Jewish relations was the noted Scripture scholar John Dominic Crossan, then a priest of my order. While I have significant disagreements with some of his present positions, Crossan instilled in his students a tremendous respect and an appreciation for Sacred Scripture and, in me, a special concern for the long history of Christian antisemitism, which he saw as rooted in New Testament interpretation. He delivered one of the earliest lectures on antisemitism and the New Testament in light of *Nostra Aetate* in a public series on Vatican II held at Chicago's Loyola University.[1] I was in the audience that evening as a proud student. It was only later on that I would recognize that, despite his deep commitment to the elimination of antisemitism, his approach to the interpretation of Jesus' parables, rooted in the views of Rudolf Bultmann and his disciples such as Norman Perrin, contained the seeds of theological anti-Judaism with an emphasis on the displacement of "those who first heard the word."

Reflecting later on this dual experience of Crossan as both a persuasive critic of antisemitism and at the same time a purveyor of theological anti-Judaism, it became apparent to me how deep-seated antisemitism remains in Christian self-understanding, so that even those who staunchly oppose its outer manifestations sometimes remain unaware of its subtle dimensions. Despite this inconsistency I shall always be grateful to him for instilling in me a profound concern for antisemitism and a deep commitment to developing a new constructive theology of Christian-Jewish relations. Without his encouragement I doubt I would have ever made Christian-Jewish relations such a central part of my academic and ministerial career.

Another professor who influenced me in this area was Edward Gargan, a Catholic historian from Loyola University who was deeply influenced by his faculty colleague Gordon Zahn, the author of the first study in English on the Catholic Church during the Nazi era.[2] As a seminarian, I took Gargan's popular course on twentieth-century German history, which included an extensive segment on the Church and the Holocaust. Gargan was adamant that the Church must confront its failures during the Nazi period. While the course did not go into the history of Christian-Jewish relations, it did introduce me to a failure of the Church that can only be understood in terms of classical Christian antisemitism.

One other experience during my seminary years also had a role in strengthening my involvement in Christian-Jewish dialogue. While a third-year seminary student, I enrolled in a Hebrew course with another Catholic seminarian. The enrollment itself proved an interesting experience. The College of Jewish Studies (now Spertus Institute of Jewish Studies) had never had Christian students attempt to register for any of its courses, and the registrar was not sure she could accept us. It took a decision by an incoming school president to assure our enrollment in the course. The elderly Orthodox Jewish professor who taught the course took a very real interest in us, as did the Jewish students in the class, save for one convert from Christianity for whom we obviously constituted a bit of a faith challenge. Not only did our professor instill in us a deep appreciation for the Hebrew Scriptures (even though he insisted the text in Isaiah about a "virgin" giving birth to a son could not be translated as "virgin"), but he established a sense of respect for us as Christians that has never left me. I completed the course firmly believing that Christians and Jews could enjoy a sense of religious solidarity despite their theological differences.

Later, my years as a graduate student at the University of Chicago provided further formative influences on my commitment to Christian-Jewish dialogue. To begin with, during my very first quarter of graduate studies I took a course offered by prominent New Testament scholar Norman Perrin on Palestinian Judaism at the time of Jesus. The first day of class Perrin told us that although he really did not know very much about the subject matter, the faculty thought that such a course should be offered, so he volunteered to teach it. He then went to his briefcase and pulled out a volume I immediately recognized because I had already read it several years before in the course I took at the College of Jewish Studies. It was a popular book on Jewish festivals written for an ordinary adult audience. Perrin waxed eloquent about how profoundly the book had affected him. I thought to myself: on this topic I know much more than this world-class scholar!

I often cite this example in lectures not to demean Professor Perrin in any way, for he was a great scholar and teacher, but to show how little Judaism at the time of Jesus was included in the training programs for New Testament scholars. This made possible all sorts of arguments about the superiority of Jesus' teachings over against Judaism because there was very little knowledge among New Testament scholars of what the Jews of Jesus' time (as opposed to Jews in earlier times) actually believed. While the Jewish community in the Palestine of Jesus' time continued to be rooted in the Hebrew Scriptures, new ideas had emerged since the close of those Scriptures (around the second century B.C.E.) that paralleled the supposedly "new" teachings of Jesus and from which he in fact drew inspiration.

More positive influences at the University of Chicago came from two professors there who were to strengthen my focus on reconstructing the theology of the Christian-Jewish relationship. The first was J. Coert Rylaarsdam, one of the real pioneers in Christian-Jewish understanding. In his courses on the Hebrew Scriptures, he engendered in his students, including me, a profound appreciation of the richness of these Scriptures in contrast to the "inferior" status they had held in our previous thinking. He also took every opportunity to urge his students to confront the sin of antisemitism and to work for a new constructive relationship between Christians and Jews.

The other professor was the renowned historian Martin Marty, who was especially interested in contemporary Christian-Jewish relations, including the persistence of antisemitism in the churches. He strongly encouraged me to undertake studies of this issue as part of my doctoral work. These studies laid a solid scholarly foundation for my growing interest in the subject.

I should also mention that during my time at the University of Chicago, I had a memorable exchange with the Anglican scholar James Parkes, one of the leading scholars in the history of Christian-Jewish relations. Parkes had been a public enemy of the Nazis during World War II because of his outspoken attacks on antisemitism. In one of my courses I was encouraged to write a paper on his theological understanding of the relationship between the Jewish and Christian covenants. This proved an eye-opening experience for me and engendered an interest in covenantal theology that has remained a permanent feature of my academic work. The essay was eventually published in the *Journal of Ecumenical Studies*,[3] and Parkes wrote a response. While I had disagreements with some of Parkes' positions, the quality of this soul-searching exchange was truly soul-forming for me.

These formative experiences during my seminary and graduate school years led me to believe that Christians could transform their faith in a positive way through the encounter with Jews and Judaism. This encounter must confront the dark side of our relationship as well as highlight the ways in which the Christian faith, so deeply rooted in Judaism, can be reinvigorated by an understanding of Jewish faith perspectives. I have spent my academic and pastoral life exploring both these dimensions. It is to these matters that I now turn.

Repentance and Reconciliation

Fr. Edward Flannery, author of the groundbreaking *The Anguish of the Jews: Twenty-Three Centuries of Antisemitism*,[4] once remarked that Christians have torn out of their history books the pages most known by Jews. In my own training, except for the course with Professor Gargan that I mentioned earlier, I received no exposure to the centuries of anti-Judaism and antisemitism that have marked Christian history. It is not that I was taught to dislike Jews—quite the contrary, as my personal narrative has shown. But I was never made aware of how deeply embedded the theological and social disdain for Jews and Judaism had become in

Christian consciousness and how much this disdain had undercut Christian support for Jewish victims of the Nazis. This awareness was heightened for me through my encounter with the writings of French historian Jules Isaac, whose work was introduced to me by his translator Clare Huchet Bishop. Isaac, who helped convince Pope John XXIII to place Catholic-Jewish relations on the agenda of Vatican II, demonstrated most convincingly that antisemitism had entered the very heart of the Christian proclamation.[5]

What I have come to recognize in the last four decades is that there is no way for Christians to have honest reconciliation with Jews until we have restored to our textbooks those torn out pages. *Teshuvah*, repentance, is the first and necessary step in any process of reconciliation between Christians and Jews. As various declarations of the Catholic and Protestant churches in recent years have insisted, and as Pope John Paul II has shown in word and action, Christian moral integrity depends on the Christian assumption of moral responsibility for the anti-Judaic legacy of Christianity. Nothing short of this will do. We may have legitimate discussions about what exact role historic Christian anti-Judaism played in the Holocaust and other outbreaks of antisemitism. But we cannot deny its significant impact on members of the Christian churches at all levels, from the masses to the leaders. Only after we have confronted and expressed our profound apology can we Christians begin the process of seeing how contact with the Jewish religious tradition can help us recover our bonds with the Jewish people and constructively advance the expression of our own faith. To skip over the step of *teshuvah* is to deprive the second effort of any firm foundation.

Having made the point about the utter necessity of the Christian repentance (which is taking shape through such documents as the Vatican's "We Remember: A Reflection on the *Shoah*"[6]) we can move on to the positive dimensions of the nearly four decades of Christian-Jewish encounter generated by Vatican II's *Nostra Aetate* and parallel Protestant documents. This encounter has produced a revolution in the Church's perception of its relationship to Judaism and the Jewish people.

In the past several decades, I have come to see the intimate bond between the Church and the Jewish people, which the Church itself has increasingly recognized. This represents a further development from Vatican II in which the Church repudiated its centuries-old theology of Jewish displacement from the covenant and, instead, affirmed the ongoing covenant between God and the Jews. This link between the Church and the Jewish people has been clearly affirmed by Pope John Paul II and the Vatican Commission for Religious Relations with the Jews. The Commission, quoting John Paul II, asserts: "Because of the unique relations that exist between Christianity and Judaism—'Linked together at the very level of their identity'—relations 'founded on the design of the God of the covenant,' the Jews and Judaism should not occupy an occasional and marginal place in catechesis: their presence there is essential and should be organically integrated."[7]

A similar theme is found in the writing of Cardinal Carlo Maria Martini of Milan, who argues that deepened relations between Christians and Jews are vital to the future health of the Church itself: "What is here at stake is not simply the more or less lively continuation of a dialogue. It is the awareness of Christians of their bond with Abraham's stock and of the consequences of this fact, not only for doctrine, discipline, liturgy and spiritual life of the Church, but also for its mission in the world of today."[8] Cardinal Martini also points out that the original split between Judaism and Christianity must be viewed as a schism, not a permanent rupture. Catholicism was impoverished by the loss of the living contact with its Judaic roots. According to Cardinal Martini, such schisms throughout the history of Christianity have deprived "the body of the Church from contributions which could be very important for its health and vitality, and produces a certain lack of balance in the living equilibrium of the Christian community" and this "was especially true of the first great schism . . . in the first two centuries of Christianity."[9] With this sense of a deep and permanent bond with the Jewish people as a basic framework for Christian self-understanding, the Church has gradually moved toward a positive reappropriation of its Jewish roots in many areas of faith.

A New Appreciation of the Hebrew Scriptures

One significant area of change has been the attitude toward and use of the Old Testament. I grew up seeing these books as merely a foil or, in better moments, a prelude to the New Testament. They were not emphasized and were often even criticized for their supposed spiritual inferiority. In recent years considerable discussion has ensued regarding their role in

Christian faith. Part of the discussion has centered on how we should name the first part of the Bible. I, and some others, have argued for a change to "Hebrew Scriptures" or "First Testament." Others suggest using the Hebrew term *Tanakh*. Even if we eventually stay with "Old Testament," the important issue is how we employ these Scriptures in our preaching and teaching. The 1985 Vatican "Notes on the Correct Way to Present Jews and Judaism in Preaching and Catechesis in the Roman Catholic Church" insists that we must see the richness of the Hebrew Scriptures in their own right and not use them merely as a foil or prelude to the New Testament. More and more Christians are coming to recognize that without deep immersion in the spirit of the Hebrew Scriptures, they are left with a truncated version of Jesus' message—which in fact was deeply rooted in what the New Testament calls "the Scriptures" and what Christians came to call "the Old Testament"—and hence with an emaciated version of Christian spirituality.

We still have a way to go in really making the Hebrew Scriptures integral to Christian faith. Though for the past several decades they have been used in the Sunday liturgy (except during the Easter season), they are rarely the focus of the homily, and often the texts included in the lectionary have been chosen because in some way, peripherally at times, they are related to the gospel text for a Sunday. This means that many rich texts from the Hebrew Scriptures are not read at all in the Sunday liturgy. And the fact that they are absent from the retelling of the birth of the Church in the Easter season tends to diminish their importance.

Nor is the Old Testament given its fair due as a resource for theology, ethics, and spirituality. About the only theological disciplines that have drawn upon the Hebrew Scriptures are liturgy and sacramental theology, and even here the controlling rubric has often been an ultimately pejorative "foreshadowing" theme. If the Hebrew Scriptures are to continue their movement to the center of faith-identity for Christians—where they were for Jesus—then they must begin to assume the status of primary and not merely peripheral resources for Christian theology. For me, personally, this has led to a concerted effort to highlight sections of the readings from the Hebrew Scriptures in my Sunday preaching. It takes some effort because these texts often can be overly complex for the average parishioner. But, on the whole, people have responded well, sometimes telling me after the end of the liturgy that they had never before appreciated the spiritual richness of some of these texts from the Hebrew Scriptures.

Moving from generic considerations relative to the Hebrew Scriptures to specific themes, I would highlight the following as of growing importance for my own faith-identity and expression. All are themes that have been virtually missing, or at least seriously downplayed, during much of Christian history since what Cardinal Martini has termed the Church's schism with the Jewish people.

The Primacy of Community

The first of these biblical themes is that of peoplehood or the primacy of community. Judaism has generally maintained a strong sense that individual salvation must take second place to the salvation of the community. This sense of peoplehood is an integral part of the covenantal tradition of Sinai in which the revelation of God's presence was given to Moses for the well-being and mission of the whole people rather than simply for the good of the individual.

As we examine Christian history, we see that very often Christian faith degenerated into an almost exclusively individualistic sense of divine-human encounter. Personal salvation assumed a primacy it never had for Jesus—or even for Paul, contrary to later interpretations of his thought. This individualistic approach to Christian faith often was accompanied by an other-worldly, a-historical, and at times anti-historical interpretation of spirituality. The world for Christians frequently became a place from which they longed to escape rather than one they were called to transform as a people along with their Jewish partners. This was certainly the spiritual approach that dominated my spiritual formation as a novice in the Servite Order.

This individualistic tendency even infiltrated the most central religious act of the Catholic tradition, the Eucharist. The origins of this primal sacrament are directly rooted in the Pharisaic communal meals that formed a crucial part of Jesus' constructive appropriation of Judaism in the period of the Second Temple. The Eucharist tended in later Christianity to become an occasion when the individual Christian believer offered personal prayers to God while the priest performed a sacrifice on the altar. Such a tendency weakened any communal consciousness among the individual believers assembled for worship. It was only with the liturgical reforms of Vatican II that this began to change. Picking up on its definition of the Church as "the people of God," a notion that was central to the re-form produced by Vatican II, the Council restored Catholic Christianity's historical and communal orientation that had been attenuated as a result of the original break with Judaism. This is clearly seen in the priority the Council gave to eucharistic practice. Many key liturgical scholars who shaped the reform were significantly influenced by new contacts with the Jewish liturgical tradition beginning with the Hebrew Scriptures and the sacred meals that formed a core element in Second Temple Judaism.[10]

This is but one example of how the enhanced Christian-Jewish dialogue not only has benefited intergroup understanding but also has positively influenced the general renewal of Christian life. The only word of caution I would introduce here is the same one voiced by New Testament scholar Gerard Sloyan, who has warned that an appropriation of the term "people of God" can easily breed a new form of theological imperialism, in which both the Church's Jewish roots and the continued flourishing of the Jewish people are overlooked. Thus Sloyan suggests that the problem is "as much of an understanding in depth of Christian origins as it is of ecumenical relations with Jews."[11] Clearly, for the term "people of God" to contribute to a constructive re-Judaization of Christianity, it must be used with the concomitant assertion that the Jewish people also remain "people of God."

Liberation theology, which has contributed significantly to the renewal of the Church in Latin America, and to some degree in Africa and Asia, has shown some positive appropriation of Judaism's communal/historical sense. Several of the leading theologians who set the framework for liberation theology turned to the Exodus covenantal tradition as the inescapable starting point for the ongoing process of human liberation from all forms of oppression. One cannot fully understand the liberating mission of Jesus, according to theologians such as Gustavo Gutiérrez and José Miguez Bonino, without seeing how it flows from the liberation of the people of Israel recorded in the Hebrew Scriptures. Without this positive connection to the Exodus tradition of liberation, interpretations of Jesus' preaching frequently become a-historical and overly individualistic—the "Jesus as my personal Savior" approach.

To be candid, there also have been disturbing views of Judaism in liberation theology that cannot be ignored. Not all the theologians related to this movement have seen the covenantal tradition in Exodus as positively as Gutiérrez and Bonino. Examples of this weakness are evident in the writings of Leonardo Boff and, especially, Jon Sobrino. Not only are they silent about any link between the liberating spirit of Jesus' proclamation and the liberating spirit of Exodus, but they reintroduce the notion of Jewish responsibility for Jesus' death in a way that reminds us of the tragic days prior to Vatican II's repudiation of the deicide charge in *Nostra Aetate*. Even Gutiérrez and Bonino are not above criticism for their inadequate understanding of the role of Torah in biblical Judaism and the unsatisfactory way they tie the Exodus tradition of liberation to Christ. But given the long history of Christian neglect of the Hebrew Scriptures as a resource for Christian faith, the positive use of the Exodus covenantal tradition by Gutiérrez and Bonino, though in my judgment in need of substantial reformulation regarding Judaism, represents a step forward in the re-Judaization of Christian theology.

Human Co-creatorship with God

Another important dimension of the Jewish covenantal tradition that has influenced my understanding of Christian faith is that of human co-creatorship with God. Particularly in our time, when human beings are gaining more and more power over creation, this notion assumes a new importance for Christian ethics. The theme of co-creatorship emerges from both the biblical tradition and the later Jewish mystical tradition. Rabbi Irving Greenberg captures this theme when he writes: "God has invited us . . . to join fully in the task of perfecting the universe."

Christian theology has tended to accentuate the omnipotence of God, which in turn has intensified the impotence of the human person and the rather inconsequential role played by the human community in maintaining the sustainability of creation. But the idea of human co-creatorship with God has been gaining prominence among Christian thinkers. For example, it is a major theme of Pope John Paul II's encyclical *Laborem Exercens*. With his understanding of human co-creatorship, John Paul strikes the balance between the respective roles of God and the human community in sustaining the continuation of life at all levels. In the Pope's view, human co-creatorship is a gift from God that helps fulfill the dynamics of creation. This model, because of its stress on genuine human creativity, goes beyond the model of "stewardship," in which the emphasis is almost exclusively on preserving what God has already set in place.

The idea of human co-creatorship with God is also found in the Canadian Catholic bishops' statement on economics and in the United States Catholic bishops' statements on energy, peace, and economic justice. It is especially prominent in the last of these, where the bishops draw exclusively upon this motif in the book of Genesis for a spirituality that can undergird an indispensable sense of human co-creational responsibility in our day. In doing so they acknowledge, albeit indirectly, the basic poverty of the New Testament and the strength of the Hebrew Scriptures in this area.

A More Positive Image of the Human Being

Another way in which exposure to the Jewish covenantal tradition has been affecting my theological perspective has to do with theological anthropology. Judaism generally has maintained a more positive image of the human being than has Christianity. Catholicism has been somewhat better in this regard than Protestantism, but both have tended to stress sinfulness much more than goodness in their theological anthropology. Judaism has not been ignorant of a deep-seated sinful drive within the human person, but its stress on this sinful drive has been far less prominent than has generally been the case in Christianity.

Most Christian theologians have lacked contact with Jewish biblical, rabbinic, and mystical viewpoints on basic human goodness, and this has resulted in a distorted emphasis on certain statements in the Pauline writings without the counterbalance of relevant themes in the Hebrew Scriptures and other statements from the New Testament. New Testament scholars such as Bishop Krister Stendahl have even argued that later Protestant theologians projected back into Paul guilt feelings arising from their own introspection, which would have been foreign to Paul. While Judaism may need to do some rethinking of its classical position regarding the power of evil in light of the *Shoah*, Christianity's approach stands in need of greater review. Since so much of the Christian approach to human sinfulness, particularly in Catholicism, has been related to sexuality, increased encounter with the Jewish tradition may help restore a far more positive outlook on sexuality as an avenue for experiencing the divine presence, a notion that is deeply rooted both in the Hebrew Scriptures and the later Jewish mystical tradition.

A related issue is that of the Christian understanding of the forgiveness of sin, and for sacramentally-based Christian denominations such as Catholicism, the celebration of penance and reconciliation. As some liturgical scholars, such as my late colleague Ralph Keifer, have emphasized, a rather truncated interpretation of forgiveness and the sacrament of penance developed over the centuries in Christianity. This interpretation, which had its origins largely in the teaching of Irish monks, overemphasized sinfulness and depravity to the exclusion of the joy of reconciliation. In so doing the Church severed its understanding of forgiveness from its roots in the Jewish tradition where it involved reconciliation with the person or persons affected by one's sinful action far more than it emphasized inner cleansing. The New Testament, in its parable of the return of the prodigal son and its injunction not to dare to offer gifts at the altar until one has made amends with the person against whom the sinful act has been committed, carries on this authentic Jewish spirit. We can hope that Christians will continue to recover this understanding of forgiveness and penance through the present-day encounter with Judaism.

A More "Landed" Faith

The final issue I want to raise in relation to the biblical part of the Jewish covenantal tradition is the potential impact on Christian faith of the Jewish tie to a land. Christian scholars Walter Brueggemann and W. D. Davies have done important studies on this question. Both assert that failure to grasp the insights of the Jewish land tradition not only leaves Christians with a falsified picture of Judaism, but also deprives Christianity of a vital rootedness in history and a full appreciation of the role of non-human creation in the reign of God.

I certainly wish to maintain some significant differences between Christianity and Judaism regarding the present meaning of the land tradition. It is my firm belief that one result of the Christian theology of the incarnation is an equalization of all land in terms of sacredness. Jerusalem is, from this theological perspective, no holier than Geneva, Rome, the *favelas* of Rio, or the inner city of Chicago. (It should be said that some Jewish historians, such as Ellis Rivkin, note that there was in fact a certain universalization of land as an integral element in the Pharisaic revolution during the Second Temple period.) But having made the above assertion of personal faith, I wish to proclaim with equal vigor my firm conviction that the Church's faith expression must likewise be firmly rooted in the earth. By reason of the Church's recent affirmation of the ongoing significance of the Jewish covenant, there is need for Christians to respect the land theme in Judaism, even though Christian interpretations of this theme may take different paths. Christian faith must always remain firmly planted in the earth. Far too often, concentration on the "heavenly Jerusalem" as a supposed replacement for the "earthly Jerusalem" has led to an excessively ethereal spirituality in the churches.

There is another way in which contact with the land dimension of the Jewish covenantal tradition has assumed special significance for me. As a social ethicist deeply involved in the ecological challenge of our day, I recognize the severe limitations of the Christian tradition in terms of an authentic spirituality of the land. So much popular piety in Christianity has drawn Christians away from their earthly home, which is viewed as "exile." Such a mindset in Christianity has severely undercut the commitment to the sustainability of creation. In much of Christian liturgy we have lost almost all consciousness of the need to proclaim the glory of God's creation.[12] Unlike Judaism, with its festivals such as *Sukkot,* the fall festival when Jews annually reconnect with nature, the Christian liturgical cycle is virtually bereft of celebrations that highlight God's continuing presence in all of creation. Personal experience of this creation-oriented aspect of Judaism has proven immensely beneficial to me in work on ecology and ethics.

A New Understanding of Jesus, the New Testament, and the Emergence of Christianity

My abiding involvement in the Jewish-Christian dialogue has also profoundly affected my understanding of Jesus, the New Testament, and the emergence of Christianity. We are witnessing a genuine revolution in New Testament scholarship, made possible in part by a much greater understanding of Hebrew and Aramaic and an increased reliance on Jewish materials from the Second Temple or "intertestamental" period. I have personally welcomed the rapid end to the dominance of the exegetical approach associated with the German scholar Rudolf Bultmann and some of his disciples. This exegetical approach to the New Testament seriously eroded Jesus' concrete ties to, and dependence upon, biblical and Second Temple Judaism. The negative effect of this type of biblical exegesis is clear in the personal stories I related above with regard to my own experience of being a student of Norman Perrin and John Dominic Crossan.

My experience of the depth of Jewish faith through my many encounters with Jews over the past four decades has made the new New Testament scholarship on Jesus' Jewishness personally meaningful for my faith, and not just of academic interest. So when scholars increasingly portray Jesus as a person deeply imbued with Jewish spirituality, my appreciation of Jesus is enhanced, not diminished. I now recognize the richness of Jesus' ties to Judaism, a richness that I must affirm in my own faith perspective if I am truly to say that I am an authentic disciple of Jesus. Such an understanding also leads me to recognize that the separation of Judaism and Christianity came only gradually and that something precious in terms of faith was lost by Christians when the ties were severed several centuries after Jesus' death.

I can now appreciate the understanding put forth by many biblical scholars that Jesus did not establish a new, independent religion in his lifetime. Jesus died on the cross as a faithful "son of Israel." This is now part of the bedrock of my Christian faith and theology.[13] I must now begin to rethink the theological understanding of the gradual separation of Christianity and Judaism as scholars lay it out.

The Christian scholars now engaged in rethinking the Church's relationship to the Jewish people certainly do not concur on all points. Major source problems and ambiguities virtually assure the continuation of these disagreements for the foreseeable future. Nonetheless, there is a growing consensus emerging among those scholars who have examined the question in some depth. This new consensus might best be expressed in the words of Cardinal Martini: "In its origins Christianity is deeply rooted in Judaism. Without a sincere feeling for the Jewish world, therefore, and a direct experience of it, one cannot understand Christianity. Jesus is fully Jewish, the apostles are Jewish, and one cannot doubt their attachment to the traditions of their forefathers."[14]

There is now a growing willingness within Christianity, a willingness I share with prominent church leaders and scholars such as Cardinal Martini, to acknowledge that in the rupture with the Jewish community led by Gentile Christians, or on their behalf, the late first century Christian community may have made some serious mistakes. Most Christians have tended to cheer for Paul, not Peter and James and the Jewish-spirited Jerusalem church, at the so-called Council of Jerusalem. The enhanced appreciation of Jesus' Jewishness now forces me and other scholars to take a second look at the situation. From the new perspective it now appears that Peter and James were trying to retain something precious, however inadequately they might have stated their case. In deciding to begin to sever links with Judaism, a part of Christianity's soul was deadened. This "hero modification" with respect to the Council of Jerusalem story is but one example of the fundamental attitudinal shift in my own thinking that has resulted from my immersion in the study of Judaism at the time of Jesus and the early Church.

It is my firm conviction that the restoration of Jesus and his teachings to a fully Jewish matrix will not reach its full potential until it moves beyond the parameters of New Testament scholarship and begins to penetrate other theological disciplines. Most of the other areas of theology, especially systematic or dogmatic theology, still operate on the basis of the older exegetical approach dominated by Rudolph Bultmann. This accounts for the continuation of a fairly widespread, though often subtle, theological anti-Judaism among many contemporary systematic theologians who still present Christianity as the replacement for an "outmoded" and "spiritually inferior" Judaism.

The restoration of Jesus and his teachings to their Jewish matrix must also extend beyond the theological disciplines to Christian preaching. In my own Sunday preaching I have made attempts over the years to show how Jesus' perspectives on so many issues, and how the parables he used to convey his perspectives, are rooted in an important segment of the Judaism of his day. Because so often in the Sunday readings from the New Testament Jesus appears to be standing over against the Jewish community of his day, I find it necessary to make an explicitly positive connection between what he proclaimed and what the Pharisees and other Jews were teaching at that time.

Appreciating Post-biblical Judaism

It is not only a positive appropriation of the Hebrew Scriptures and an enhanced appreciation of Jesus' Jewish context that constitute the re-

Judaization process within contemporary Christianity. As the Vatican Commission for Religious Relations with the Jews has emphasized, post-biblical forms of Jewish faith need to be taken seriously by Christian scholars as well. This includes the Jewish mystical tradition and Jewish reflections on the covenant in the modern era. If we truly believe what the churches increasingly have been saying in a variety of documents about the enduring links between Judaism and Christianity, as I certainly do, then it is impossible to express the theological and ethical meaning of Christian covenantal life without explicit reference to the ways in which various Jewish scholars have interpreted covenantal responsibility in our time.

In light of this conviction, it has become apparent to me that contemporary Jewish reflections on such basic religious issues as the meaning of the God of the covenant, or Jewish deliberations on such pressing ethical issues as abortion and peace, assume the status of an indispensable resource for Christian theology. It is not simply a matter of taking such contemporary Jewish resources seriously because of interreligious sensitivity or a commitment to religious pluralism, as important as these considerations continue to be. In light of the renewed theology of the Christian-Jewish relationship, Jewish theological and ethical reflections now have become integral to my methodology as a Christian theologian. No longer can I regard them merely as extra resources from a parallel community to be incorporated in a peripheral way. In a real sense they have become "in house" resources that I cannot ignore in formulating my reflections on theological and ethical issues within the Church.

To conclude, I should mention that I have learned much from my experience of a deeply rooted sense of hope in the Jewish tradition, which is partly responsible for the Jewish community's remarkable ability to build anew upon the ashes of the *Shoah*.[15] This sense of hope, I have come to see, is closely tied to the Jewish sense of humor. One person who exposed me to the tradition of Jewish humor was my late colleague of thirty years at the Catholic Theological Union, Rabbi Hayim Goren Perelmuter, to whom I owe more in terms of understanding the depth of Judaism than I can fully express. Rabbi Perelmuter often spoke and wrote about Jewish humor, and he expressed it in our own personal exchanges. From his writings and our conversations, I have come to appreciate how integral humor is to the Jewish sense of being a religious person in the world.

Notes

[1] Dominic M. Crossan, o.s.m., "Anti-Semitism and the Gospel," *Theological Studies* (June 1965) 180–214.

[2] Gordon Zahn, *German Catholics and Hitler's Wars: A Study in Social Control* (New York: Sheed & Ward, 1962).

[3] John T. Pawlikowski, "The Church and Judaism: The Thought of James Parkes" *Journal of Ecumenical Studies* (Fall 1969) 573–97.

[4] Edward H. Flannery, *The Anguish of the Jews: Twenty-Three Centuries of Anti-semitism* (New York: MacMillan, 1964; rev. ed.: New York: Paulist Press, 1985).

[5] Jules Isaac, *The Teaching of Contempt: Christian Roots of Antisemitism* (New York: Holt, Rinehart & Winston, 1964) and *Jesus and Israel* (New York: Holt, Rinehart & Winston, 1971).

[6] Vatican Commission for Religious Relations with the Jews, "We Remember: A Reflection on the *Shoah*," *Catholics Remember the Holocaust,* ed. Secretariat for Ecumenical and Interreligious Affairs, National Conference of Catholic Bishops (Washington, D.C.: United States Catholic Conference, 1998) 47–56. While this and other ecclesial documents have some major limitations, they nonetheless set forth acknowledgement of the Christian anti-semitic tradition. See John T. Pawlikowski, "The Vatican and the Holocaust: Putting *We Remember* in Context," *Dimensions: A Journal of Holocaust Studies* 12:2, 11–22, and "*We Remember:* Looking Back, Looking Ahead," *The Month* (January 2000) 3–8.

[7] Vatican Commission for Religious Relations with the Jews, "Notes on the Correct Way to Present Jews and Judaism in Preaching and Catechesis in the Roman Catholic Church" (1985), *Origins* (July 4, 1985) 103; quotations from Pope John Paul II are from an address made to an international catechetical meeting in Rome, 1982.

[8] Cardinal Carlo Maria Martini, "The Relation of the Church to the Jewish People," *From the Martin Buber House* (September 1984) 9.

[9] Ibid., 13.

[10] For more on the Jewish roots of Christian liturgy, see Eugene J. Fisher, ed., *The Jewish Roots of Christian Liturgy* (New York: Paulist Press, 1990) and John T. Pawlikowski, "Do This in Memory of Me: Interreligious Reflections on Remembrance in Christianity," *Commitment and Commemoration: Jews, Christians, Muslims in Dialogue,* ed. Andre LaCocque (Chicago: Exploration Press, 1994) 83–93.

[11] Gerard Sloyan, "Who are the People of God?" *Standing Before God,* eds. Asher Finkel and Lawrence Frizzell (New York: KTAV, 1981) 113.

[12] See Richard N. Fragomeni, "Liturgy at the Heart of Creation," *The Ecological Challenge: Ethical, Liturgical, and Spiritual Responses,* eds. Richard N. Fragomeni and John T. Pawlikowski (Collegeville: The Liturgical Press, 1994) 67–82.

[13] My own writings on the subject include: John T. Pawlikowski, *Christ in the Light of Christian-Jewish Dialogue* (New York: Paulist Press, 1982); *Jesus and the Theology of Israel* (Wilmington, Del.: Michael Glazier, 1989); "Christology, Antisemitism, and Christian-Jewish Bonding," *Reconstructing Christian Theology,* eds. Rebecca S. Chopp and Mark Lewis Taylor (Minneapolis: Fortress Press, 1994) 245–68; "The Search for a New Paradigm for the Christian-Jewish Relationship: A Response to Michael Signer," *Reinterpreting Revelation and Tradition: Jews and Christians in Conversation,* eds. John T. Pawlikowski, O.S.M. and Hayim Goren Perelmuter (Franklin, Wis.: Sheed & Ward, 2000) 25–48.

[14] Cardinal Carlo Maria Martini, "Christianity and Judaism: A Historical and Theological Overview," *Jews and Christians Exploring the Past, Present, and Future,* ed. James B. Charlesworth (New York: Crossroad, 1990) 19.

[15] My own writings on the theological and moral implications of the *Shoah* include: John T. Pawlikowski, *The Challenge of the Holocaust for Christian Theology* (New York: Anti-Defamation League, 1962); "Christian Theological Concerns After the Holocaust," *Visions of the Other: Jewish and Christian Theologians Assess the Dialogue,* ed. Eugene J. Fisher (New York: Paulist Press, 1994) 28–51; "The Holocaust: Its Impact on Christian Thought and Ethics," *New Perspectives on the Holocaust,* ed. Rochelle L. Millen (New York: New York University Press, 1996) 344–61; "Penetrating Barriers: A Holocaust Retrospective," *From the Unthinkable to the Unavoidable: American Jewish and Christian Scholars Encounter the Holocaust,* eds. Carol Rittner and John K. Roth (Westport, Conn.: Greenwood Press, 1997) 99–109; "Divine and Human Responsibility in Light of the Holocaust," *Humanity at the Limit: The Impact of the Holocaust Experience on Jews and Christians* (Bloomington, Ind.: Indiana University Press, 2000) 15–26; "God: The Foundational Ethical Question After the Holocaust," *Good and Evil After Auschwitz: Ethical Implications for Today* eds. Jack Bemporad, John T. Pawlikowski, and Joseph Sievers (Hoboken, N.J.: KTAV, 2000) 53–66.

e i g h t

EUGENE J. FISHER

Enriching Christian Life
Through Encounter with Judaism

Learning from the Detroit Immigrant Milieu

I attended my first Christian-Jewish dialogue in my mother's womb. It was 1943. My father, having been rejected by every branch of the American military because he had had asthma as a youth, was helping to defeat Nazism in any way he could, working as an air raid warden, planting a victory garden, raising funds for the war effort—a typical story of "the greatest generation." At the time, he was the Grand Knight of the Gabriel Richard Council of the Knights of Columbus, and he and my mother organized a joint banquet with the local Masonic and B'nai B'rith lodges to raise money to support the American military. I still have the old Knights of Columbus bulletins that announced and reported on the event. Interestingly, there is a letter in there from the chancellor of the Archdiocese of Detroit reassuring the K of C members that it was OK to be doing this with the Masons, despite their rather ominous history toward the Catholic Church in Europe. (It helped, too, I suspect, that the chancellor was my father's cousin.) Eating with the B'nai B'rith members posed no such spiritual problem, though my parents talked for years about the delicate (and humorous) negotiations they had over the menu. Through this and other activities, the Catholic, Protestant, and Jewish lodges together raised large sums of money to support the American troops during World War II.

Though we had non-Catholic neighbors, I grew up in a very Catholic environment (some would call it a Catholic ghetto) in pre-Vatican II suburban Grosse Pointe, which is on the east side of the city, a fact the significance of which native Detroiters will instantly appreciate. At that time, Detroit was in a sense two cities divided by Woodward Avenue, a major artery extending outward from downtown. The Jewish community, for reasons that had to do with both immigration patterns and patterns imposed by socioeconomic discrimination against immigrants, lived in certain areas of the west side, while, for similar reasons, Italians and Poles lived in certain areas of the east side. This pattern prevailed even when the communities moved out to the suburbs, with eastsiders moving eastward and westsiders to the west. In any event, I do not recall having met any Jews while growing up, much less learning anything about Judaism beyond what was necessary for understanding Jesus (and there was very little of that, in point of fact, in the Baltimore Catechism). I was most likely given the same negative portrait of New Testament-era Judaism as every other Christian in the world.

The fact that I knew no Jews had, I suppose, good and bad sides. On the negative, there was no reality to test the stereotypes against. On the other hand, I was never taught to connect all those bad things the Pharisees allegedly did with anybody living in modern times. In many ways I was a *tabula rasa* with regard to contemporary Jews and Judaism until graduate school. My father, an attorney, did have some Jewish colleagues, I now realize. But since, in our immigrant-oriented environment, being Jewish was no more exotic than being Italian or Lebanese or Czech, this fact would not have been something called to my attention.

If anything, there was a sense of shared immigrant experience. My father, as I was told at his funeral, was the first Catholic to have joined a major law firm in the city's history, and I knew that we Catholic kids were not welcome in the public schools unless we went there full time. I figured this out when I got taunted and beaten up (not severely, but enough to make me feel very down on myself for a while) one day on the way home from school. I never walked home that way again. My father, too, had his experiences with anti-Catholic prejudice. As a rising young attorney shortly after the War, he applied for membership in the Detroit Athletic Club, a downtown facility where big business was done and deals were made over lunch and in the locker room. He was blackballed, however, when it was discovered that despite his English name, he was really mostly Irish and very Catholic. It would not do to have "them" polluting the club with papism, now, would it?

There are other stories, but I think the point is made. I played happily with all the kids in our neighborhood. "Protestant" and "Catholic" didn't matter much to us kids. But in the larger environment the process of breaking down the social barriers among ethnic and religious groups was only beginning. To grow up Catholic in the 1940s and 1950s was to know you were "different" and had to prove yourself to the world at large in ways that others did not. Following the football fortunes of the University of Notre Dame, for example, gave pride to a community of families, each of which had an incident or two in recent experience such as those I have described. The same, of course, was true of American Jews. Catholics and Jews both were, after all, America's "ethnics," the unwashed immigrants of Emma Lazarus' poem on the Statue of Liberty. A Catholic as president of the United States? Impossible—at least until the 1960s. A Catholic as president of Harvard? Impossible—that took until the 1970s to occur. A Jewish vice-presidential candidate? Not until the year 2000!

It was World War II that began the process by which society's invisible but well-understood social barriers were gradually broken. The reasons are doubtlessly complex. The underlying one, I believe, was simply that America desperately needed immigrants to win the war. Hence, the culture became far more accepting of those asked to die to save it. One can see this reflected in the war movies of the period: A WASP lieutenant heads a small platoon composed of an Irish guy, an Italian (or Jew or Hispanic), and a Black, one of whom will die saving the WASP's life. I saw a lot of these movies on television as a kid. In any event, the soldiers came home to the G.I. Bill (a kind of Marshall Plan for ethnic America) and many of them became the first in their family's history to go to college.

Learning from the Civil Rights Movement and the Second Vatican Council

I graduated from Austin Catholic Prep in 1961 and entered Sacred Heart Seminary College, having attended Catholic schools for everything except kindergarten. In the seminary I became intensely involved in the civil rights movement, at one point spending a week with a classmate, John

Clark, living in the apartment-home of a Black family in Chicago. Coming back, we organized the Student Human Relations Education in Action Committee. We put together a daylong race relations conference at the seminary and invited Dr. Hubert G. Locke to give the keynote address on the theme of slavery. (I did not know it for years, but he was even then co-founding with Franklin Littell the annual Scholars' Conference on the Churches and the Holocaust that has produced so much good work over the years.)

Wishing to share what had been for us a seminal experience in Chicago, John Clark and I also organized a weekend experience for the whole seminary, putting pairs of seminarians into homes of Black families for the weekend. Each host family invited in friends and neighbors for a visit with the guests. There is nothing like personal experience to bring about a breaking down of stereotypes. When Martin Luther King, Jr. came to Detroit, virtually the entire student body and faculty marched as a group to meet up with him, proudly bearing both the American and papal flags, down the very streets that were to explode into race riots some years later when King was assassinated.

While I was in college, Vatican II was held. It could not have come at a better time for me. The Council's documents, which we read and studied and debated as they came out in stately procession from Rome, blew away my childhood impression of what Catholicism was all about and replaced it with a more dynamic sense of a community chosen by God to change history itself and to improve the lot of all humankind. Salvation was not just a spiritual, personal thing anymore, but a challenge to humanity to overcome its own evil. During these college years, which are for many of us a crucial time of choosing our life's values, the Council thoroughly and irreversibly permeated my thinking. The Council's statements on ecumenism *(Unitatis Redintegratio)* and interreligious understanding *(Nostra Aetate)* became, along with the rest of the Council's teachings, part of the fiber of my being.

After college I attended St. John's Seminary for two years. There, I took some optional Scripture and biblical Hebrew courses from Fr. John J. Castelot, who had written a popular series of introductions to the Bible. There were only two or three of us in these classes, which he held informally in his room in the evening. His evident love of Scripture and joy at probing its depths infused me. But what astonished me was the fact that the Hebrew Bible, read in its original, had a whole lot more in it than any translation can really convey. Genesis, for example, even its elegant and poetic creation accounts, is filled with puns and delightful and provocative word plays that satirize elements of the common world-view of the ancient Near East and give the reader a sense of the ironies of life. In Scripture, tragedy and comedy constantly intertwine. The Bible is a far more sophisticated (and funny) set of books than our rather straight-laced approach to it as Christians allows us to see. It's no wonder that Jews are over-represented in American comedy. They have a three-millennia long tradition going for them!

Learning Jewish by Immersion[1]

Leaving St. John's Seminary but wishing to pursue theology, especially what I then called Old Testament studies, I enrolled in a master's degree program in Catholic theology at the Jesuit-run University of Detroit. One of my teachers was Professor Shlomo Marinoff, who was, for all practical purposes, the university's entire department of ancient languages. I took every course I could with him and, as with Father Castelot, I was usually one of only a couple of students in them. He was the first Jew I ever really got to know, a brilliant and gentle man of letters whom I admired greatly.

After earning my master's degree, I wanted to go for doctoral studies. Since the University of Detroit had no doctoral program in theology or Scripture, Dr. Marinoff suggested I write to his good friend, David Rudavsky, at New York University's Institute for Hebrew Studies. I found the idea of studying the Hebrew Bible with the descendents of people who wrote it quite appealing, so I dashed off a résumé. Dr. Rudavsky responded with a generous scholarship covering not only tuition but modest living expenses as well. On a warm day in early September 1968, I walked out of New York's Grand Central Station with the address of the school in my pocket and two large suitcases. I did not know where I would spend the night, but I did know that my relatively sheltered midwestern life was about to change. I set the bags down for a moment to take it all in. A young man promptly picked one up and began to walk off with it, mumbling something about carrying my luggage for me. I chased after him, carrying the other bag, and would have lost the race if a policeman had not intervened. Welcome to New York!

The changes and challenges in lifestyle, intellectual environment, and religious perspective I experienced in New York were dramatic. This was the period of massive antiwar demonstrations (which I enthusiastically joined). I had been in the seminary just at the right time to go through Vatican II as it was happening, and had been fortunate to be quite actively involved in the civil rights movement in Detroit during the same period. The winds of social change promised a new and more equal American society, as the open windows of theological *aggiornamento* promised a reformed and more open Roman Catholic Church. For many of us in those days, change represented hope, not something to be feared. We could acknowledge freely the shortcomings of the past, whether in society or the Church, because both were actively engaged in rectifying what had gone wrong. Admitting American racism and Christian antisemitism, then, was not for the purpose of dwelling on the guilt of the past, but rather for the purpose of opening a way of hope for a better future.

Most, and sometimes all, of my classmates at New York University were Jewish. The tone, style, and content of the discussions were entirely Jewish. People wrangled over what it meant to be Jewish, and the questions that framed the issues for debate were Jewish. I found this both refreshing and fascinating. If one is raised within a holistic worldview such as that provided by rabbinic Judaism or Roman Catholicism, entire sets of interrelated frameworks make sense of and give coherence to reality, even to the often-fractious internal debates that can divide a community.

Fortunately, it was just at the right time of my life for me to be immersed, with my solid grounding in integral Catholicism, in an entirely different, but no less coherent, religious culture. Virtually everything I had ever learned—spiritually, culturally, philosophically, historically, or biblically—was viewed from a very different perspective. Of all the religious traditions that had flourished in the ancient Roman Empire, Judaism alone had been allowed to survive Christianity's triumph in Europe. Jewish communities often predated Christian communities in southern and western Europe and were founded alongside Christian communities in northern and eastern Europe. The Jewish memory of Christendom, therefore, is invaluable as the one non-Christian but still "insider" perspective on Western civilization over the past two millennia. These Jewish communities, I was to discover with a sense of infinite loss, held the memories and embodied the unique spiritual witness that the Nazi genocide sought to end.

Before immersing myself in the New York Jewish experience, I had known nothing about being Jewish, save what I had learned in biblical studies under Catholic auspices. While academically sound, this perspective was only marginally useful for understanding how Jews today read their Scriptures, understand their history, and live their traditions. It was all new to me.

I did not at first encounter the Holocaust with great intensity at NYU. It was discussed as pertinent to a given topic of study. It did not dominate either the formal course work or the informal discussions of my classmates. Rather, it seemed to brood behind and beneath them, dwelling in the silence of the unspoken though not unthought. This was in 1968, well before the numerous books and movies about the Holocaust broke open the repressed memories and fears of so many in the Jewish community. What I encountered, rather, was the vibrancy of American Jewry, especially the New York variety.

I encountered the Jewish tradition as a coherent and spiritually enriching way of life. It was profoundly different, yet not necessarily contradictory to my own faith life. I learned to respect Judaism and its traditions, while also being introduced to the traumas of Jewish history. I had already known about the destruction of the Temple in 70 C.E. It was, after all, of great significance to the authors of the New Testament. I learned for the first time what happened to the Jews of the Rhineland during the first Crusade in 1096 and about the expulsion of Jews from virtually all of western Europe over the succeeding centuries, culminating in their expulsion from Spain in 1492. If these and so many similar events had been taught in my Catholic education, they had hardly been highlighted. I had missed them. In effect, the words of Fr. Edward Flannery introducing his classic 1965 book (which I was not to read until later) were very apt for me: "The pages Jews have memorized have been torn from our histories of the Christian era."[2] I did not deeply reflect on this then. It was a relatively minor theme of my major endeavor, learning about Jews and Judaism—a new world for me, a new reality that meant I had to reorganize nearly everything I had ever learned, historically and theologically, into a new overall pattern that would be faithful to the coherent vision in which I had been trained and which gave meaning to my life, and yet faithful to this other, compellingly different yet almost oddly familiar pattern. For with all the differing perspectives on ultimate issues, it was, after all, the same God and the same sacred history being studied. The tragic, suffering elements of that ancient, sacred history were there, to be sure. But they did not predominate for us at NYU in the late 1960s with civil rights and the peace movement capturing the lion's share of our nonacademic attention.

Launching My Career in Christian-Jewish Dialogue

I finished the course work for my doctorate in 1971, having by this time met and married my wife Cathie, who had taken a course on Martin Buber that I taught in the summer of 1970 at the University of Detroit. Cathie and I returned to our native Detroit in the summer of 1971. I obtained a position as director of catechist formation for the Archdiocese of Detroit, and my wife, who had completed her master's degree in theology at the University of Detroit, took a position as director of religious education for a large parish in the city. I also volunteered for the archdiocesan ecumenical commission, and was accepted.

In 1973 a Catholic-Jewish "living room dialogue group" in Dayton decided to hold a conference. Fr. Jack Kelley of the University of Dayton called Father Edward Flannery, then executive secretary of the Secretariat for Catholic-Jewish Relations of the National Conference of Catholic Bishops, and suggested it be called "The First National Workshop on Catholic-Jewish Relations." Cathie and I joined Fr. Alex Brunett (now Archbishop of Seattle), the ecumenical officer of the Archdiocese, at the workshop where I met many of my heroes for the first time: Fr. Flannery, Dr. Eva Fleischner, Rabbi Irving (Yitz) Greenberg, Msgr. George Higgins, Dr. Joseph Lichten, Msgr. John Oesterreicher, Father John Pawlikowski, Fr. John Sheerin, Rabbi Marc Tanenbaum, Sr. Rose Thering, and so many other pioneers of Catholic-Jewish dialogue. I was, I must admit, in awe, and I was stunned when both Fr. Pawlikowski and Rabbi Greenberg cited works of mine approvingly.

Father Brunett was delighted, too, to have a member of his committee so praised, and he was so impressed with the quality of the presentations and discussions in Dayton, that he arranged to have Detroit host the third National Workshop on Christian-Jewish Relations. He also approved my idea of developing archdiocesan guidelines for Catholic-Jewish relations, modeled on, but much more detailed than, the 1967 "Guidelines for Catholic-Jewish Relations" issued by the National Conference of Catholic

Bishops (NCCB), which were the first official guidelines for relations between the Church and the Jewish people issued by any Christian group in the history of Christianity. My Detroit guidelines took advantage not only of the NCCB's guidelines, but also of statements made by several episcopal conferences (notably, the French bishops, 1973) and other dioceses, especially in New Jersey and New York, as well as the 1974 Vatican "Guidelines and Suggestions for Implementing the Conciliar Declaration *Nostra Aetate* (no. 4)" and the NCCB's 1975 "Statement on Catholic-Jewish Relations."

The 1977 National Workshop was a high point in my career. Not only was something we had worked hard on a success, but it was there that I was "discovered." Fr. Edward Flannery was recently retired, so the NCCB was looking for a replacement while I, having recently finished my dissertation (finally!) for NYU,[3] was looking for an academic position. In fact, I had found one teaching Bible and education at Villanova University; the contract was in the mail.

At the Workshop, however, when I gave my own presentation on Jesus and the Pharisees, I noticed three priests in the back of the room assiduously taking notes and conferring softly with one another. "My," I thought to myself, "I must be giving a very good talk." One of the three, Fr. John Sheerin, whom I knew because he was editing the book I had just written,[4] approached and asked if I had a résumé handy. I did, having just been on a yearlong job search. That evening, Father Sheerin again approached me, this time in the speaker's lounge in the hotel, and asked if I would be interested in the position of director of the Secretariat for Catholic-Jewish Relations of the National Conference of Catholic Bishops.

Interested? I could hardly contain myself! I did so long enough to let Father Sheerin know that there was a contract from Villanova in the mail for me—so, in fairness to Villanova, the decision should be made soon. The very next week I found myself on a plane bound for Washington and facing a full day of interviews with NCCB officials, including Fr. John Hotchkin, the director of the Secretariat for Ecumenical and Interreligious Affairs, and the general secretary himself, Fr. Thomas Kelly (now Archbishop of Louisville) who wanted to be certain that I was making a "long term" commitment. The job was too important and relied too heavily on the building of close personal bonds with Jewish leaders to have people coming in and out of it. Indeed, yes, I responded. And so it has been.

Enriching Christian Life
Through Encounter with Judaism

Over the course of many years now, my interfaith involvement with Jews and Judaism has immeasurably transformed and enriched my understanding and practice of Christian faith. Among the many valuable lessons I've learned through Christian-Jewish dialogue, perhaps the most important has to do with the religious significance of family life.[5]

Judaism celebrates the family as the site of essential liturgical practice. The Sabbath, as a day of sacred time with God, appears to have been from its beginning a home festival as well as, under the priestly legislation of Leviticus, "a day for sacred assembly of the larger community" (Lev 23:3). It can be said, I believe, that there existed in ancient Judaism a certain creative tension between centering the religion around the family and centering it around the Jerusalem Temple. (In the post-Temple era this tension has persisted between a home-centered and a synagogue-centered approach to Judaism.) The prophets, though fully supportive of the Temple, inveighed against reducing the people's covenant obligations to Temple ritual, suggesting that what went on in the Temple was meaningless, and even abhorrent to God, unless the people observed in daily life the covenant's mandate of love for neighbor.

The reform of Josiah (seventh century B.C.E.), reflected in the book of Deuteronomy, attempted to centralize Israel's worship in the Jerusalem Temple, apparently because pagan practices were creeping into the people's worship in the hill shrines that at one point dotted the Judean landscape. The Babylonian Exile, however, soon drove home to the people that their God was a different sort of deity, one who could not be localized, one who was always with them, loving them and accessible to them wherever they were. Some scholars thus see in the Exile the origins of the synagogue movement, which was already widespread by Jesus' time (and provided the international network that was the basis for the Christian missionary movement among the nations of the Mediterranean).

The Jews who returned from Babylon brought with them this sense of the immediacy of the divine presence. Even before the Exile, any notion of restricting Israel's worship to the Temple had difficulties, as can be seen, for example, in the fact that the Passover celebration had a family orientation. Josiah's attempt to centralize worship in the Temple had to respect the essential family orientation of the Passover feast. Those assembling in the Temple for the Passover were ordered to "take [their] places by families" (2 Chr 35:4-5). Today, the proper liturgical setting for the Passover meal is not the synagogue but the Jewish home. Services conducted at the synagogue are distinctly secondary in nature.

After the Babylonian Exile, which initiated the Diaspora, the study of Torah, prayers apart from the Temple precincts, and other good deeds gained increasing prominence among Jews as expressions of their religious life and identity. Therefore, after the Temple was destroyed by Romans in the year 70 c.e., it was not difficult for the emerging rabbinic movement to replace the Temple ritual with a system of Torah study, prayers, and good deeds as the central elements of Jewish religious life. Whereas early Christianity replaced the Temple sacrifices with the one sacrifice of Jesus' death, rabbinic Judaism, drawing on insights going back to the prophets, made the life of each Jew a daily offering to the one universally present God.

In Judaism, the family is the primary worshipping community. The synagogue began as a *Beth ha-Midrash,* a house of study (which is, in Judaism, a form of worship). It only gradually evolved into a gathering place for communal prayer. Also, in the Jewish tradition, the Sabbath is officially ushered in not by the rabbi in the synagogue, but by the mother at home when she lights the Sabbath candles. Every week, when the blessings are uttered and the songs sung to welcome the Sabbath, the Jewish home is consecrated anew as a sacred place, virtually the Holy of Holies.

In order to understand the power and significance of home rituals and practices in Judaism, it is necessary to situate them within the concept of Torah, for an essential part of their power is that they are commanded of Jews by God. They are not simply optional pious practices taken on in addition to official religious observance; they are part of the official liturgical life itself, vital to the covenant between God and the people. Since private home rituals performed by Christians are not considered essential liturgical practices, it is wrong to assume that these practices will automatically perform the same family and people-defining function for Christian families as the home rituals do for Jewish families.

The Septuagint and the New Testament both translated the Hebrew term *Torah* into the Greek *nomos,* which in English is "law." Hence, we Christians are used to describing the relationship between the Hebrew Scriptures and the New Testament in legalistic terminology such as the "Old

Law" vs. the "New Law." While the translation is to some extent valid, much of the richness of the original Hebrew *Torah* is lost in the Greek *nomos,* a reductionism greatly exaggerated by centuries of Christian anti-Judaic apologetics.

Torah might be more properly translated as "teaching" rather than as "law." Strictly speaking, it refers to the first five books of the Bible, which contain *halakhah,* the covenant-laws, but also *agadah,* stories that help to define Jewish history and peoplehood. Contrary to Christian apologetics, in Judaism there is no such concept as the "burden of the law." That is a Christian concept derived, I am convinced, from a misreading of St. Paul.[6] There is only joy in the freedom bestowed by Torah, God's gracious gift to the people of the covenant. Indeed, the day on which the annual cycle of Torah readings in the synagogue is completed and a new cycle begun is the profoundly beautiful feast of *Simchat Torah,* "Rejoicing in the Torah," celebrated with joyous songs, processions with the sacred Torah scrolls around the sanctuary, and, in the Hasidic tradition, exuberant dancing with the scrolls. As with *Hanukah, Purim,* and *Pesach,* the merriment of the children is prominent in the celebration of *Simchat Torah.* Those of us who are Catholic could use a bit of this sense of exuberant joy in our own rituals, whether at home or in church. We tend to take our religion far too seriously, even grimly at times.

In any event, to retrieve a sense of family spirituality, Christians ought to look with care and respect on the rabbinic tradition. Jews are bound and yet paradoxically freed by the commandments of the Torah. The Jewish tradition is able to take very seriously what goes on in the home and the marketplace as a "fulfillment" of Torah. These obligations are not general and exhortative, as so often understood in Christian religious life, but quite specific and prescriptive. What one eats, how one travels, when one works, when one rests, all become for the observant Jew opportunities to give praise to God by living as an "image of God" in and for the world. Catholics too often relegate to those officially recognized as "religious" this radical sense of the sacred in ordinary life. So-called "lay" life, Judaism teaches us, can and should be no less God-intoxicated than "religious" life. Christianity should permeate the lives of Christians no less than Judaism permeates the lives of observant Jews.

In appropriating the term "people of God" for the Church, Vatican II opened up exciting new possibilities for Christian self-understanding. Many of these possibilities were not easily discerned in the traditional monarchical model of the Church that applied the terminology of the state rather than that of community to the mystery of the Church. In the context of its meditation upon the Church as a people called into being by God, the Council was able to reactivate the ancient notion of the family as a form or type of the Church: "The family is, so to speak, the domestic Church. In it, parents should, by their word and example, be the first preachers of the faith to their children."[7]

From this conciliar perspective, it is theologically inappropriate to make too strict a distinction between the parish church as a "sacred place" and the home as a "secular place." The Christian home, no less than the Jewish home, is capable of becoming a sanctuary. David Thomas is to the point when he writes: "The mystery of the Church is lived out on many levels. . . . Therefore, the family ought to manifest liturgically its ecclesial status."[8] I believe this. But for such a vision to come true, real ecclesiastical teeth must be put into the movement, and this will require more involvement by Catholic liturgists, theologians, and, yes, canon lawyers. Home rituals put into practice by those interested in family ministry are laudable and perhaps will pave the way for what is needed. But they will remain simply pious practices of a small minority of families unless they are officially tied into the liturgical life of the Church as universal practices recognized on our liturgical calendars. Family spirituality needs some "law" in it to find its full freedom of expression as a reality in the Church's life.

In Judaism many of the concepts that we Christians normally take to be polar opposites are understood more profoundly as correlatives, differing facets of one deeper reality. Law and grace are not, in Judaism, the opposites that Christians often make them out to be. In fact, the greatest grace is Torah—not only the *agadah* of Torah but also the *halakhah*, the covenant-laws or commandments. And the greatest freedom is the freedom to observe the Torah's commandments. There is wisdom here from which we Christians can learn much about the immense potential of our own religious tradition.

What we can learn, then, is relatively simple, but no less crucial for its simplicity. Unless the concept of the "domestic church" is institutionalized it will remain a marginal footnote to the texts of Vatican II. Unless home rituals are universalized, made part of the official liturgical calendar of the Church, they will remain optional pieties for a tiny minority. Official rituals for the home need to be developed and given due weight in our liturgical lives. *Lex orandi lex credendi:* the law of prayer, liturgy, is the law of belief. If we believe that family is the root of community, of *ecclesia*, we must embody that belief liturgically, so that the action of the family at prayer is the action of the Church universal at prayer.

The denial of Christian "rootedness" in living Jewish tradition resulted in an impoverishment of Christian understanding of its own ritual practices. Since theology involves a meditation upon and an articulation of faith and liturgy, Christian theology has been impoverished over the centuries by its artificial and unnecessary denial of its own natural tie to living Judaism. Today, after Vatican II, Catholics are rightly trying to retrieve that fuller sense of the Christian tradition lost in the de-Judaizing process of the early Christian centuries. Judaism has a number of essentially home-oriented feasts, which, as such, define for Jews what it means to be a people in covenant with God. Christian ways of rooting peoplehood in family will necessarily differ from Jewish ways. But Christianity needs this rooting, which is more likely to occur when and where Christians draw inspiration from Jews and Judaism.

Notes

[1] This section includes an adaptation and expansion of some paragraphs in my "Being Catholic, Learning Jewish," *From the Unthinkable to the Unavoidable: American Christian and Jewish Scholars Encounter the Holocaust,* eds. Carol Rittner and John K. Roth (Westport, Conn.: Greenwood Press, 1997) 41–55.

[2] Edward Flannery, *The Anguish of the Jews: Twenty-Three Centuries of Anti-Semitism* (New York: Macmillan Publishing Co., 1965) xi. Cf. the revised edition of that book (New York: Paulist Press, 1985) 1: "Those pages of history Jews have committed to memory are the very ones that have been torn from Christian (and secular) history books."

[3] Eugene J. Fisher, *A Content Analysis of the Treatment of Jews and Judaism in the Current Roman Catholic Textbooks and Manuals on the Primary and Secondary Levels* (Ph.D. diss., New York University, 1976; Ann Arbor, Mich.: University Microfilms International).

[4] Eugene J. Fisher, *Faith Without Prejudice: Rebuilding Christian Attitudes Toward Judaism* (New York: Paulist Press, 1977; rev. ed., New York: Crossroad, and Philadelphia: The American Interfaith Institute, 1993).

[5] The remainder of this essay is an adaptation of excerpts from my article "Creation, Family, and People of God: What Catholics Can Learn from Jews," *Religion and Intellectual Life* (Spring 1987) 118–32.

[6] Cf. Philip A. Cunningham, *Jewish Apostle to the Gentiles* (Cambridge, Mass.: Twenty-Third Publications, 1986).

[7] Vatican Council II, *Lumen Gentium,* Dogmatic Constitution on the Church (1964) no. 11.

[8] David Thomas, quoted in National Conference of Catholic Bishops, *Pastoral Plan for Family Ministry* (Washington, D.C.: United States Catholic Conference, 1978) 18.

nine

MICHAEL B. McGARRY, c.s.p.

The Path to a Journey

Nothing dramatic, but still memorable. My first girl friend was a Jew. Joan and I "sealed our love" by drinking from the same gutter when we were both four years old in Los Angeles. Then she and her family moved to Washington, D.C., and I was heartbroken. Not really, of course; I was too young. I begin my story here because Joan was the only Jew I knew while growing up in Los Angeles or studying in Baltimore, Washington, and Toronto.

Although we parted in early childhood, much later there was one moment of attempted meeting. In 1969 when I was studying in Washington, my mother suggested that I contact Joan's family with whom she had kept in contact over the years. So I telephoned them and they were gracious enough to invite me over to their home for Passover. I was excited at the prospect of seeing Joan again after all these years. When I arrived and saw she wasn't there, I queried: "Where's Joan?" The answer was disappointing: "She's following some guru over in Afghanistan." Those were the years.

A Fortuitous Introduction

My introduction to Jewish-Christian relations was never so personal, never so poignant as that of many of my colleagues. It happened quite fortuitously one day in graduate school at the University of St. Michael's College, Toronto, in the early 1970s. Even from my youngest years, I had wondered about the eternal fate of those who were not Catholic. Although I was always taught that you did not have to be Catholic to be saved, I still wondered. So I enrolled in an elective course titled "Salvation Outside the

Church." One day the professor said, quite offhandedly, "It would be an interesting study to examine the christology of the Christian participants in the Jewish-Christian dialogue." At that time, I was much more interested in completing my studies for the priesthood than in pursuing a lifelong academic career. I had witnessed my fellow graduate students spend weeks, even months, trying to find an interesting thesis topic, only to discover that someone had found it before them. I grabbed that professor's sentence out of the air and made it my own, planning a systematic series of steps leading to the completion of my thesis. I was confident that I would objectively, systematically, and dispassionately pursue this thesis to its completion, and go on from there. But I was wrong. Never did I imagine how much this work would alter the course of my life.

In the early 1970s, what we now smoothly refer to as "the Jewish-Christian dialogue," especially in its Catholic expression, was in its incipient stages. The Second Vatican Council (1962–1965) had recently concluded and, among its sixteen promulgated documents was *Nostra Aetate,* the Declaration of the Church's Relationship to Non-Christian Religions, which, with its section on the Church's relationship to Jews and Judaism, signaled a new direction in Catholic-Jewish relations. So my thesis work would begin with a study of the christological perspectives—both explicit and implicit—discernible in those parts of the council documents, particularly *Nostra Aetate,* which speak of Judaism and the Jewish people. I would then proceed to examine the christologies discernible in other official church statements, both Catholic and Protestant, issued since Vatican II that addressed Christian-Jewish relations. After that I would explore the christologies operative in the writings of Christian theologians who, as one of their primary organizing principles, self-consciously engaged contemporary Jews and Judaism.

I set off into the considerable holdings of the University of Toronto Library and into the various denominational archives in the Toronto area. It soon became obvious to me that there were relatively few official church statements to examine and that the number of contemporary Christian theologians who self-consciously engaged Jews and Judaism was rather limited. But there were pioneers in this endeavor, and I was to meet them through their writings and some also in person. Among the Protestants who had begun to cut paths that others would follow in this field of Christian-Jewish relations were Alan Davies, A. Roy Eckardt, James Parkes, and J. Coert

Rylaarsdam. The Catholic scholars who influenced my early thinking in this area included Gregory Baum, Edward Flannery, Eva Fleischner, Monika Hellwig, Harry McSorley, John Oesterreicher, John Pawlikowski, Rosemary Ruether, John Sheerin, and Thomas Stransky.

As I pursued my graduate research, two significant reference points soon emerged: first, the phenomenon of dialogue, in particular interreligious dialogue, and, second, the *Shoah,* which we then uniformly referred to as the "Holocaust." I will deal with each in turn.

Exploring the Phenomenon of Dialogue

During the early 1970s the University of Toronto was vibrant with the thought of truly significant theologians, including Gregory Baum (one of my professors and thesis readers), Leslie Dewart, and Bernard Lonergan, and the influence of the University's great neo-thomists Etienne Gilson and Jacques Maritain could still be felt. On the theological periphery, but known in much wider circles, was Marshall McLuhan, the great communications theorist. His presence, sometimes profound, sometimes puckish— but never dull—reminded us to be keenly alert to the communication process itself. Accordingly, in my studies I became aware of the use of language in dialogue, especially of the language used in the presence of, and, to a degree, because of, "the other." In other words, I became aware of the phenomenon of dialogue.

Before the 1960s, with few exceptions, the Catholic Church felt it had much to say to people of other religions, but not much to learn from them. The proposition that "error has no rights" hung over the Church as a legacy in many forms and poses. This was not to say, of course, that no Catholics were involved in dialogue with people of other religions, but interfaith dialogue was certainly was not a *corporate value* within the Church. Nevertheless, there were some pioneers in this area and, though my own work at this point did not include much experience of interfaith dialogue, I was able to study the religious and theological language of those Christians who were actively engaged in the Jewish-Christian encounter.

Dialogue, by definition, requires alternate moments of speaking and listening. Concerning the speaking, those who are sensitive to the phenomenon of dialogue are careful with their language in order to clearly and accurately express their beliefs. At the same time, they are careful with their language in order not to offend their dialogue partners. Many communication theorists have insisted that language not only describes a universe but also creates one. Genuine interfaith dialogue requires great care to articulate beliefs of a cherished tradition, and it requires further caution to avoid offending people from other traditions. Such care and heightened awareness may slowly but irreversibly change a participant's theological universe.

What I found in my study of those Christians involved in interfaith dialogue with Jews was that they were indeed careful about the language they chose when articulating their beliefs. I assumed that this was out of respect for their dialogue partners and out of a desire to represent accurately what they believed. They avoided certain simplistic and exclusivistic words and phrases, and they instead used more inclusive and flexible expressions. It seemed to me that these theologians realized that, in the presence of others who were not of their faith, some of their "business-as-usual" theological expressions were no longer appropriate. In this regard, language that suggested that only Christians could be saved, that the Jews killed Christ and all succeeding generations were guilty of that crime, that the Jewish religion of the first century was excessively legalistic and moribund, and that the Church had replaced the Jews as God's chosen people— all such traditional Christian claims now appeared inappropriate and had to be scuttled, or at least "softened."

The notion that the Church had replaced the Jews as God's chosen people was and remains especially important for Jewish-Christian dialogue since it epitomizes the theme of "supersessionism," which is that cluster of theological affirmations asserting that the role of the Jewish people in salvation history has been taken over—superseded—by the Christian Church. Thus, from a supersessionist perspective, God no longer has a covenant with the Jewish people, but has shifted into a covenantal partnership with Christians instead. According to this view, Judaism no longer has reason to exist—which is to suggest that the continued existence of the Jews as a people is without purpose. This, for centuries, had been the claim of the Church triumphant, the Church that had much to teach others but little, if anything, to learn from them. But with the advent of interreligious dialogue as an ecclesial posture, the Church had to begin to reform its language and, indeed, to supersede its supersessionist theology.

The shift away from a supersessionist position involved, in my view, both negative and positive movements. Negatively, it meant that the Church had to divest itself of its supersessionist teachings, which had become so central to the Church's self-understanding. It was imperative that the Church repudiate its supersessionist teachings because, in the first place, these teachings have given Christians the excuse and the ammunition to be prejudiced against Jews and even to persecute them. Second, these teachings had to be renounced simply because they have misrepresented Judaism and the Jewish people and, likewise, because they have distorted Christian self-understanding. The spiritual beauty and depth of Judaism have not been reflected in traditional Christian teachings about Judaism. Moreover, essentially Jewish characteristics of Christianity have been either ignored or expunged from the understanding and practice of Christian faith.

Positively, a post-supersessionist Church needed and needs Christians to dialogue with Jews, to study Judaism with them, in order to learn how Jews understand and practice their faith. Thus the charge of the Vatican Commission for Religious Relations with Jews: "Christians must therefore strive to acquire a better knowledge of the religious tradition of Judaism: they must strive to learn by what essential traits Jews define themselves in light of their own religious experience."[1] This endeavor will not only help us as Christians to gain a more accurate view of Jews and Judaism; it will also help us to better understand the source of many essential features of Christianity and to retrieve lost or forgotten treasures bequeathed to us from Judaism.

One feature of a more accurate understanding of Jews and Judaism that Christians can acquire from Jewish-Christian dialogue is the realization that Jews do not define themselves in terms of "denying Christ" (which is so often how they are defined by Christians) but rather in terms of the revelation central to what we call our "Old Testament" and also in terms of post-biblical rabbinic writings such as the Talmud and the Midrash. Down through the ages, in response to various historical circumstances (the destruction of the Second Temple being one of the most dramatic examples), Jews have had to reinterpret God's perennially valid biblical revelation to them. This Jewish tradition of reinterpretation is exceedingly rich, and for us Christians to ignore it is our loss. We should study this Jewish tradition, and the best way to do this is in dialogue with Jews who know it. Moreover, our study of this tradition should not be something we do merely out of archeological or historical interest. Rather, it should be for the purpose of understanding a living tradition—and a living people. In turn, this study of Judaism, with its rich tradition of scholarship and religious practices, may enrich and transform our Christian self-under-standing and faith.

Dialogue and its attendant appreciation for past and contemporary Jewish thought and practice are critical parts of the Christian move away from its supersessionist past and its persistent supersessionist inclination. Supersessionism has flourished in an atmosphere of monologue—where we Christians have imagined what Jews believe, or where we have projected onto them notions culled, for example, from polemical passages in the New Testament or in the writings of the Church Fathers. In an atmosphere of mutual respect, hearing how Jews define themselves and experience their tradition, Christians can readily conclude that Jews have developed a bountiful tradition after the New Testament period and have continued to be nourished by both biblical and post-biblical thought. Particularly influential for my own development in this regard have been the writings of such Jewish thinkers as Franz Rosenzweig, Abraham Joshua Heschel, Emil Fackenheim, Leon Klenicki, Irving Greenberg, and Harold Kushner. The fact that these are modern and contemporary thinkers illustrates the point that, for me, the Jewish tradition is a living, life-giving tradition that continues to draw from its past and creatively address contemporary issues.

I believe that the turn to Jewish history and to contemporary Judaism, to how Jews have coped and continue to cope with successive challenging circumstances, will reveal to Christians that God has not abandoned the Jewish people—that theirs is not a superseded religion, nor they an obsolete people. To the contrary, Christians who engage in interfaith dialogue with Jews will discover a vibrant people with a dynamic religious tradition. Furthermore, for those of us who have been overwhelmed by studying the history of Christian antisemitism and the *Shoah,* the encounter with contemporary Jews and with living Judaism will help us to avoid despair and will restore our hope in the resiliency of the human spirit. To be sure, studying the tragic history of Christian antisemitism and the *Shoah* is an important enterprise, no matter how overwhelming and demoralizing it is. But tragedy does not define Judaism and the Jewish people. Yes, the story of the Jews is a story replete with tragedies, but it is also a story

of overcoming tragedies. It is a story filled with blessings—of God's blessings on the Jewish people and of the Jews blessing God in good times and in
bad. This is a story we Christians need to know, and when we know it we
will never again tell our story—the story of Christian self-understanding and
faith—in supersessionist terms. Such is the fruit of interreligious dialogue.

Confronting the Shoah

While my study of the phenomenon of dialogue was of crucial importance to my developing an appreciation of Jews and Judaism as well as a
post-supersessionist Christian theology, my study of the *Shoah* had an
even greater impact on my theological perspective. For a number of years
after the end of World War II, the Jewish community, both in the West and
in Israel, found itself nearly paralyzed in facing what had happened to the
Jewish people in the *Shoah*. Similarly, but for different reasons, Christians
only very slowly came to grips with the effects of the *Shoah* on Christian
self-understanding and faith. I was no exception. In my nearly twenty
years of Catholic education, I had not studied the *Shoah* at all. Because of
this lacuna in my education, the work on my graduate thesis came to a full
stop when I faced the *Shoah* in my exploration of Jewish-Christian dialogue. As the bare and almost unbelievable facts began to form a mosaic
for me, I wondered, "How could it have happened? How could it have happened that in a Christian country, indeed on a continent where the vast
majority of people were Christian, one group of people sought to destroy
another people *just because they were that other people?* How could it have
happened?"

In the early stages of my reading about the *Shoah,* an answer
emerged: the Christians were simply not Christian enough; if they had
only followed the teachings of their Master by loving their brothers and
sisters, they would never have perpetrated such horror. But, I should have
known, a quick and facile answer to a profound and disturbing question is
often an inadequate answer.

As I continued my study of the *Shoah,* I was struck by an insight
found on the first page of Fr. Edward Flannery's groundbreaking book
The Anguish of the Jews: Twenty-Three Centuries of Anti-Semitism: "The
pages Jews have memorized have been torn from our histories of the Christian era."[2] In Toronto I began to read those pages, which happen to be

about Christian anti-Judaism and antisemitism. In reading them I realized that my first answer as to how the *Shoah* could have happened in a Christian country and on a Christian continent—that Christians were simply not Christian enough—now needed to become more nuanced. As a result, the answer was to become more troubling.

Most influential in my research on Christian anti-Judaism and antisemitism was a study done by Fr. Gregory Baum. Originally published in 1961 as *The Gospel and the Jews,* his book was slightly revised and received wider distribution in 1965 under the title *Is the New Testament Anti-Semitic?*[8] The question of antisemitism, it seemed, had to be pursued even into the Gospels themselves—and that was a most disturbing idea for me to accept. I knew that, for a long time, scholars who employed historical-critical methods in biblical studies had questioned ideological and polemical dimensions of the Bible. But it was frightening to discover that the possible source of the nearly two millennia of Christian anti-Judaism was to be found in Sacred Scripture.

In his book Baum acknowledged that "Christianity [including the New Testament] wrongly understood offers a constant temptation for hostility against the Jews,"[4] but he nonetheless concluded that Christian antisemitism was a later development in Christian history. But by the early 1970s Baum had changed his mind. In his introduction to Rosemary Radford Ruether's *Faith and Fratricide: The Theological Roots of Anti-Semitism,* Baum claimed that the Vatican II's "acknowledgment of the Jews . . . as spiritually alive was against the teaching of Christian Scripture and tradition."[5] This did not lead him to suggest that this Vatican II teaching should be repudiated or even revised. On the contrary, he suggested that Christian theologians might "submit the gospel to a radical critique . . . in obedience to God's Word in the present," a Word that summons us "to remove the elements of death from the Christian message of life and to reinterpret . . . the self-understanding of the Christian Church."[6]

For my part, I concluded in my thesis that "whether the New Testament is antisemitic or not, there is no dispute that it was read in an antisemitic way by some in the Church."[7] I might have said that it has been read and continues to be read in an antisemitic way by *many* Christians. Nevertheless, since writing my thesis, I have been persuaded by the evidence to a less radical conclusion than the one reached by Baum in the early 1970s. I now side with those who claim that the Gospels, written *within* the matrix of the Jewish world, reflect intra-community disputes rather than the Christian anti-Judaism and antisemitism that came later.

Although Baum came to believe that the New Testament contained antisemitic elements, he did not suggest, as some scholars eventually did, that there was a "straight line" from passages in the New Testament to the gas chambers of the *Shoah.* While acknowledging that traditional Christian teachings about Jews and Judaism "aided Hitler's purposes," Baum believed "it would be historically untruthful to blame the Christian Church for Hitler's anti-Semitism and the monstrous crimes committed by him and his followers."[8] Here I agree with Baum. In my view, with the Nazi project there was a qualitative shift from religiously-based antisemitism to a racially-based antisemitism. At the same time, however, I fully grant that the constellation of church teachings—often referred to as the "teaching of contempt" for Jews—created an atmosphere within which this new deadly mutant of antisemitism was not adequately challenged, let alone squelched, by Christians.

Examining Post-Shoah Christologies

While I was deeply concerned during my Toronto studies with the questions of whether the New Testament is inherently antisemitic and whether some of its teachings led directly to the *Shoah,* my thesis focused not on these questions but on post-*Shoah* christologies. I began with a study of the christological perspectives discernible in those parts of the documents of the Vatican II that mention Judaism and the Jewish people.[9] It was clear that the council fathers, in the Declaration on the Relation of the Church to Non-Christian Religions, committed the Church to a posture of dialogue with no mention about missions to the Jews. However, in the documents other than *Nostra Aetate* where reference is made to the Jewish people, Christ is presented as the fulfillment of Israel's hopes. Moreover, in *Ad Gentes Divinitus,* the Decree on the Church's Missionary Activity, where there is no reference to Jews, the traditional universal character of the Christian mission to convert all people to Christ is affirmed. While Vatican II opened the door of interfaith dialogue for the Church, the preponderant christology expressed by the council affirmed Christ as the fulfillment of Israel's hopes and as the sole mediator of salvation. I found it significant, however, that statements affirming the latter were not found in those parts of the council documents that made explicit reference to Christian-Jewish relations. I wondered if it was possible to formulate a christology that did not compromise traditional christological beliefs and, at the same time, acknowledged the continuing validity of Judaism.

After examining the documents of Vatican II, I turned my attention to subsequent church statements, both Catholic and Protestant, that addressed Jewish-Christian relations, and I noted some definite christological drifts in those statements.[10] While for centuries Christians tended to ignore the fact that Jesus was a Jew, all the statements I examined suggested that Jesus could only be properly understood as a Jew. Although many mentioned that Jesus was the fulfillment of Israel's messianic hopes, the later documents tended to speak of partial fulfillment in Jesus and of complete fulfillment—the object of both Christian and Jewish hopes—coming only in the end times. None of the statements claimed that Jesus broke away from Judaism, but they saw in Jesus a new beginning or a new covenant which did not abrogate the Jewish covenant. Some statements suggested that Jesus was the sole mediator of salvation while they also tried to leave theological room for the abiding validity of Judaism, but they did not delineate how these beliefs might co-exist.

Next I focused on the christological perspectives of Christian theologians who were involved in Jewish-Christian relations.[11] Some theologians, while deploring antisemitism and calling for a Christian appreciation of the Jewish heritage, believed there was a radical difference between Judaism and Christianity and claimed that there was no possibility for a "bridge theology." Others articulated a bridge theology that maintained the theological integrity and validity of both religious traditions. Many located the foundation for their bridge theology in a proper understanding of Jesus Christ.

As an analytical tool in my investigation, I adapted the schema that Roy Eckardt used to describe theologies that account for the relationship between Christianity and Judaism—theologies of discontinuity and continuity.[12] The theology of discontinuity, applied to christology, stresses the uniqueness and finality of Christ; the universality of Christ as the sole mediator of salvation; Christ as the fulfillment of Jewish hopes and prophecies; Christ as the leader and embodiment of the New Israel, successor to Judaism; and the necessity of preaching Christ to the Jewish people. The theology of continuity, applied to christology, stresses Christianity as the continuation of Israel's covenant, which Christ does not abrogate but rather opens up to the Gentile world. This christology speaks of the abiding validity of the covenant with Israel; the positive Jewish witness to the unredeemed character of the world and, therefore, the positive witness of the Jewish "no" to Jesus; Christ as *partial* fulfillment of Jewish messianic prophecies; and the eschatological unification of all God's people.

In the conclusion of my thesis, I noted Eva Fleischner's claim that various christologies existed already in the New Testament period, to say nothing of the christological pluralism after apostolic times.[13] I suggested that some form of *Logos*-christology, which emphasizes that Jesus incarnated the *Logos* (Word) of God revealed also apart from Jesus, may prove fruitful as a way for Christians to recognize the validity of Judaism (and other religions).[14] From the perspective of *Logos*-christology, properly understood, Judaism may be seen as not only preparing the way for Christianity but also as one of God's ways of continuing to communicate the divine *Logos* to the world. We Christians do claim to have a vision of the truth—a vision we treasure and want to share. But many of us who have been involved in Jewish-Christian relations have come to see this vision as including the ongoing validity of Judaism. A *Logos*-christology, which is able to account for Jesus as incarnating God's Word for Christians while also accounting for the abiding validity of the Jewish tradition, may, in the end, bring about a new rapprochement between Christians and Jews.

Reconsidering Roman Catholic Understandings of Mission

Certainly a most important motivation in my early years of studying the Jewish-Christian encounter was my own rich, though parochial, Roman Catholic upbringing. A shadow side of this parochialism was the sometimes not-so-subtle suggestion that Catholicism was the only true religion and Catholics would be the only ones saved.

As mentioned above, my early graduate studies moved me to take the course "Salvation for Non-Christians," which prompted the questions I addressed in my thesis. My membership in the Missionary Society of St. Paul the Apostle, better known as the Paulists, brought into focus dimensions of this problematic issue. As a community, the Paulists are committed to spreading the Gospel in North America. So I found myself wondering what "mission" could mean for the Church now that it is committed to dialogue with its Jewish brothers and sisters. I sought to address the following questions: Just what do we believe about the salvation of others, in particular the Jews? What might be the significance of Jesus Christ for the salvation of non-Christians? What might be the salvific efficacy of non-Christian religions, in particular Judaism? If non-Christians can be saved, what is the purpose of Christian missionary activity? These questions led me to explore the tension between the traditional Roman Catholic missionary rationale and the Church's newly emerging dialogical relation with the Jewish people.[15]

Since Vatican II, the Roman Catholic Church has vigorously pushed the missionary life. Nevertheless, from my study of recent church documents that deal specifically with evangelization, it is clear that the Catholic Church at this time does not wish to mount a mission directed at the Jews.[16] The favored term for the Church's address outside itself—according to the repeated usage of Pope John II—is *ad gentes,* which is arguably best translated as "to the Gentiles."

My own efforts to reconcile mission and interreligious dialogue have been animated by at least two beliefs. The first belief is that dialogue is not only about "setting the record straight" about sins of the past, but also about finding God's truth in the present and for the future. For some Christians who are new to Christian-Jewish dialogue, learning about our conflicted history often provokes a paralyzing sense of guilt for what our Christian ancestors did to Jews. They understandably conclude that we should no longer try to convert Jews but, after all that has transpired, we should just leave them alone. In my view, this is not enough. Interreligious dialogue should not simply expose the sins of the past but, ideally, create new avenues to share truths in the present and to foster new possibilities for the future. The second belief that animates my efforts to reconcile mission and dialogue flows from the first. It is my conviction that we must refrain from missionizing Jews, not out of guilt, but rather out of a realization that the Jews remain in covenant with God.

Much theology that is sympathetic to the relationship between Christianity and Judaism seems to be motivated by guilt for what Christians have done to Jews throughout history. At times this theology appears to be driven by the commitment to never allow another *Shoah.* As noble as that motivation is, it is more important and ultimately more lasting that we base our newly developing relationship with the Jewish people on what we believe God has revealed about the permanent validity of God's covenant with the Jewish people. Like Judaism, Catholicism values tradition just as it does Scripture, and this tradition can be used to correct former teachings. The new interfaith relationship between Christians and Jews requires faithful imagination about what we hold most dear even as we listen for the Spirit's guidance as to where we need to go.

We Christians hold dear the conviction that God wants all people to know of God's steadfast love for them, but in the last half century we have come to realize that Jews know of God's steadfast love precisely in the context of their own covenantal relationship with God. We Christians believe with all our hearts that Jesus Christ mediates God's saving love, but we also believe deeply that God's redemptive love is made available to Jews in their covenant with God. Thus, the Roman Catholic Church can exempt the Jews from their missionary aims not because of any timidity or lack of faith, but because it believes passionately what has been revealed: that salvation is God's work, not ours, and that God is faithful to God's covenant with the Jews.[17] From the Catholic perspective, Jewish life and faith are crucial for the very notion of God that we profess. That is, we believe our God is ever faithful. Thus, God's covenant with the Jews is a commitment from which God has never backed away. If during the first centuries of the common era, Christians felt the need to develop an apologetic of Jewish hard-heartedness and wickedness to explain why all Jews did not become Christian, now after Auschwitz we Christians must retrieve and develop a fresh apologetic of God's faithfulness to the Jews and of Jewish faithfulness to God by way of their covenant. In a post-*Shoah* world we Christians must not seek the end of the Jewish people by means of conversion. To the contrary, we must seek to support the survival of Jews *as Jews*. Our new relationship to the Jewish people must be one of dialogue, not proselytism—and we refrain from proselytizing Jews not because we are fainthearted, but precisely because we believe passionately in the God who is forever faithful.[18]

Preaching in a Post-Shoah Context

A second direction in my own thinking and pastoral work has been a growing passion for how my work affects pastoral preaching. Vatican II sparked in Catholics a new interest in the Scriptures, one which we have learned from our Protestant brothers and sisters. This new appreciation of Scripture has, in turn, inspired more biblically-based preaching by Catholic priests and deacons. I have been particularly concerned that the Church's newly emerging teaching about Jews and Judaism reach "the people in the pews," as the cliché puts it—and the way that most teaching might get to the people in the pews is by way of the pulpit.

For more than a decade now I have been privileged to participate in the regular gatherings of the National Workshop on Christian-Jewish Relations, which have featured practical sessions on the implications of the new relationship between Christians and Jews. At many of these workshops, I have offered sessions for local clergy and other preachers about how to preach the Scriptures without being anti-Jewish and antisemitic. The question with which I began my study of Christian faith in relation to Jews and Judaism— the issue of anti-Judaism and antisemitism in the Scriptures themselves— finds its most practical application in how these Scriptures are read and interpreted within the Christian community as it gathers for Sunday worship.

In my own Roman Catholic tradition, the weekly scriptural homily has become a fixed part of our worship and has assumed greater importance since Vatican II. As a preacher, I have devoted myself to the practical task of sharing the Scriptures with the people. I have been particularly attentive to scriptural passages that have been commonly read in anti-Jewish ways—passages that depict the Jewish people as the opponents of Jesus, that seem to contrast Jesus' teachings with other Jewish teachings, and that appear to underscore Jesus' rivalry with particular groups of Jews (e.g., the Pharisees). These passages require a sophistication about how they might be heard and applied in a post-*Shoah* world, and they require creative responses and interpretations—which I have done my best to employ. This dimension of my own journey has not found its way into print other than through occasional homilies written for national homiletic services in the United States, but it has been a very important feature of my journey.

Living and Working in Israel

In 1985 I had a sabbatical during which I pursued Jewish studies at the Hebrew University, and this acquainted me with two places that would abide in my consciousness and alter the course of my life: the State of Israel itself and Tantur Ecumenical Institute located in the southern part of Jerusalem, just north of Bethlehem.

I was thoroughly intrigued with Israel as a place of multiple layers and unending complexity. Between 1985 and 1998 I made six trips to Israel to attend scholarly conferences and to visit friends and holy sites. There was something in the land that kept drawing me back. When, in the early 1990s I visited Israel for a conference held partly at Tantur, something deep in me told me that I would return, for I wished to work for Christian-Jewish reconciliation in the Jewish state. I spoke of my dream with fellow Paulist Fr. Tom Stransky, then rector of Tantur. He laughed, "Oh, so you want my job, do you?" In a rare moment of modesty I replied: "No way. I have too much to learn. I want to apprentice with you." So it was that even in 1993 as I took a position as pastor of Newman Hall, the Catholic parish serving the University of California, Berkeley, I held on to my dream of someday living and working in Israel.

When in 1998 Tom Stransky announced that he would retire the following September, I received permission from my Paulist superiors to apply for his position. After an international search, culminating in interviews at Tantur's sponsoring institution, the University of Notre Dame, I was chosen for the position of rector.[19] I began my preparation even as I finished out six years as pastor in Berkeley.

Beginning in September 2000, the Al Aksa Intifada brought to a bitter close what had been a joyful and extraordinary observance of the Jubilee in the Holy Land. The highlight of that year, without a doubt, was Pope John Paul II's pilgrimage to the primary places of salvation history, culminating in a weeklong visit to the Holy Land itself. With vivid memories of the Pope's visit and with the spiral of violence seemingly unabating, I reflect on this phase of my life in the Holy Land, *Eretz Israel,* the land of Jesus. My thoughts focus on two issues: the papal visit in March 2000 and Jewish-Christian dialogue in this land.

In 1904, Theodore Herzl, the father of modern Zionism, approached Pope Pius X, looking for an encouraging word and a blessing upon the Jewish return to the Land. He was stung by the Holy Father's reply: "We cannot encourage this movement. . . . The Jews have not recognized our Lord, therefore, we cannot recognize the Jewish people. . . . And so, if you come to Palestine and settle your people there, we will be ready with churches and priests to baptize all of you."[20]

It would, of course, be an exaggeration to say that every Jewish Israeli has studied the history of relations between the Holy See and the
State of Israel. But they all know at least in a vague way the historical es-
trangement between the Catholic Church and the Jewish state. While Pope
John Paul II consistently emphasized the *spiritual* purpose of his journey
to the Holy Land, the *educational* power of his trip on average Jewish Israelis was extraordinary. Throughout the Pope's visit, Israelis witnessed
moving examples of the new relationship of the Catholic Church to the
Jewish people, and this was particularly vivid in three iconic moments: (1)
John Paul shaking hands with Israeli Prime Minister Ehud Barak, a reverse of the scenario suggested by Pius X; (2) the Pope greeting survivors
of the *Shoah,* painstakingly one by one, at Yad vaShem, the Holocaust
memorial in Jerusalem[21]; and (3) the Pope shuffling to the Western Wall
where, in that most holy of Jewish places, he placed a request for forgiveness for all the offenses Christians had inflicted on "the people of the Covenant" through the centuries.[22]

It was my privilege to help frame and interpret the papal trip to the
Holy Land for an American television network. Such efforts have become
part of my work at Tantur Ecumenical Institute: to interpret the Church,
in all its wondrous and frustrating diversity, to the similarly complex Israeli public.

At the same time a new challenge (actually there are many, but here
I mention only one) has emerged in my journey: how to work with local
Christians, mostly Arab, and local Jews.[23] In this relationship the mindsets
and practices that reflect Western societies often do not find immediate
correspondence. As one local priest cautioned, "Dialogue is a Western im-
port; it does not apply in the Middle East." For communities who have not
gone through the cultural movement we call the "Enlightenment," approaching "the other" as partner with whom one may share and from whom
one may learn can be daunting. The imposing shadow of Israeli-Palestin-
ian *political* relations always impinges on anything so "pure" as *religious*
dialogue. Indeed, in this part of the world, religion and politics are not so
easily separated. So we struggle.

Here in Jerusalem, I am reminded on a daily basis that I carry an
American passport, that I come from the West—and that I have much to
learn. At the same time, I believe that the course of improved Jewish-
Christian relations, which Western churches have charted over the last

fifty years, needs to find local, indigenous expression here in the Land called Holy. With humility appropriate to a newcomer and outsider, I hope to contribute something to the local peoples in this marvelous, fascinating, perplexing, and frustrating land. The violence of recent years must be replaced by life-giving reconciliation in order to help the peoples of this land live together in dignity, justice, and security—however that may be worked out politically by the parties themselves. Here at Tantur we work to bring members of the still divided Christian family together to work against the scandal of our disunity. At the same time, we as Christians, even in our disunited state, reach out to our Jewish and Muslim brothers and sisters, striving to foster dialogue and mutual understanding. The way is not clear or easy, but my life so far in relation to my Jewish brothers and sisters tells me that the way will be rich and, ultimately, of God.

Notes

[1] Vatican Commission for Religious Relations with the Jews, "Guidelines and Suggestions for Implementing the Conciliar Declaration *Nostra Aetate* (no. 4)," (1974) Preamble.

[2] Edward A. Flannery, *The Anguish of the Jews: Twenty-Three Centuries of Antisemitism* (New York: Macmillan, 1964) xi. Cf. the rev. ed. (New York: Paulist Press, 1985) 1: "Those pages of history Jews have committed to memory are the very ones that have been torn from Christian (and secular) history books."

[3] Gregory Baum, *Is the New Testament Anti-Semitic?* (New York: Paulist Press, 1965).

[4] Ibid., 329.

[5] Gregory Baum, "Introduction," in Rosemary Radford Ruether, *Faith and Fratricide: The Theological Roots of Anti-Semitism* (New York: Seabury Press, 1974) 6.

[6] Ibid., 8, 9.

[7] Michael B. McGarry, *Christology After Auschwitz* (New York: Paulist Press, 1977) 4.

[8] Gregory Baum, "Introduction," *Faith and Fratricide,* 7.

[9] See *Christology After Auschwitz,* 13–28.

[10] See Ibid., 29–55.

[11] See Ibid., 56–98.

[12] See A. Roy Eckardt, *Elder and Younger Brothers: The Encounter of Jews and Christians* (New York: Charles Scribner's Sons, 1967) 50–51.

[13] See Eva M. Fleischner, *Judaism in German Christian Theology Since 1945: Christianity and Israel Considered in Terms of Mission* (Metuchen, N.J.: Scarecrow Press, 1975) 134–37.

[14] See *Christology After Auschwitz,* 101–03.

[15] See Michael B. McGarry, "Contemporary Roman Catholic Understandings of Mission," in *Christian Mission/Jewish Mission,* eds. Martin A. Cohen and Helga Croner (New York: Paulist Press, 1982) 119–46; "Interreligious Dialogue, Mission, and the Case of the

Jews," in *Christian Mission and Interreligious Dialogue*, eds. Paul Mojzes and Leonard Swidler (Lewiston, N.Y.: Edwin Mellen Press, 1990) 102–12; and "Can Catholics Make an Exception? Jews and 'the New Evangelization,'" www.bc.edu/bc_org/research/cjl/articles/mcgarry.htm, 1–12, paper presented at the conference "Remembering for the Future II" (Berlin, Germany, March 1994).

[16] In my essay "Contemporary Roman Catholic Understandings of Mission," I analyze the four documents from Vatican Council II (1962–1965) that most explicitly bear on the question of the Church's missionary activity—Dogmatic Constitution on the Church *(Lumen Gentium)*, Decree on the Church's Missionary Activity *(Ad Gentes Divinitus)*, Declaration on the Relationship of the Church to Non-Christian Religions *(Nostra Aetate)*, and Declaration on Religious Freedom *(Dignitatis Humanae)*—and two subsequent papal documents—the apostolic exhortation On Evangelization in the Modern World (*Evangelii Nuntiandi*, 1975) by Pope Paul VI, and the encyclical Redeemer of Humankind (*Redemptoris Hominis*, 1979) by Pope John Paul II. In "Can Catholics Make an Exception?" I again analyzed On Evangelization in the Modern World and also the encyclical Mission of the Redeemer (*Redemptoris Missio*, 1991) by Pope John Paul II, "Dialogue and Proclamation" (1991) by the Pontifical Council for Interreligious Dialogue and the Congregation for the Evangelization of Peoples, and "Go and Make Disciples" (1992) by the National Conference of Catholic Bishops.

[17] See "Contemporary Roman Catholic Understandings of Mission," 142.

[18] See "Can Catholics Make an Exception?" 9.

[19] Tantur was initiated by Pope Paul VI in the late 1960s to continue the stimulating discussions he and other Catholic leaders had with Protestant and Orthodox theologians at Vatican II. The University of Notre Dame underwrites and administers Tantur on land leased to it from the Vatican.

[20] Conversation cited in Sergio I. Minerbi, *The Vatican and Zionism: Conflict in the Holy Land 1895–1925* (New York: Oxford University Press, 1990) 100–01.

[21] Here one should note that the Holy Father, in his frail condition and contrary to papal protocol whereby visitors approach *him*, went to each of *them*. In Israel, there was a corporate emotional gasp as this old man's hands were clasped—indeed locked—in embrace by one woman who claimed that, as a young priest in Poland, he had carried her a number of kilometers to safety.

[22] The text of Pope John Paul II's message in the Western Wall reads: "God of our fathers, you chose Abraham and his descendants to bring your Name to the Nations: we are deeply saddened by the behaviour of those who in the course of history have caused these children of yours to suffer, and asking your forgiveness we wish to commit ourselves to genuine brotherhood with the people of the covenant."

[23] To this, I must add the blessing and challenge of working among Muslims for new bridges of understanding.

ten

MARY C. BOYS, s.n.j.m.

The Road Is Made by Walking

> Walker, walker, there is no road.
> Walker, walker, there is no road.
> The road is made by walking.
> *Antonio Machado*

As people on a voyage talk over the experiences and the purpose of their trip, the church engages in conversation on its journey through history. We talk as we walk, and theology is a part of such conversation . . . in which we reflect on what we have been saying, try out more adequate ways to speak and clarify the criteria for making such corrections. . . . The flow of our talk depends on the movement of our feet. If we stumble over rough terrain, we cannot pretend that this does not cause gaps in the conversation. If we are out of breath from the steepness of the Way at some moment, we may have to walk a while in silence. The concrete humanity of our conversation is brought home to us by such limitations. There are other activities as human as theology, but there is not one that is more human.[1]

The road to reconciliation between Jews and Christians is made one step at a time. This is one walker's story.[2]

Setting Out on the Road

I belong to the generation of U.S. Catholics initially raised on the Baltimore Catechism, then enveloped in the thinking of the Second Vatican Council (1962–1965) in adolescence. While the Council's theologies have profoundly reshaped my understanding of Catholicism, many of the questions and answers of that catechism seem eternally etched in my brain. Ask any Catholic of similar background, "What is a sacrament?" and we will all respond without hesitation, "A sacrament is an outward sign instituted by Christ to give grace." Yet I have no recall of the following question and answer, which I discovered a couple of years ago while preparing a class on the history of Catholic religious education:

Q. Why did the Jewish religion, which up to the death of Christ had been the true religion, cease at that time to be the true religion?

A. The Jewish religion, which, up to the death of Christ had been the true religion, ceased at that time to be the true religion because it was only a promise of the redemption and figure of the Christian religion, and when the redemption was accomplished and the Christian religion established by the death of Christ, the promise and figure were no longer necessary.[3]

The long, clumsy sentence would have made memorization difficult. Moreover, I suspect our teachers had little curiosity about Christianity's relationship with Judaism, since the Jewish population at that time in the Pacific Northwest, where I grew up, was small. Learning that Christianity had made Judaism obsolete was not nearly as important as being able to refute the more numerous Protestants. Our vocabulary had not yet expanded to include "ecumenism" or "interreligious dialogue."

If the catechism's perspective on Judaism had little effect, it nonetheless provides a snapshot of the supersessionist theology that suffused Church life prior to Vatican II. The solemn liturgy of Good Friday included a prayer for the "perfidious Jews" until Pope John XXIII removed it in 1959. Texts presented the Old Testament as mere promise, the New Testament as fulfillment. Sermons suggested that the gospels' depiction of legalistic Pharisees represented the emptiness of Judaism at the time of Jesus. Our formation in faith entailed a disparagement of Judaism, even if it avoided (as did mine) maligning Jews as "Christ-killers." Of course, the world included Muslims, Buddhists, and Hindus, (and a host of other religious peoples) but they were too exotic to figure in our parochial religious landscape. At any rate, the catechism informed us, "true religion was not universal before the coming of Christ. It was confined to one people—the descendants of Abraham. All other nations worshiped false gods."[4]

I am grateful that my socialization through ritual, symbol, and story provided a rich sense of Catholic identity that complemented the propositions of the catechism and compensated in large measure for its dry didacticism. It is clear, nonetheless, that our identity was formed *over against* the religiously other, all of whom conveniently fit under the rubric "non-Catholic." Only Catholics, we were told in the pulpit and classroom, "had" the "true" faith.

The realities of family and neighborhood, however, often undermined the theological absolutes presented to us with such assurance. The catechism's claim that Judaism was no longer a true religion could not compete with the positive associations I already had with Judaism, thanks to our close family friend Pauline Lee, a Jew who—most impressive to me—owned a candy store! On a more profound level, her friendship with three generations of our family implicitly taught me about accepting differences. While my maternal grandfather was not religiously affiliated, my grandmother was actively involved in Catholic life in Seattle, and three of her four children (including my mother) were lifelong, practicing Catholics. None seemed to have had the slightest thought of converting Pauline, despite the theology of the time—a fact my eighty-eight-year-old aunt confirmed when I phoned her to check the accuracy of my perception.

My father, a man of integrity and generosity but no religious affiliation, offered another challenge to absolutist theological claims. He has thus played an important role in my thinking about belief and salvation. One of my few distinct memories as a first-grader is the sure knowledge that my teacher, whom I otherwise adored, was wrong in asserting that "only Catholics went to heaven." I could never believe in a heaven that would not include my father. Interacting with neighbors, family, and friends of moral integrity who belonged to other Christian denominations—or none at all—contributed to further cognitive dissonance.

Fortunately, the burgeoning ecumenical movement provided impetus during my high school years to explore religious differences and to engage with those whose perspectives differed from my own. The advent of Vatican II made it an exciting time to be a Catholic. Belonging to a Church opening its windows to let in fresh air animated my interest in religion, and provided a major motivation for my lifelong professional work in religious education. In 1965, during my senior year, a group of us in the Sodality sponsored an afternoon of conversation with the youth group from a nearby synagogue. It was my first step on the journey of dialogue.

Religious Life: A "Blue Highway"

That journey, however, took a circuitous route, as I joined a women's religious community, the Sisters of the Holy Names of Jesus and Mary, in 1965, spending the initial years of formation near Portland, Oregon, and then in Spokane, Washington. As a congregation known historically for its commitment to education and to the arts, its members were then principally involved in the consuming work of running schools, with little opportunity for sustained interaction outside the Catholic realm.[5] Yet living in the religiously variegated and relatively "unchurched" Pacific Northwest meant we had more frequent contact with "non-Catholics" than would have been the case in places where Catholicism was dominant (especially the cities of the eastern seaboard).[6] We also interacted more with the religiously unaffiliated than would have been the case in places where Christianity suffused the culture, such as the South. The geographic location of my province also meant less knowledge of anti-semitism than was characteristic of places such as Quebec, where our congregation originated in 1843 and where many members still live.[7]

Moreover, religious life, as I have come to discover, offers distinct possibilities for engaging beyond the borders of one's denomination. By entering a community of women religious, I had seemingly set out on a "blue highway," a back road removed from society's major thoroughfares.[8] Indeed, as Sandra Schneiders observes, members of religious communities occupy a marginal position.[9] We have renounced marriage and the creation of a family, personal ownership and pursuit of corporate wealth, and full and independent participation in political life and processes. We choose this marginality for the sake of prophecy, not escapism. Religious life exists at the edge of society's system in order to recognize and repair how that system harms those it excludes.

This marginality bears significance for involvement in the interreligious terrain today. It offers the impetus for and freedom to recognize the Spirit of God wherever it may be moving, a point to which I shall return in the concluding section. Moreover, there is power in the margins—as a doctoral student once commented to me after I returned a draft with numerous comments penned in the margins! Only the professor, she observed, gets to write in the margins.

In the late 1960s, however, we were more concerned with moving from the confines of the cloister to the wider venue of the world. What should be our role? Though still immersed in the Catholic world, the momentum of Vatican II provided energy for us to look outward. During this period, I also discovered Rabbi Abraham Joshua Heschel's work, initially his book on the prophets,[10] which contributed significantly to my love not only of the prophetic writings but also of the "Old" Testament (as I then called it). It is a book to which I return regularly, particularly to reflect on his profound insight into God's pathos, which has been so formative for my understanding of God.[11] I also engaged in some modest ecumenical activity with local evangelical churches. Those were the early days of the Catholic charismatic movement—Pentecostalism in liturgical dress—and I participated in a number of prayer meetings, only to grow disillusioned by the anti-intellectualism.

The Educational Path

After finishing my B.A., with majors in religion and in English, and fulfilling the requirements for certification as a secondary teacher in Washington State, I remained in Spokane to teach high school. It was all consuming, with classes and extra-curricular activities—sports, retreats, student council, debate—and I loved it! I hoped to go to graduate school for a doctorate in New Testament, but without question, I knew that I should first get experience in teaching.

Those five years of teaching made an enormous difference. I became a student of the educational process as well as the Bible, and this dual commitment decisively shaped not only my graduate studies but also my entire professional life. Teaching has graced me by opening new horizons, raising challenging questions, and expanding my world. Even as teaching demands incredible energy and creativity, it is immensely life giving.

Entering the doctoral program in 1974 in religion and education jointly sponsored by Union Theological Seminary and Teachers College, Columbia University, provided me ample space to study those two disciplines—and proximity to Jewish Theological Seminary of America, where Heschel had taught before his death in 1972. As I walked the streets of my new Morningside Heights neighborhood, I regretted that it was no longer possible to meet Heschel on the street. While my forays into Jewish Theological Seminary were few—I felt very much a stranger then—my studies in Christian origins and biblical hermeneutics at Union opened a new world of thinking about the relationship of Judaism and Christianity. I began to grapple with the complexity of the Church's emergence from formative Judaism, and realized how simplistically we had learned (and taught) this development. I realized with increasing dismay the chasm between the findings of biblical scholars and theologians and what preachers and teachers were saying. In particular, I became more critical of the motif of "salvation history," which we had used in introducing our students to the Bible in those high-school religion classes. It became the subject of my doctoral dissertation, and my first sustained theological contribution to the conversation between Jews and Christians.[12]

Most of those theological conversations at that juncture, however, were with other Christians, most notably with my mentor, Fr. Raymond E. Brown, S.S. His enormous erudition, eagerness to learn from Jewish scholars, dedication to scholarship in the service of the Church, support for women, and great kindness exercised a profound influence on me.

Yet, if in those days I learned theology principally from Christians, a few Jewish classmates from Teachers College became my instructors in Jewish life. Intense conversations after classes, supplemented by exposure to New York's Jewish culture, such as expeditions to the Lower East Side, expanded my education. Because one of my friends worked long hours to help organize the Israel Independence Day Parade, she insisted not only that I come but also that I sit in the viewing stand, where, to my mortification I was the only one who did not know *Hatikvah,* the Israeli national anthem. A year later she invited me to her family's *Seder* in Dayton, Ohio. Again, I was the only non-Jew, but her family's hospitality enabled me to feel comfortable.

Meanwhile, Boston had become home to me, where I began teaching at Boston College in the fall of 1977. The city is justly famous for its labyrinthine streets and gridlock. It opened new horizons, however, in the interreligious realm. Invited to join the Catholic-Jewish Committee, which met monthly to discuss an array of issues, I became part of a network of men and women from various walks of life who cared deeply about the relationship of our two communities. I made my first trip to Israel in the late 1970s with a group of Jews and Catholics from the Boston area led by long-time members and friends Rabbi Murray Rothman (a part-time colleague in the Boston College theology department who died in 1999) and Fr. Robert Bullock, a local pastor. The scholarship of colleagues at Boston College, particularly Anthony J. Saldarini and later Donald Dietrich, furthered my knowledge of Judaica and of the Holocaust.[13] I wrote my first article on the implications of Jewish-Christian dialogue in the early 1980s, "Questions Which 'Touch on the Heart of Faith.'"[14] I remember how important the essay became to me as I was working on it, but I had no sense of how the questions I took up then would persist and intensify.

A sabbatical in 1983 gave me the privilege of spending a semester in Israel at the Ecumenical Institute for Theological Research at Tantur, on Jerusalem's southern boundary. Living in Israel allowed me to experience being a member of a minority religion, and revealed the tortuous complexity of the Arab-Israeli relationship and the politics of the Middle East. It also exposed me to diverse Christianities (e.g., Arab-speaking Greek Orthodox, Copts, Armenians), provided entrée into various groups of Jews and Christians engaged in dialogue (e.g., the Rainbow Group in Jerusalem), and provided occasion for more contact with the Sisters of Sion, who have become increasingly important to me because of their communal commitment to the Jewish people.[15] My experience during that sabbatical, reinforced by many subsequent trips, has given me a feel for the importance of the Land in Jewish life. Above all, Israel itself became a tangible reality—a tiny nation state in which two peoples struggle to live together—not simply the rarefied "Holy Land." While praying for the peace of Jerusalem, I frequently think of Zechariah's vision of what peace might mean:

> Thus says the LORD: I will return to Zion, and will dwell in the midst of Jerusalem; Jerusalem shall be called the faithful city, and the mountain of the LORD of hosts shall be called the holy mountain. Thus says the LORD of hosts: Old men and old women shall again sit in the streets of Jerusalem, each with staff in hand because of their great age. And the streets of the city shall be full of boys and girls playing in its streets (Zech 8:3-5).

Forging New Educational Pathways

When I returned from Israel, I became increasingly involved in integrating the scholarship of the Jewish-Christian dialogue with pastoral and educational matters in the Church. In many ways, it was (and remains) a lonely pursuit. With the exception of Gabriel Moran and, more recently, Padraic O'Hare, few of my colleagues in the Association of Professors and Researchers in Religious Education (APRRE) seemed to consider it relevant.[16] I found it ironic that a number who were pursuing the implications of liberation theologies for the educational and pastoral realms seemed disinterested in the scholarship that posed such fundamental questions about Christian self-understanding. Even more problematic were the unacknowledged anti-Jewish elements in most of these liberation theologies.

My lack of clarity about how to pursue the dialogue *as a religious educator* meant I had to "walk my thought." That is, I had to pursue the questions in my own way, which is through teaching, with its imperative to study and to approach knowledge with an eye toward making it accessible. While not ready to teach a full course on the subject (suspecting as well that my colleagues would have viewed it as peripheral to the curriculum), I increasingly integrated concerns into my courses. In "Biblical Interpretation in Education and Ministry," the relationship between the testaments became a major component. We studied ways that the Church had understood that relation over the ages, and how the liturgy enacts it, primarily through the lectionary and the literary-theological technique of typology.

Mindful that many Christians regard the "Old" Testament as virtually irrelevant to their lives, I gave priority to its texts in the course "Biblical Spiritualities for the Educational Ministry" in order to reclaim them for Christian spirituality. Among many other passages, we pondered anew the Ten Commandments ("Ten Words," in Hebrew; Exod 20:1-17 and Deut 5:6-21). In considering the imperative to "keep holy the Sabbath," we drew upon Heschel's *The Sabbath,* which challenged us to think more deeply about what Sabbath might mean for Christians today. For many it was also an initial encounter with the profundity of Jewish thought on Sabbath observance—and a hint at the riches of thought Christians might uncover if they removed the layers of supersessionism obscuring an adequate portrayal of Judaism.[17]

Paging through the files of those courses for this essay, I realize how much they enriched me—and, I hope, those who took them. Mindful I was teaching those committed to ministry in the Church, I always kept my eye on the question, "What difference does this make?" I was not then, nor am I now, a specialist in Judaica or in Jewish-Christian relations. My approach has always been that of a religious and theological educator seeking to understand and practice Christianity.[18] What I have learned while walking is that "conversation with Jews is indispensable to understanding the Christian faith." History demonstrates that "apart from listening to and talking with Jews, we will misunderstand the Christian faith and act on our mis-understandings."[19]

My most intense experiences of "listening to and talking with Jews" has come through my collaboration with Sara S. Lee, director of the Rhea Hirsch School of Education at Hebrew Union College-Jewish Institute of Religion, Los Angeles. We met in the spring of 1985, when Sara, a Boston native, came to brief me about an upcoming speaking event she was or-ganizing. We connected from the start, and began involving one another in projects. Each of us was immersed in her own religious tradition, and con-vinced learning about the other was vital to that tradition—a remarkable conviction in light of Sara's experience as a child of antisemitism at Catholic hands. Each of us had a passion for teaching and shared the language of education, thus enhancing our professional collaboration. As our friend-ship deepened, so too did the foundation of trust necessary for the work of dialogue.

When we wrote a grant proposal in 1991–1992 to the Lilly Founda-tion to engage in a multi-year "Catholic-Jewish Colloquium" for twenty-two leaders in religious education, our ideas were still inchoate. We had a good sense of the issues, but realized we were setting out into uncharted territory. We believed educational leaders in the synagogue and church could widen the circles of dialogue if they became knowledgeable, but no one before us had mounted a sustained program for Jewish and Catholic educators to study together in a systematic fashion. We knew the resources, both texts and scholars, but we had no overarching vision of a curricu-lum. Sara and I invested hundreds of hours of preparation. We had to make this road by walking, one session at a time.

What distinguished our walk was our determination to make educa-tional process central to dialogue. We drew upon our professional exper-tise as teachers to give depth and texture to dialogue. We provided excellent resources for the participants to *study,* and sent them questions and exer-cises to prepare for each session. We structured generous stretches of time (never enough, they told us) for discussion with one another as well as with guest scholars—and spent hours crafting questions for these discus-sions. We honored the formative aspect of education by investing signifi-cant time in building community in each session. We also structured the sessions for participants to share their own deep attachments to Judaism or Catholicism by exploring rituals and practices. Studying together and conversing about what mattered most in our respective religious traditions was a profound experience for all of us.[20]

Our first project (1992–1995) left us with the question of how religious educators might educate in ways that stimulate a deep and learned commitment to their own tradition of faith while simultaneously impelling persons to participate in building a religiously pluralistic society. We are pursuing this question through our current project, "Educating for Religious Particularism and Pluralism." It has been slow going: The issues are more complex, and the literature more diffuse; we have even less of a map to follow than we did previously. We, however, have enjoyed what novelist Wallace Stegner calls a "moment of complicated clarity," and I shall draw upon some of our insights in the final section of this essay.

What we learned by "walking" in these projects is that educational process, particularly study and conversation in the presence of the other—"interreligious learning"—is the key to transformation. We are convinced that interreligious learning takes dialogue to a greater depth by involving persons in a *relationship* of mutual study. Interreligious learning gives pride of place to substantive conversation. It moves beyond the exchange of "tea and sympathy" in which differences are glossed over, and avoids adversarial modes in which differences become points of competition and contention.[21]

My experience in collaborating with Sara, and my more recent team teaching with Professor Carol Ingall of the Jewish Theological Seminary, heightens my belief that educational process is a necessary component of Jewish-Christian dialogue.[22] Leading such educational processes involves far more than skills. It depends upon practicing what Nicholas Burbules has called the "communicative virtues," general dispositions and practices that help support successful communicative relations with a variety of people over time.[23] They include tolerance, patience, an openness to give and receive criticism, a readiness to admit that one may be mistaken, the desire to reinterpret or translate one's own concerns so that they will be comprehensible to others, the self-imposition of restraint in order that others may speak, and the willingness to listen thoughtfully and attentively. Dialogue, then, is not only an outcome of careful educational process, but also a way of life that requires a great deal of work. I find it a deeply religious activity, a theme to which I shall return.

Little did I realize when I began teaching how profoundly ecumenical and interreligious dialogue would affect my life, both personally and professionally. After seventeen years on the faculty of a large Catholic university, I have been teaching for the past nine years in a historically Protestant seminary remarkable for its diverse racial, ethnic and denominational mix. Ecumenical dialogue is implicitly part of the daily work, whether in classes or in the myriad activities beyond the classroom. Because my appointment also involves serving as an adjunct professor at Jewish Theological Seminary, I work with colleagues and students primarily through its William Davidson School of Jewish Education. Since 1998, I have served as an outside consultant (and the only non-Jew) at the Hebrew Union College/Jewish Institute of Religion in rethinking its rabbinic curriculum across its four campuses (New York, Cincinnati, Los Angeles, Jerusalem). Thus, in my day-to-day life I engage constantly with those who, to varying degrees, have different religious sensibilities, practices, and beliefs. The encounter is, of course, two-sided, as many of those with whom I interact have had relatively little encounter with Catholics.

Few of these encounters constitute dialogue in the formal sense. Much of what we do together is mundane—planning courses and conferences, writing papers together, attending a seemingly endless round of meetings, and forming coalitions around common concerns. We seldom bring to an explicit level what we are absorbing from working across boundaries of difference or how our experiences take us out of our comfort zones. When, however, we do have occasion to reflect, we realize that we have changed each other.

Viewing the Road from the Other's Side

The vitality of Judaism graces my life. It is my study partner, as it were, in the arduous process of discerning God's voice in the cacophony of our times. I cannot imagine practicing Christianity without loving Judaism as I have learned it from friends as well as from study. Encounter with Judaism has breathed new life into the dry bones of my compulsions by energizing me to keep Sabbath each Sunday. It has given me new appreciation for the power of Catholic liturgical life, has enabled me to uncover new layers of meaning in sacred texts, and has bequeathed me friendships that enrich my life immeasurably.

Christian life without engagement with Jews is impoverished. When, as I occasionally hear a student relegate the religious other to the category of the "unsaved," or I hear Christians claim that the way of Jesus Christ is the *only* true way to God, I feel deep sorrow. I feel a similar regret when I find a contemporary catechism asserting: "By celebrating the Last Supper with His apostles in the course of the Passover meal, Jesus gave the Jewish Passover its definitive meaning" and "The Sabbath, which represents the completion of the first creation, has been replaced by Sunday."[24] I grieve not only because of the supersessionist theology that has been so disparaging of Judaism but also because of the absence of any encounter with *living* Judaism that such claims reveal. I suspect the authors have never been privileged to participate in a *Seder* or share in a *Shabbat* meal or experience interreligious learning. Consequently, they perpetuate a form of catechesis that shapes religious identity in an oppositional manner—as if the profound meaning of the Eucharist and the significance of Sunday were lessened by Jewish thought and practice of Passover and *Shabbat*. This catechesis seems all too reminiscent of that older catechism's declaration that Judaism had ceased being the "true religion" with the death of Christ.

Dialogue demands reconstruction of Christian self-understanding precisely because so much of how we think about Christianity is built upon a distorted portrait of Judaism. This daunting task is at once the great challenge and vital gift of relationships with knowledgeable Jews. At the heart of such relationships is the discovery of the *living* Jewish tradition, a disclosure in tension with the way many of us learned about the "Jewish roots" of Christianity. This discovery necessitates reexamining conventional understandings, and may, as in the case of the distinguished Episcopal theologian Paul van Buren (d. 1998), stimulate a fundamental reorientation: "I set about reconstructing how Christian theology might look if it incorporated an acknowledgment of the Jewish people as continuing, living Israel."[25] My own encounter with the living Jewish tradition inspires a passion to develop ways of educating in faith that foster religious commitments that are clear and rooted—grounding persons in their tradition's way of life—yet simultaneously ambiguous and adaptive, recognizing the inadequacy of any one expression of faith in the infinite God. It compels me to develop more adequate ways of interpreting Scripture, celebrating liturgy, and drawing upon our symbol systems.[26]

Reconstructing our theology may *seem* like a cerebral task—and, without question, it *is* intellectually demanding. Insofar as it entails revising our religious self-understanding, it is also a deeply emotional process, forcing us to wrestle with our own ignorance, misunderstanding, bias, and finitude. On occasion, it requires leaving the familiarity of our own tradition to enter as strangers into the other's world. It entails developing not only a new perspective on the other, but also on ourselves.

Revelation at the Crossroads: Finitude and Power

As Judaism and Christianity have met in my life, I have come face-to-face with the finitude of my own tradition. I have also experienced its power anew.

My visceral sense of the finitude of Christianity has deepened as my knowledge of Jewish-Christian relations over time has developed. If we are to heal the "still open wounds" of history and ameliorate the "teaching of contempt," we must probe the ways in which theology has legitimized the vilification, denunciation, and persecution of Jews.[27] Facing this history is a humbling task. For example, recently I spoke to a group of Holocaust survivors in tandem with the author of a novel about the impact of the Spanish Inquisition on Jews.[28] Yes, I could explain (at least in part) the factors that shaped the Church's mentality of sixteenth-century Spain—but *this* audience sitting before me knew far better than I that the prejudices and persecution of the late medieval Church provided fertile ground on which "the venomous plant of hatred for the Jews was able to flourish"[29] in *their* lives. As one member of the audience asked me after another lecture: "How could those who believed in the Gospel of Jesus Christ have done such atrocities in his name?" For such questions our catechisms provide no answers.

Although many Christian churches, and the Catholic Church in particular, have recently expressed sorrow and repentance for past sins against the Jews, and resolved that the "spoiled seeds of anti-Judaism and antisemitism must never again be allowed to take root in any human heart,"[30] such expressions do not sufficiently permeate Christian self-understanding. Catholics and other Christians have some excellent documents about our relationship with the Jewish people and tradition, but too frequently the insights of those documents remain isolated from other doctrinal statements. The message of the documents has yet to suffuse Christian life.

Interreligious encounter reveals the incomprehensibility of God, who alone is infinite and absolute. God's incomprehensibility exposes the limited perspectives of one's own religious tradition. Even as I believe ardently in the Way of Christianity and aspire to live it as a practicing Roman Catholic, I know it does not exhaust the paths by which God draws us— and I cannot believe it is *the* superior way by which God calls *all* to walk. In the theological realm this means reexamining the traditional affirmations of Christianity regarding Jesus as Lord and Savior of all in light of the knowledge and wisdom gained through interreligious encounter in our time. Traditional doctrinal formulations are important; they express the continuity of faith over the ages, and should not be swept aside in mere fervor for what is new. Neither, however, should they become idols. The Church articulated them in particular times and cultures in response to specific crises; they must be interpreted in their historical contexts. It is the Church's task to discern the Spirit's movement in every age.

Surely we must detect the movement of the Spirit in the dissolution of walls of misunderstanding, intolerance, and enmity between religious groups. Surely, also, when women and men of deep, if differing, faith come together in our time, the Spirit's presence inspires us to conceptualize our relation to other religions in terms our ancestors in faith could not have imagined. Those who speak in the name of the Church must listen attentively to those at the forefront of interreligious dialogue who have spent years pondering its meaning. Like many others, I am troubled by a document such as the recent declaration from the Congregation for the Doctrine of the Faith, *Dominus Iesus,* which approaches dialogue from above, judges pluralist theologies in sweeping generalizations, assumes the posture of omniscience and objectivity, and reasserts traditional formulations without nuanced appraisal of present developments.[31] In conflating pluralism with relativism, *Dominus Iesus* ignores the work of significant theologians who insist that interreligious dialogue necessarily includes attention to difference.[32] We may not yet have fully adequate theologies of pluralism, but their blanket condemnation in *Dominus Iesus* overlooks promising pathways, prematurely settles complex issues, and places learned, creative theologians under a cloud of threat.

My involvement in Jewish-Christian dialogue fosters an intense interest—and stake—in this question of pluralism. While I make no pretense of having worked out a fully satisfactory understanding from a Catholic perspective, my current project with Sara Lee, to which I alluded earlier, provides a useful conceptual scaffold. By beginning with two sets of differentiations, we have tried to avoid the extremes of fundamentalism and relativism. We first distinguished different modes of "religious particularism," that is, practicing a specific religious way of life. An *impoverished* particularism is synonymous with parochialism; it is superficial, provincial, and religio-centric, if relatively benign. In contrast, an *adversarial* particularism diminishes, caricatures, or even demonizes the other. Ignorant of the other, it gives rise to bigotry and serves as a foundation for discrimination (e.g., white supremacist groups and the Taliban). An adversarial particularism rightly gives religion a bad name—but it ought not to be confused with a *textured* particularism that is rooted in the rich images, practices, symbols and stories of one's religious traditions.

Textured particularism is fundamental to our project. A rich and receptive particularism is necessary for developing a religious identity that is simultaneously rooted and adaptive, assured and ambiguous—one that allows for engagement with pluralism. A textured particularism is passionate, implying deep, even visceral connections to one's religious tradition. It requires a serious immersion in the community's life—in those symbol-rich moments in which the divine presence and the power of the faith community are experienced. At the same time, the requisite knowledge of one's tradition contributes to a profound humility about the tradition—the ways in which the community of faith has been unfaithful to its vision of God, and the finitude of its beliefs and practices.

While we discern a threefold differentiation of particularism, we suggest that *pluralism* needs to be distinguished from *universalism, absolutism,* and *relativism.* In *universalism,* differences are diminished or even repressed. So much attention is devoted to commonalities that differences are overlooked, dissolved, or reduced to the lowest common denominator (e.g., Hanukkah/Christmas cards in which Santa Claus lights a menorah). *Absolutism,* in contrast, regards one's own belief as superior to all others, and thus judges entirely from within one's standpoint. Whatever differs from the "absolute truth" is in error. *Relativism* recognizes differences, but levels them in such a way that there are no criteria for distinguishing the ethical stance from the unethical position, the good practice from the harmful practice.

To our way of thinking, then, pluralism implies a careful attention to differences. This means recognizing, appreciating, studying, and valuing differences—not simply regarding the other as a curiosity or phenomenon. The requisite attentiveness results in the realization that my lens on the world (or my tradition's set of beliefs) is not the only lens (or belief

system), and allows differences to penetrate one's taken-for-granted beliefs. Thus, pluralism transcends mere tolerance. Rather, it *implies a desire
to learn from differences without adopting or absorbing the other.*

To learn from difference means not only seeing the limitations of
one's tradition, but also appreciating its power in a new way. Dialogue with
Jews has heightened my interest in Christianity's distinctive doctrines and
practices (e.g., the Trinity and the Eucharist), and deepened my appreciation for its modes of contemplative prayer and discernment. It has renewed
my commitment to Catholic social teaching and fostered a far deeper grasp
of the importance of practices in sustaining a religious way of life.

In my experience, dialogue with Jews deepens appreciation for mystery, for the ungraspable nature of truth, for the "more than" of religious
experience. It has stimulated me to ponder more profoundly the One Beyond All Names and to probe more seriously who this God is who "saves"
and "redeems." It has challenged me to wrestle with painful questions of
God's absence or powerlessness that arise out of reflection on the *Shoah*.
Thus, I find that Judaism, particularly as Jewish friends and colleagues
mediate it, reveals new layers of meaning in my vocation insofar as it opens
up new—if often unsettling—vistas on God.

At the same time, my immersion in a women's religious congregation provides a sort of compass for walking along the interreligious road.
The relativism and indifferentism the Vatican fears do not surface. To the
contrary, engagement with the religious "other" has intensified my desire
to be a learned and committed Catholic. It may be that my location in a
community—albeit one with few involvements with Jews and Judaism—
contributes to this. Sandra Schneiders suggests that because members of
religious communities are absorbed in the God-quest as the primary concern of their lives, they are "sensitively attuned to religious and spiritual
developments inside and outside the Church." Belonging to a religious order
allows one to be "at once very deeply involved in institutional Catholicism
and often widely and deeply involved in the experiences of spirituality beyond its denominational boundaries."[33]

The religious needs of the postmodern world require doctrinal flexi-
bility and conversation across boundaries of faith and practice. Yet, boundaries remain necessary for cross-fertilization. Rather than "chain link fences
guarded by Dobermans," boundaries can be "loci of interaction," as Rachel
Adler suggests. They are like the cell membrane, the perimeter at which

the cell conducts its interchanges with other cells. In a religious tradition with such a living, permeable boundary, "the contacts, the flowings in and out . . . maintain its life within its environment." Adler holds that for Jews the notion of *Tzedek* (justice as righteousness) enables persons to understand themselves as subjects with "permeable boundaries, contiguous with the boundaries of neighbor-selves."[34]

Religious life provides me an atmosphere in which permeable boundaries can be developed and maintained. Sandra Schneiders argues that a religious community can embody a vital Catholic Christian spirituality that is able to "provide a stable and secure base for interaction with currents of spirituality that are not explicitly Catholic and, equally importantly, a wisdom context within which to discern what is and what is not compatible with and enriching of Christian faith." She points out that members of a religious community "can celebrate in the power of age-old Catholic liturgical ritual even as they develop new forms of prayer suitable for this cultural setting" and "can draw on and learn from the wisdom of the Catholic mystical tradition even as they learn from the prayer traditions of other faiths."[35]

The "blue highway" of religious life has proved an excellent site from which to join the march of Jews and Christians on a pilgrimage of reconciliation and renewal. Along the way, I have had many memorable conversations with learned, committed men and women. We have all stumbled a few times, and found the hills more challenging than we had anticipated. The road we are making by walking, however, leads to new vistas. Like the road to Emmaus, conversation with the stranger makes all the difference for following the Way.

Notes

[1] Paul M. van Buren, *Discerning the Way: A Theology of the Jewish-Christian Reality* (San Francisco: Harper & Row, 1980) 13, 15.

[2] An earlier, briefer version of this essay appeared as "The Transformative Power of Interreligious Dialogue," SIDIC *[Service International de Documentation Judéo-Chrétienne]* 33/1 (2000) 2–7.

[3] *A Catechism of Christian Doctrine Prepared and Enjoined by Order of the Third Plenary Council of Baltimore,* no. 3 (New York: Benziger Brothers, 1921) 79; Q & A 391. This is the Baltimore Catechism, first published in 1885, and revised in 1941; Q & A 391 unchanged in the 1941 revision.

[4] *A Catechism of Christian Doctrine,* 97; A. 487.

[5] In its earliest years, the congregation conducted schools for girls from families of limited means. Educating the poor and disadvantaged remains a central focus of our mission.

[6] The states of Oregon and Washington have the highest percentage of persons who do not affiliate with a church. See Martin B. Bradley and others, *Churches and Church Membership in the United States 1990* (Atlanta: Glenmary Research Center, 1992).

[7] See Michael Brown, "From Stereotype to Scapegoat: Anti-Jewish Sentiment in French Canada from Confederation to World War I," and Pierre Anctil, "Interlude of Hostility: Judeo-Christian Relations in Quebec in the Interwar Period, 1919–39," *Antisemitism in Canada: History and Interpretation,* ed. Alan T. Davies (Ottawa: Wilfrid Laurier University Press, 1992) 39–66 and 135–66, respectively. In general, Jews were regarded as outsiders and a threat to the status quo of the Anglo-Protestant and French-Catholic arrangement.

[8] See William Least Heat-Moon, *Blue Highways: A Journey into America* (New York: Little and Brown, 1999); originally published in 1982.

[9] Sandra M. Schneiders, *Finding the Treasure: Locating Catholic Religious Life in a New Ecclesial and Cultural Context,* vol. 1 (New York: Paulist Press, 2000) 138–44, 348.

[10] Abraham Joshua Heschel, *The Prophets* (New York: Harper & Row, 1962).

[11] Schneiders draws upon Heschel in her theology of religious life. Heschel viewed the prophet's fundamental experience as a "fellowship with the feelings of God, a sympathy with the divine pathos." Schneiders argues that the immediacy to God and marginality to the social order fundamental to religious life cultivate "participation in the divine pathos." "To feel the pathos of God," she continues, "is not a warm and comfortable religious experience; it is an experience of the howling wilderness driving one to protest" (*Finding the Treasure,* 139, 141).

[12] Mary C. Boys "*Heilsgeschichte* as a Hermeneutical Principle in Religious Education" (doctoral diss., Teachers College, Columbia University, 1978). This was later published in revised form as *Biblical Interpretation in Religious Education: A Study of the Kerygmatic Era* (Birmingham, Ala.: Religious Education Press, 1980). For further development, see my "Kerygmatic Theology and Religious Education," *Theologies of Religious Education,* ed. Randolph Crump Miller (Birmingham, Ala.: Religious Education Press, 1995) 230–54.

[13] See especially Anthony J. Saldarini, *Pharisees, Scribes and Sadducees in Palestinian Society* (Wilmington, Del.: Michael Glazier, 1988 and *Matthew's Christian-Jewish Community* (Chicago: University of Chicago Press, 1994); Donald J. Dietrich, *God and Humanity in Auschwitz: Jewish-Christian Relations and Sanctioned Murder* (New Brunswick, N.J.: Transaction Publishers, 1995).

[14] Mary C. Boys, "Questions 'Which Touch on the Heart of Faith,'" *Religious Education* (November-December 1981) 236–56. Earlier, I had written an essay on the work of Holocaust survivor Elie Wiesel, but I had not yet grappled with implications for religious education; see Mary C. Boys, "Contending With God: The Meaning of Faith in Elie Wiesel," *NICM Journal* (Spring 1978) 75–85.

[15] The Sisters of Our Lady of Sion were founded in France in the 1840s for the work of converting Jews, so their present commitment represents a dramatic reversal of their founding vision. I see them as a sort of parable for the Church today. See my "The Sisters of Sion: From a Conversionist Stance to a Dialogical Way of Life," *Journal of Ecumenical Studies* (Winter/Spring 1994) 27–48.

[16] See especially Gabriel Moran, *Uniqueness: Problems and Paradox in Jewish and Christian Traditions* (Maryknoll, N.Y.: Orbis Books, 1992); Padraic O'Hare, *The Enduring Covenant: The Education of Christians and the End of Antisemitism* (Valley Forge: Trinity Press International, 1997).

[17] See Abraham J. Heschel, *The Sabbath* (New York: Farrar, Straus and Giroux, 1951). See also Irving Greenberg, *The Jewish Way: Living the Holidays* (New York: Summit Books, 1988). The superb essay of Dorothy C. Bass, "Keeping Sabbath," in her edited book, *Practicing our Faith: A Way of Life for a Searching People* (San Francisco: Jossey-Bass, 1997) 75–89, was not yet available. See also Dorothy C. Bass, *Receiving the Day: Christian Practices for Opening the Gift of Time* (San Francisco: Jossey-Bass, 2000).

[18] "Religious" educator refers primarily to my concerns to make accessible the knowledge and wisdom of religious traditions, and especially that of Christians. "Theological" educator denotes my interest in the education and formation of professional theologians, clergy and others who serve in pastoral positions.

[19] Clark Williamson, *A Guest in the House of Israel: Post-Holocaust Church Theology* (Louisville: John Knox/Westminster, 1993) 9.

[20] Sara Lee and I have written about this at length in the journal for which we served as guest editors, *Religious Education* (Fall 1996), an issue devoted to "Religious Traditions in Conversation" that includes our analysis of the colloquium, and commentary by eighteen authors (eight of whom were participants).

[21] Leon Klenicki uses "tea and sympathy" to image the initial stage of dialogue that allowed Jews and Christians to see each other as human beings trying to overcome medieval views of each; he sees this stage now to be an interlude between historical moments, and a prelude to a new stage of the dialogue. See his "A Jewish Reflection on the Year 2000," *A New Millennium: From Dialogue to Reconciliation,* eds. Eugene Fisher and Leon Klenicki (New York: Anti-Defamation League, 2000) 66.

[22] Professor Ingall and I taught a course in fall 2000 on "Faith Journeys and the Religious Education of Adults." Students from our respective institutions studied contemporary memoirs and autobiographies by Jews and Christians. While the course did not explicitly revolve around the theological issues in the Jewish-Christian dialogue, we were nevertheless engaging in dialogue.

[23] Nicholas C. Burbules, *Dialogue in Teaching: Theory and Practice* (New York: Teachers College Press, 1993) 42.

[24] *Catechism of the Catholic Church* (Washington, D.C.: United Sates Catholic Conference, 1994) nos. 1340 and 2190, respectively.

[25] Paul M. van Buren, *According to the Scriptures: The Origins of the Gospel and of the Church's Old Testament* (Grand Rapids, Mich.: Eerdmans, 1998) 6.

[26] I have taken up this task in *Has God Only One Blessing? Judaism as a Source of Christian Self-Understanding* (New York: Paulist Press, 2000).

[27] "Our still open wounds" is taken from the statement of the French bishops, "Declaration of Repentance," *Catholics Remember the Holocaust,* ed. Secretariat for Ecumenical and Interreligious Affairs, National Conference of Catholic Bishops (Washington, D.C.: United States Catholic Conference, 1998) 34. Historian Jules Isaac coined the phrase "teaching of contempt" to summarize the way Christianity had taught about Jews and Judaism. This French survivor's audience with Pope John XXIII in 1960 apparently helped to place the

Church's relations with Jews on the agenda of Vatican II. See the account in Michael Phayer, *The Catholic Church and the Holocaust, 1930–1965* (Bloomington and Indianapolis: Indiana University Press, 2000) 203–08.

[28] Lewis Weinstein, *The Heretic* (New York: goodnewfiction.com, 2000).

[29] French bishops, "Declaration of Repentance," *Catholics Remember the Holocaust,* 34.

[30] Vatican Commission for Religious Relations with the Jews, "We Remember: A Reflection on the Shoah," *Catholics Remember the Holocaust,* 55.

[31] The Vatican's Congregation for the Doctrine of the Faith, headed by Joseph Cardinal Ratzinger, promulgated *Dominus Iesus* on September 5, 2000; text in *Origins* (September 14, 2000) 209ff.

[32] See, e.g., Michael Barnes, *Christian Identity and Religious Pluralism: Religions in Conversation* (Nashville: Abingdon, 1989); James Fredericks, *Faith among Faiths: Christian Theology and Non-Christian Religions* (New York: Paulist Press, 1999); and S. Mark Heim, *Salvations: Truth and Difference in Religion* (Maryknoll, N.Y.: Orbis, 1995).

[33] Schneiders, *Finding the Treasure,* 348.

[34] Rachel Adler, "A Question of Boundaries: Toward a Jewish Feminist Theology of Self and Others," *Tikkun* (May/June 1991) 43.

[35] Schneiders, *Finding the Treasure,* 349.

e l e v e n

JOHN C. MERKLE

Faith Transformed
by Study and Friendship

Nearly three decades ago I began to read books about Judaism by Jewish authors. I was in graduate school at the Catholic University of Louvain in Belgium. As an undergraduate I had attended two Catholic seminaries, so I already had read numerous works of Christian theology. When I began reading Jewish sources about Judaism, I was stunned by the radical difference between the Judaism portrayed in those sources and the Judaism depicted in the classical Christian literature with which I had become familiar. There was almost no resemblance between the two.[1]

It soon became evident to me that the Judaism of Christian theology was not anchored in knowledge of Judaism. This caused an acute theological, even spiritual, crisis for me. The problem was not simply that the Church to which I belonged had misrepresented another faith. It went deeper than that, cutting to the very core of Christian self-understanding, for I was all too aware of the fact that, from very early on, the Church had defined its faith in relation to Judaism.

Having emerged as a Jewish sectarian movement, and then having gone its separate way, the Church attempted to legitimize its independent status by presenting itself as the "new Israel" that had displaced the Jewish people, who were thereby relegated to the position of "old Israel." It was now becoming clear to me that for such a claim to be considered true by Christians, Judaism had to be presented as something inferior to Christianity, as an outmoded religion that deserved to be replaced by Christianity. But the Judaism that I was encountering in Jewish sources—and eventually came to encounter in Jewish homes and synagogues—was very much alive and bearing the fruit of holiness. It was a noble and vital faith that had spiritually sustained countless Jews amidst untold persecutions—so often at the hands of Christians. Soon I came to realize that the antisemitism manifested in Christian history was rooted in the anti-Judaism of Christian theology.

Related to the grave moral problem of antisemitism, there was a profound theological problem I knew I had to face. Since the Church's identity had been built in large part upon misinformation about Judaism, I wondered if there was a way of explaining Christian identity apart from anti-Judaism. I wondered how the Church might legitimize its mission other than by portraying itself as the "new Israel" that had replaced the "old Israel." And this was not solely an academic question, but a personal spiritual problem—for I was shaken to the foundations of my spiritual life by the realization that my Church had established its identity over against a misrepresented Judaism.

It wasn't long before I found out that other Christian theologians—though not many of them—were also confronting this issue. And soon after I began studying Judaism, the Vatican Commission for Religious Relations with the Jews, in 1974, issued guidelines for Catholic-Jewish relations, urging Catholics to understand how "Jews define themselves in the light of their own religious experience."[2] I understood this to mean that we Catholics should strive to understand Judaism as Jews define it, not as Christians have defined it. Then another Church document caught my attention. In a 1975 statement, the National Conference of Catholic Bishops emphasized the seriousness of the new Christian encounter with Jews and Judaism. The bishops claimed that "the brief suggestions" on Catholic-Jewish relations of the Second Vatican Council (1962–1965) "have been taken up by some theologians, but their implications for theological renewal have not yet been fully explored."[3] To a large extent, my own theological enterprise has been a response to the challenge of the American bishops to explore these implications. In what follows, I explore a few of these implications as I also convey something of my encounter with Jews and Judaism.

Antecedents of a Transformed Faith

My first real encounter with Judaism came at Louvain through the study of Jewish authors. I had known Jews when I was growing up in New

Jersey, but I hadn't known anything of their Judaism. When I think about it now, I'm surprised I didn't develop a more positive image of Judaism in my childhood than the one I absorbed from religion classes. After all, as a boy I liked and respected the Jews I met—and not only because the ones on my paper route were more generous in tipping me for my service than were my fellow Christians. (Ironically, this was the case especially at Christmastime!) I liked the Jewish children on my paper route as much as their parents, as also the Jews I met at a Jewish Community Center my family joined in order to use its indoor pool one winter. I recall respecting Jews not only because they tipped so well but also because it seemed to me that, in general, they were more knowledgeable and they were better musicians than most people I knew. Given these impressions, shouldn't I have suspected that Judaism fostered generosity, learning, and aesthetic sensitivity? Shouldn't I, therefore, have formed a more positive image of Judaism than the one I was taught at school?

Yes, it was at school, and perhaps also from the pulpit, but not at home, that I was taught that Judaism, after the birth of Christianity, was no longer a means of grace. While I never knew my parents to challenge church teachings, I also never knew them to reinforce negative teachings about Judaism. Besides, they were the only Christian parents I knew who joined a Jewish Community Center! Still, I learned my lesson well at school: the validity of Judaism came to an end with the emergence of Christianity as the one valid pathway to God. (I learned also that Catholicism was the one valid Christian way to God.) It's not that I dwelt on the idea of Christianity replacing Judaism, but being theologically inclined from an early age, I did feel the need to justify my Christian commitment. It made sense to me that there was only one true religion, and I felt secure in knowing I belonged to it. This didn't mean I thought non-Catholics couldn't "get to heaven" (which was the main issue of religion as we were taught it in those days). Still, I believed what I was taught about Catholicism being the only true religion. But since I liked the Jews I knew (and some other non-Catholics as well), I took solace in the admission of my religion teachers, if they were pressed, that God *could* save even non-Catholics if they honestly didn't know the error of their beliefs.

Even when I was in college I believed my religion fulfilled and surpassed Judaism. In my junior year I heard that someone I knew had recently converted from Catholicism to Judaism, and I recall thinking to myself "that was a step backward." Not even my positive encounters with Jews kept me from being a supersessionist! Still, I suspect those encounters pre-disposed me to perceive the grandeur of Judaism once I encountered it in the Jewish books I read while in graduate school. Having read those books, I would be unable to ever again think that converting from Christianity to Judaism "was a step backward."

Faith Transformed by Study

During my years at Louvain, 1972–1976, I read many modern Jewish religious philosophers, especially Leo Baeck, Martin Buber, Franz Rosenzweig, Emmanuel Levinas, Will Herberg, and Abraham Joshua Heschel, as well as several from earlier periods. While all of them helped to foster in me a new appreciation of Judaism, it was Heschel who inspired me the most. Before ever reading Heschel I had read many Christian authors, and though I loved some of their writings, not one of them evoked in me as much as Heschel did such a deep sense of the reality of God.

Soon I learned that many Christians had been similarly inspired by Heschel. To be sure, many Jews have effectively represented the grandeur of Judaism, but Heschel seems to have succeeded in communicating it to a larger Christian audience than anyone else. Living the last decade of his life (1907–1972) in the midst of an interfaith revolution, when Christians more than ever before began to reevaluate their perspectives on Judaism, Heschel had the opportunity to reach the Christian world in ways unknown to Jews of previous generations. And while he was one of many Jewish religious thinkers of the twentieth century to influence Christians, he more than others has been regarded by Christians, at least American Christians, as a spokesman for his tradition.

By reading Heschel and other Jewish theologians, I perceived Judaism in a way completely opposite to how it has been portrayed in Christian polemics. No longer did I see it as "the religion of the Old Testament," as so many Christian writers put it. I came to see how Judaism has developed as a rich and diverse tradition from biblical times onward to this very day. Also, I learned that what unites the diverse forms of Judaism is the fact that each in its own way represents faith in God, expressed by some degree of adherence to the Torah, within the context of the covenant of Israel.

Since God, Torah, and the covenant of Israel are three central categories of Judaism, it makes sense that when Christian theologians have attempted to demonstrate the superiority of Christianity over Judaism they have claimed that the Jewish understanding of God, the way of Torah, and the covenant of Israel have been superseded by the Christian view of God, the Gospel of Christ, and the new covenant in Christ. But through my study of Judaism I came to believe that various Jewish understandings of God as they have developed through the centuries are every bit as profound as what Christian theologians usually have claimed can be attained only by means of Christian faith; that the way of Torah, which in traditional Christian literature has been declared abrogated, continues to bear the fruit of holiness; and that the Jewish people, whose "old covenant" with God supposedly had been replaced by the "new covenant" in Christ, have endured for more than three millennia precisely because of the enduring vitality of Jewish covenantal life. In coming to these beliefs I was, of course, developing a new understanding of Judaism, one very different than the traditional understanding I had been taught. As a result, I inevitably had to develop a new understanding of Christian faith in relation to Judaism, also radically different than the traditional one I previously held.

Faith Transformed by Friendship

While my first real encounter with Judaism came by way of study, it wasn't long before friendship with Jews nurtured my appreciation of Judaism even more than had my study of Jewish texts. My time and study with Jews have left me with the same question that Protestant theologian Robert McAfee Brown raised after his encounters with Rabbi Heschel. He asked "What have I got to tell this man about God?" Brown confessed that he "never found an answer" to that question and "at this stage of Christian-Jewish dialogue" he remained "content to learn."[4]

This is precisely how I have felt after some of my encounters with Jewish friends. Brown confessed that his experience with Rabbi Heschel left him "disquieted." My experiences with Jews have often left me disquieted as well, destabilizing my previous understanding of Judaism and of Christian faith in relation to Judaism. These encounters have convinced me that Judaism provides my Jewish friends with the spiritual resources and insights that Christian theologians typically have claimed are available only through faith in Christ. Through study, I had already concluded that Judaism enabled Jews to be as close to God as Christians could be in the context of their faith. The presence of Jewish friends in my life set the seal on that conviction.

Rethinking Christian Faith in Relation to Judaism

Disheartened by the awareness that Judaism had been terribly misrepresented in traditional Christian theology, disillusioned by the knowledge that the Church had established its identity over against this caricature of Judaism, shaken by the obvious connection between theological anti-Judaism and antisemitic persecution of Jews, unsettled by my new conviction that Judaism provided just as much intimacy with God as did Christianity, and immeasurably enriched by my study of Judaism and my friendships with Jews, what was I to do?

I realized that much of what I formerly believed about Judaism and about Christianity in relation to Judaism was no longer credible. But I also realized that, despite its anti-Judaism, Christianity was the religion through which God graced my life and the lives of countless others. Long before I learned of anti-Judaism and its dreadful effects, I knew well that many sins had been committed in the name of Christianity. But those sins were not intrinsic to Christian faith. What about anti-Judaism? Was there a way to affirm Christian faith without implying that Jews were in error for not affirming it? Even if I thought so, how would the Church respond?

I was fortunate to be studying at Louvain when these questions were emerging for me. For centuries it had been one of the great intellectual centers of Catholicism, and at the time there was a vibrant sense of Church renewal in the air. I had marvelous professors, some of whom had inspired the rethinking of Catholic faith that found expression at Vatican II. I was especially blessed to have as my mentor Professor Benjamin Willaert, the most creative thinker I have ever met. He was the best read but least published of my professors. He just didn't take time out from reading, thinking, and conversing to put his thoughts in print. But his classes in doctrinal theology were always fascinating intellectual adventures. He welcomed, even encouraged, all sorts of questions, and he imagined many possible answers to each. He and other professors at Louvain were completely supportive of my inquiries into Jewish thought, and I couldn't have had a more thoughtful guide than Professor Willaert as I wrote my doctoral dissertation on Heschel's understanding of the sources and antecedents of faith in God.[5]

The post-Vatican II renewal in the Church, particularly in regard to Christian-Jewish relations, heartened me as I pursued my graduate studies. Already at Vatican II, in *Nostra Aetate* (the Declaration on the Relation of the Church to Non-Christian Religions), the Catholic hierarchy began to reverse the Church's anti-Jewish teachings. Along with repudiating the timeworn charge of collective Jewish guilt for the crucifixion of Jesus, *Nostra Aetate* notes "the spiritual bond" linking Christians and Jews, claims that "the Jews should not be presented as repudiated or cursed by God," and promotes "mutual understanding and respect" between Christians and Jews.[6] While the final version of *Nostra Aetate* was considerably weaker than earlier drafts in rejecting anti-Judaism and in affirming the abiding validity of the Jewish covenant, it nevertheless signaled a revolutionary turn in the Church's understanding of Christian faith in relation to Judaism.

Official church statements have become stronger ever since Vatican II. In its 1975 "Statement on Catholic-Jewish Relations," the National Conference of Catholic Bishops claimed that "one of the most hopeful developments in our time . . . has been the decline of old anti-Judaism and the reformation of Christian theological expositions of Judaism along more constructive lines."[7] In its 1985 "Guidelines for Catholic-Jewish Relations," the NCCB recognized "the permanent vocation of the Jews as God's people" and claimed that "together, the Church and the Jewish people are called upon to witness to the whole world."[8] In the same year the Vatican Commission for Religious Relations with the Jews issued a document affirming "the permanence of Israel" as "a sign to be interpreted within God's design," and it reminded Catholics that "the permanence of Israel is accompanied by a continuous spiritual fecundity."[9] While some passages in this document did not measure up to the ones here quoted, these passages reassured me that the Vatican really was confronting the Church's anti-Jewish heritage and was now perceiving Jews and Judaism in an entirely different light than had been the case throughout Christian history. This new Catholic perspective had largely to do with Pope John Paul II who has spoken frequently of the abiding validity of God's covenant with the Jews, and has pointed out how Catholics can find "help in better understanding certain aspects of the Church's life . . . by taking into account the faith and religious life of the Jewish people."[10]

But despite this new approach to Jews and Judaism, many Christians still think of Judaism as superseded by Christianity. Many other Christians, while accepting Judaism's validity, consider Judaism inferior to Christianity, a position still reflected in some official church documents and in the writings of many Christian theologians. This view is rooted in the belief that Jesus is the Messiah of Jewish expectations through whom the Jewish covenant has been fulfilled and a new covenant established. According to this view, although Judaism is valid, Jews would do well to accept Christ and thereby embrace Christianity as the fulfillment of Judaism. But have the messianic expectations of Israel been fulfilled? And did Jesus really establish a new covenant apart from the Jewish covenant?

I believe that the new covenant of which Jesus spoke (Luke 22:20) was not a covenant that would replace or be an alternative to the Jewish covenant. Rather, it was the new messianic form of that covenant envisioned by the prophets Jeremiah and Ezekiel (Jer 31:31-34; Ezek 16:59-63). However much Jesus anticipated this covenant and realized it in his life, the messianic expectations of Judaism that inspired his hopes—the end of all idolatry, war, and suffering—have not been fulfilled. Must we not admit that the messianic form of the covenant—anticipated by Jeremiah, Ezekiel, and Jesus—is still but a hope, and not a reality, for Christians as well as for Jews?[11]

Here's how I see it: We should acknowledge that Christianity is valid because it, like Judaism, fosters covenantal life with God. The same God who formed Israel into a people by way of the covenant, and who regards this people and their covenant as irreplaceable, also called into being the Church with its new form of covenantal life. Surely this was not to make of the Church a "new Israel" that would usurp the role of the Jewish people. It was not to have a new covenant replace an old one. Rather, in accord with the divine promise to Abraham (Gen 12:3), it was to extend the blessings of covenantal life—albeit in a new form—to Gentiles.

My dear friend Rabbi Hershel Matt, of blessed memory, helped me form this perspective. He saw Judaism as representing "the original (form of the) Covenant" and Christianity as carrying on "the new (form of the) Covenant." He said "whatever is claimed by the Christian to be provided through Christ, the Jew had already received a thousand years and more before the Christ of Christians ever appeared." But he suggested that through Christianity "God's covenant promise and providence have been opened up to extend beyond the People Israel."[12]

Jews keep their covenant with God alive by way of Torah. We Christians have come to know God through the gospel of and about Jesus, so in keeping our form of the covenant alive, we recall Jesus' ministry, commemorate his death, and celebrate his resurrected presence. If we truly reject a supersessionist understanding of Christianity in relation to Judaism and, instead, affirm the abiding validity of the Jewish covenant, this will affect *how* we recall Jesus' ministry, *how* we commemorate his death, and *how* we celebrate his resurrection.

When recalling Jesus' ministry, we should acknowledge that, contrary to those who have portrayed it as in opposition to the way of Torah, it was a specific way of interpreting and enacting the teachings of the Torah. It was a redemptive ministry *not* because it represented an alternative to the covenantal life of Torah but because it made the healing power of that life come alive for so many of those to whom Jesus ministered. While his ministry was "only to the lost sheep of the house of Israel" (Matt 15:24), it turns out that many others have been served by it as well. Since "faith comes from what is heard" (Rom 10:17), those who have heard of, and been inspired by, Jesus' ministry have experienced God's redeeming grace. But we who have come to know divine grace through Jesus need not assume that Jewish knowledge of God's grace is less real or profound than ours.

When commemorating Jesus' death, we should be aware that, contrary to the timeworn Christian claim that "the Jews killed Christ," contemporary biblical scholars have convincingly shown that Roman authorities ordered Jesus' execution because they viewed him as a challenge to their rule in Judea. Jesus must have known how these authorities perceived him. Yet Jesus was faithful to his divinely ordained ministry to the end, unto death on a Roman cross, when infidelity could have spared his life. So it makes sense that we Christians speak not only of the redemptive significance of his ministry but also of his redeeming death. This does not mean we have to think that God required Jesus' death as a condition for salvation; we need only acknowledge that, in witnessing or hearing the news of the death of this faithful Son of God, countless women and men have been moved to repent before God. Again, we need not believe that Jesus sought death or even intended to die in order to reconcile the world to God; we need only believe he willingly gave his life in service to God and to the "reign of God," and that in doing so he inspired innumerable people to turn away from sin and toward God. We who have been inspired by Christ's fidelity unto death to commit ourselves to God need not assume that Jews have been any less inspired by other means.

When celebrating Jesus' resurrection, we should remember that, contrary to the traditional Christian claim that his resurrection vindicates Christian faith over against Judaism, Jesus' faith was in fact Jewish faith. The Jewish people knew of God's fidelity long before the resurrection of Jesus; indeed many of them believed in the resurrection of the dead before God raised Jesus. Since then Jews have continued to know and celebrate God's fidelity to the living and the dead apart from any reference to Jesus and his resurrection. Might we not see in Jesus' resurrection a sign of God's affirmation of the Jewish covenant in which Jesus lived and for which he died,[13] even though Jesus' resurrection is the source of faith for Christians and not for Jews? We Christians believe that Jesus' resurrection is a sign that God will raise us to new life beyond the grave, but we need not assume that Jewish hope for redemption is any less real or meaningful than ours.

Having encountered the grandeur of Judaism in Jewish books and, more importantly, in Jewish lives, I have become convinced that Judaism has an indispensable role to play in the sanctification and redemption of the world. I believe with all my heart that God wants Judaism and the Jewish people to flourish every bit as much as God wants Christianity and the Church to thrive. Abraham Heschel acknowledged that "conversion to Judaism is no prerequisite for sanctity,"[14] and I am convinced the same applies to Christianity. But Christianity, like Judaism, is a means to sanctity, and a way by which people may help God sanctify and redeem life.

While at first I had found it unsettling to believe that Judaism provides just as much intimacy with God as does Christianity, in time I found it more unsettling to think otherwise. Hershel Matt's approach to his faith inspired me in this regard. He was passionately steadfast in his Jewish faith while affirming the validity of Christianity. This is because for him Judaism was not the object of his faith but the means by which he lived his faith in God. This was Abraham Heschel's approach as well. Unwavering in his commitment to Judaism, Heschel nonetheless claimed "religion is a means, not the end" and, therefore, "to equate religion and God is idolatry."[15] My encounter with Hershel Matt, and my reading of Abraham Heschel, forced me to realize that Christianity must never be the object of my faith but the means by which I express my faith in God. I became convinced that genuine faith in God demands a relativizing of one's own religion;

that faith in God is incompatible with the absolutizing of anything other than God, including a cherished tradition that fosters faith in God.

Rethinking the Doctrine of the Trinity in Relation to Jewish Monotheism

Rethinking Christian faith in relation to Judaism inevitably includes rethinking the doctrine of the Trinity in relation to Jewish monotheism, and this has been a principal concern of mine.

Perhaps the most hallowed of all Jewish claims about the reality of God is this: "Hear, O Israel, the Lord is our God, the Lord is one" (Deut 6:4). This idea of God's oneness means not simply that there is only one true God, but also that God possesses inner unity, which, in turn, is the necessary precondition for whatever unity is achieved in this world.

The one God of Jewish faith transcends the world while being present to it. There have been those who have challenged the idea of divine transcendence, claiming that it is impossible for us to have a relationship with a reality that transcends the world. This would be true if transcending the world meant being remote from it. But the Jewish idea of divine transcendence suggests that God is greater than the world, not removed from it. In fact, it is God's transcendence that enables God to be omnipresent, unconfined by finite limitations, and thereby able to relate intimately to all beings. But, in Judaism, the presence of God is not thought of only in terms of omnipresence but also in terms of specific moments of presence, manifested and depicted in many ways. The God of Jewish faith is no remote deity dwelling in splendid isolation but a versatile presence dwelling in the midst of people. God's oneness, then, is dynamic, not static, a unity with a diversity of manifestations.

Christianity owes its monotheism to Judaism, but Christianity has its own distinctive version of monotheism. While the God of Christian faith and Jewish faith is one God, Christians speak of this God as being triune: three in one. I am convinced that Christians can affirm this trinitarian monotheism without regarding it as superior to, or even incompatible with, Jewish monotheism. I readily acknowledge that some religious affirmations are not merely different, but irreconcilable, and I believe some religious doctrines are truer than others; even that some are true while others are false. But I am convinced that in certain instances different religious affirmations, often thought to be mutually exclusive, merely represent different perspectives; that each in its own way, from its own vantage point, apprehends something of the incomprehensible God and of the divine-human encounter. With regard to Christian and Jewish versions of monotheism, it might be that they not only represent different perspectives on the same reality, but that they also represent different emphases on what both Christians and Jews alike perceive.

Christians traditionally have spoken of the one God as "Father, Son [Word], and Holy Spirit." (There is a traditional view in both Christianity and Judaism that God transcends gender even though gendered terms are used to speak of God. I agree with the view that if God is referred to as "Father" then God should also be called "Mother." I also believe that though Jesus was a male, the Word of God that he incarnated should not be identified as masculine. But this is for another essay.) This trinitarian formulation need not be understood as contrary to a Jewish approach to God but as a way of emphasizing the versatility of God recognized also by Jews. The Jewish people knew of God as Father long before Christians, following the lead of Jesus, addressed God as Father. They listened in faith to God's Word in the Torah and the prophets centuries before that Word moved the prophet from Nazareth. And long before Christians spoke of God as Spirit the Jewish people knew of God's presence as Spirit, cleansing and fortifying the human spirit. All this the Jewish people knew from of old, and to this very day still know. But what they have emphasized is the oneness or unity of God who relates to the world in a variety of creative and redemptive ways.

So while Jews do not speak of God as triune, they do speak of God as Father (and often today also as Mother), and they speak of God's Word, and they speak of God as Spirit. I do not wish to impose Christian categories on Jews but only to point out that the Christian doctrine of the Trinity has its roots in, and can be understood as compatible with, Jewish ways of speaking about God. Admittedly, Christian trinitarian language also has been and at times continues to be articulated in non-Jewish ways. Needless to say, non-Jewish forms of religious language have value, but I contend that when we Christians have employed non-Jewish ways of articulating trinitarian doctrine we have often obscured our monotheistic faith.

We Christians are true to the Jewish faith of Jesus, as also to our Christian faith, when, along with Jews, we stress the oneness of God. But this does not preclude our speaking of God as triune. We know that there is but one God and that God possesses inner unity. But given the way we Christians have come to know God, we have learned to speak of God's inner unity in terms of Trinity, tri-unity. If we understand what the fourth- and fifth-century framers of trinitarian doctrine referred to as the three *personae* of the Trinity as three *ways of being* by which God relates to creation—as Creator, Revealer, and Sanctifier—rather than as three inter-relating *Persons,* then our trinitarian perspective is compatible with Jewish monotheism. Monika Hellwig is to the point when she writes: "The Church Fathers did not intend *person* in the modern sense taken literally. That would simply mean three gods."[16] Sometimes the way we Christians have articulated our faith has sounded more like tri-theism than trinitarianism, but this is not what our tradition at its best has promoted. The risk of such tri-theism is lessened when we Christians renew and deepen our ties with the Jewish people and learn to value what they have to teach us about the dynamic oneness of God.

Inspired by Jewish Views of God's Love

As much as my encounters with Jews and Judaism have helped me to appreciate the oneness of God, they have also enhanced my appreciation for the love of God. My friendship with Jews and my reading of Jewish theologians have convinced me that what Jews understand about God's love is as profound as what Christian theologians usually have claimed could be known only through faith in Christ. To be sure, some of the deeds attributed to God in the Hebrew Bible appear, from the perspective of many Christians, to be less than godly. But such a contrast is obviously unfair. Not only does it fail to acknowledge the fact that in the Hebrew Bible God is repeatedly referred to as loving and compassionate; it also ignores the fact that Jewish views of God have developed well beyond those found in ancient Israelite religion. Post-biblical Jewish understandings of God, no less than developed Christian views, call into question some of the Bible's accounts of God's actions.

How absurd for Christians to contrast the New Testament's God of love with the supposedly remote and wrathful God of the Hebrew Bible! The fact that unloving acts are ascribed to God in the Hebrew Bible (as also in the New Testament) does not erase the fact that therein God is also repeatedly referred to as compassionate, merciful, and loving. The biblical authors may not have been consistent in their portrayals of God's relationship to human beings, but in their more inspired moments they made unsurpassed claims about God's everlasting love. Rather than be surprised that the biblical authors were inconsistent in their presentations of God's love, should we not be astonished that, given their antiquity, the Hebrew Scriptures contain so many teachings about the love of God that inspire us yet today?

As much as ancient Israelite faith celebrated the love of God, it signaled only the beginning of a developing Jewish appreciation of God's love. Concerning the sages of early post-biblical Judaism, Rabbi David Wolpe writes: "The Rabbis delighted in developing the concept of God's love for humanity in general and for Israel in particular" and this was "the central truth of their lives: the existence of a good and caring God, enmeshed in the trials and triumphs of human life, who looked on them and the world with love."[17]

While the ancient rabbis believed God was "enmeshed in the trials and triumphs of human life," they understood God's presence to be subtler than was often depicted in the Bible—less blatant but no less real! "Unlike the Bible, the Talmud makes the rarest mention of direct intervention by God in contemporary events," writes Rabbi David Hartman. Yet, "the reader who penetrates beneath the surface of talmudic discussions increasingly realizes how deeply God is present and involved in every page of the Talmud."[18] I have been particularly inspired by the fact that rabbinic reluctance to appeal to divine intervention in human events indicates no lack of faith in divine love. As confident as they were of God's abiding presence, the Jewish sages had "an assurance of God's ever-renewed love."[19] In fact, their confidence signaled a maturation of faith beyond that of biblical Judaism because, on balance, rabbinic faith in divine love was less dependent on miraculous signs than was the faith of many biblical characters. In rabbinic Judaism, God's love is known not so much through the kinds of extraordinary miracles of divine intervention attested to in the Bible but through what the Jewish Prayer Book calls "the miracles which are daily with us," the ordinary wonders of existence. "The living God of Judaism," writes Hartman, "can be experienced in a world in which [God's] providential love and guidance are discovered and felt as 'the world pursues its normal course.'"[20] Thus, God's providential love is not a matter of manipulation but of inspiration, mediated principally through the love of those who live by the rabbinic dictum: "Just as God is loving, you too must be loving" (Sifre Deut 49).

Developing Compassion for God

God's love has its consequences, not only for those loved but also for God. It means, as many Jewish sages have taught, that God is affected by the plight of creatures, even to the point of suffering. Rabbi Heschel went so far as to say that the idea of divine pathos is "the central idea in prophetic theology" because "God's participation in human history finds its deepest expression in the fact that God can actually suffer."[21]

Many Christians may think this talk of God's suffering is nothing new, since we Christians focus on the suffering of Christ whom we believe is God incarnate. But, in fact, classical Christian theology, having assimilated the Aristotelian idea of suffering as an imperfection unworthy of God, rejects the idea that God suffers. The traditional view is that Christ suffers in his human nature, not in his divine nature. True, there are Christian theologians nowadays who speak of the suffering of God, claiming that for God to be unmoved by the plight of creatures would indicate not perfection but deficiency on God's part. And there have been Jewish thinkers who have tried to explain away the biblical and rabbinic allusions to God's suffering because they, like many Christians, have been influenced by Aristotelian philosophy. But the idea of God's suffering can be found in abundance within the Jewish tradition, and even if we reject the classical Christian theological view that God cannot suffer, it is good for us Christians to realize that others, without a doctrine of the incarnation, affirm the suffering of God, suffering born of love.

Learning from Jews that God suffers *with us,* rather than focusing solely on how Christ suffers *for us,* can have a profound effect on our understanding of God and on our way of relating to God. It can help us overcome our tendency to blame God for the evils that befall us, and it can save us enormous spiritual energy that might otherwise be spent in the fruitless attempt to solve the insoluble problem of how God, thought to be not only all-good but also all-powerful, either causes or permits evils to occur. Focusing on God's suffering, we may be inclined to question the idea of divine omnipotence, just as Heschel did by claiming that this idea, "holding God responsible for everything, expecting God to do the impossible, to defy human freedom, is a non-Jewish idea."[22] Perhaps the idea of divine omnipotence should become a non-Christian idea as well. If we stop thinking of omnipotence as an attribute of the divine, we will be free to appreciate as never before that the true mark of divinity—what makes God divine and thus worthy of our worship—is not absolute power and control, but infinite compassion, unending love.

Such an understanding of God is bound to have a profound effect on our way of relating to God. If, with Heschel, we believe that "God's mercy is too great to permit the innocent to suffer," but that "there are forces that interfere with God's mercy, with God's power," we may be moved to have "compassion for God," which Heschel regards as an expression of faith in God.[23] We may also become convinced, or more convinced, that our supreme responsibility is to let the divine mercy flow through our lives to help God alleviate suffering.

Inspired by the Way of Torah

While I have thus far emphasized how my ongoing encounter with Jews and Judaism has affected my understanding of God and Christian faith, I hope the implications of this encounter for Christian spirituality are apparent. Now I'd like to be explicit about how encounter with Jews and Judaism can enrich the practice of Christian faith. I'll give three examples.

Jewish religious practice, what is also called "the way of Torah," is a *communal way of responding to God.* Jewish philosopher Martin Buber is perhaps best remembered for urging us to relate to each other and to God in a deeply personal way, as an I to a Thou (rather than in an impersonal I-It manner). But Rabbi Heschel reminds us that "our relationship to God is not as an I to a Thou, but as a We to a Thou."[24] Acknowledging that "it is in the heart of every individual that prayer takes place," Heschel nonetheless claims that "a Jew never worships as an isolated individual but as a part of the community of Israel."[25] To be a Christian is also to be a part of a community, the Church. But there has always been a stronger tendency toward individualism in Christian spirituality than in Jewish spirituality. This is evident in what is often a Christian preoccupation with personal salvation in contrast with the Jewish concern for redemption of the people Israel and the entire world. To overcome the tendency toward individualism in Christian spirituality, and to develop a healthy balance between the individual and the communal, we Christians can be helped by seeing how Jews live by way of Torah.

My second example has to do with the way of Torah as a *physical way of rendering life holy*. It is enacted in concrete deeds of justice and compassion, just as the redemption it signifies and fosters is a concrete redemption in and of this world. It is enacted also in concrete ritual observances, many of which have to do with food—abstaining from some foods, koshering others, and pronouncing just the right blessing over each type of food. Judaism is known in something as mundane as the baking and braiding of *challah* on Fridays, in the smell of that baking *challah* filling the home, and in the very enjoyment of eating it on *Shabbat*. One of the more important lessons we Christians can learn from Jews is how the gratification of carnal needs can be an act of sanctification. Of course, Catholicism and other forms of Christianity have their bodily, earthy side as well—as is evident in sacramental celebrations. But whereas the celebration of the sacred significance of the physical is deeply engrained in Jewish religious practice, it often goes against the grain of Christian spirituality, which is often a form of otherworldly piety that bespeaks an ambivalence toward, or even at times hatred for, God's good earth and the things thereof. The renowned Thomas à Kempis taught generations of Christians to strive for "perfect contempt of the world," for in his view "the soul that loves God despises all things that are less than God."[26] To be sure, there are more ecological forms of Christian spirituality than the one espoused by Thomas à Kempis. But spiritualism—the bifurcation of the spiritual and physical, and the elevation of the spiritual at the expense of the physical—has been far more of a problem in Christianity than in Judaism. So we Christians can learn from Jews just how much matter matters for a healthy spiritual life.

My final example has to do with the way of Torah as a way of sanctifying time, of welcoming the eternal into time, particularly in the form of the Sabbath. Christian spirituality, despite the Christian liturgical calendar, has often revealed a heaven-bent eagerness to be done with the temporal life. This proclivity was expressed perhaps most poignantly by Thérèse of Lisieux when she wrote of how from childhood she "dreamt of martyrdom."[27] Thérèse, like Thomas à Kempis, does not represent the whole spectrum of Christian spirituality, but she, like he, has been one of the most influential spiritual guides in the history of Christianity. To enrich our appreciation of time as a blessing, and to overcome any tendency to regard it as a curse, we Christians can learn from those who live by way of Torah, and we may try to celebrate time in ways analogous to Jewish celebrations of time, especially Sabbath time. If there is anything we and our threatened environment desperately need in this fast-paced, secularized, polluted world, where exhaustion, loneliness, and alienation abound, it is Sabbath rest, Sabbath prayer, Sabbath togetherness, and Sabbath peace.

Conclusion

Clearly, my encounter with Jews and Judaism has transformed my understanding and practice of Christian faith in many ways. Above all, it has convinced me that my faith is strengthened by my perceiving Jews as covenantal allies and Judaism as an allied faith, and that the one God desires religious diversity as well as interreligious cooperation in the divine and human task of sanctifying and redeeming the world. The task is urgent. Religious intolerance kills! And when it doesn't literally kill, it diminishes human beings. Interreligious understanding heals and enhances human lives. This is why it is so desperately needed—because it makes us more humane and thereby brings honor and glory to God.

God is so great, far greater than any of our conceptions of God, far greater than either of our traditions—and all traditions. Yet however great and glorious, this God of ours needs our help. If there is anything I have learned from Judaism, and I have learned so much, it is that God needs human cooperation to redeem human lives. So it is my prayer, as I end this essay, that Jews and Christians be together bound in covenantal partnership to help God put an end to evil and to mend this broken world by becoming vehicles of God's redeeming presence.

Notes

[1] Something of the story I tell in this essay and some of the ideas developed in it appeared in John C. Merkle, "Bound Together in God," *Religious Education* (Fall 1996) 547–54.

[2] Vatican Commission for Religious Relations with the Jews, "Guidelines and Suggestions for Implementing the Conciliar Declaration *Nostra Aetate* (no. 4)," (1974) Preamble. Since all ecclesial documents cited in this chapter can be found in a variety of publications (pamphlets, journals, and collections) and on various websites, references to them in these

endnotes indicate only the ecclesial sources, the titles, the dates the statements were made or issued, and textual sub-headings or numberings (if any), and not specific publications.

[3] National Conference of Catholic Bishops, "Statement on Catholic-Jewish Relations" (1975).

[4] Robert McAfee Brown, "Abraham Heschel: A Passion for Sincerity," *Christianity and Crisis* (December 10, 1973) 257.

[5] My book, *The Genesis of Faith: The Depth Theology of Abraham Joshua Heschel* (New York: Macmillan Publishing Co., 1985), is an adaptation of this dissertation.

[6] Vatican Council II, *Nostra Aetate,* The Declaration on the Relationship of the Church to Non-Christian Religions (1965) no. 4.

[7] National Conference of Catholic Bishops, "Statement on Catholic-Jewish Relations" (1975).

[8] National Conference of Catholic Bishops, "Guidelines for Catholic-Jewish Relations" (1985) General Principles, no 6.

[9] Vatican Commission for Religious Relations with the Jews, "Notes on the Correct Way to Present Jews and Judaism in Preaching and Catechesis in the Roman Catholic Church," (1985) no. VI, 25.

[10] Pope John Paul II, "To Christian Experts in Jewish-Christian Relations" (March 6, 1982).

[11] Cf. Rosemary Radford Reuther, *Faith and Fratricide: The Theological Roots of Anti-Semitism* (New York: Seabury Press, 1974) 243, 253.

[12] Hershel Matt, "How Shall A Believing Jew View Christianity?" *Judaism: A Quarterly Journal of Jewish Life and Thought* (Fall 1975) 394.

[13] Cf. Paul M. van Buren, *Christ in Context: A Theology of the Jewish-Christian Reality,* San Francisco: Harper & Row, 1988) 107–08.

[14] Abraham Joshua Heschel, "No Religion Is An Island," *Union Seminary Quarterly Review* (January 1966) 131.

[15] Ibid., 126.

[16] Monika K. Hellwig, *Understanding Catholicism,* 2nd ed. (New York: Paulist Press, 2002) 193.

[17] David J. Wolpe, *The Healer of Shattered Hearts: A Jewish View of God* (New York: Henry Holt & Company, 1990) 70.

[18] David Hartman, *A Living Covenant: The Innovative Spirit and Living Covenant of Judaism* (New York: The Free Press, 1985) 6–7.

[19] Ibid., 274.

[20] Ibid., 255.

[21] Abraham Joshua Heschel, "Teaching Jewish Theology," *The Synagogue School* (Fall 1969) 12; *The Prophets* (New York: Harper & Row, 1962) 259.

[22] Heschel, "Teaching Jewish Theology," 13.

[23] Abraham Joshua Heschel, "On Prayer," *Conservative Judaism* (Fall 1970) 4; *A Passion For Truth* (New York: Farrar, Straus, and Giroux, 1973) 301.

[24] Abraham Joshua Heschel, "Man's Quest for God," *Studies in Prayer and Symbolism* (New York: Charles Scribner's Sons, 1954) 45.

[25] Ibid., 55.

[26] Thomas à Kempis, *On the Imitation of Christ,* trans. Abbot Justin McCann (New York: New American Library, 1957) 45, 58. This and the next quotation are quoted by Douglas

John Hall, *Imaging God: Dominion as Stewardship* (Grand Rapids, Mich.: Wm. B. Eerdmans, 1986) 29–30. While acknowledging that "there have been forces at work in our religious past that militated against a complete otherworldliness," Hall nevertheless claims "the hagiography of Christendom abounds in demonstrations of the principle that spiritual salvation implies physical destruction" and "the allure of martyrdom, that is, of the violent destruction of 'the flesh,' has been more than an occasional trend within Christian history."

[27] Thérèse of Lisieux, *The Story of a Soul,* trans. John Beevers (Garden City, N.Y.: Image Books, 1957) 154.

A STATEMENT BY THE CHRISTIAN SCHOLARS
GROUP ON CHRISTIAN-JEWISH RELATIONS

A Sacred Obligation

Rethinking Christian Faith in Relation to Judaism and the Jewish People
September 1, 2002

Since its inception in 1969, the Christian Scholars Group has been seeking to develop more adequate Christian theologies of the church's relationship to Judaism and the Jewish people. Pursuing this work for over three decades under varied sponsorship, members of our association of Protestant and Roman Catholic biblical scholars, historians, and theologians have published many volumes on Christian-Jewish relations.

Our work has a historical context. For most of the past two thousand years, Christians have erroneously portrayed Jews as unfaithful, holding them collectively responsible for the death of Jesus and therefore accursed by God. In aggreement with many official Christian declarations, we reject this accusation as historically false and theologically invalid. It suggests that God can be unfaithful to the eternal covenant with the Jewish people. We acknowledge with shame the suffering this distorted portrayal has brought upon the Jewish people. We repent of this teaching of contempt. Our repentance requires us to build a new teaching of respect. This task is important at any time, but the deadly crisis in the Middle East and the frightening resurgence of antisemitism worldwide give it particular urgency.

We believe that revising Christian teaching about Judaism and the Jewish people is a central and indispensable obligation of theology in our time. It is essential that Christianity both understand and represent Judaism accurately, not only as a matter of justice for the Jewish people, but also for the integrity of Christian faith, which we cannot proclaim without reference to Judaism. Moreover, since there is a unique bond between Christianity and Judaism, revitalizing our appreciation of Jewish religious life will deepen our Christian faith. We base these convictions on ongoing scholarly research and the official statements of many Christian denominations over the past fifty years.

We are grateful for the willingness of many Jews to engage in dialogue and study with us. We welcomed it when, on September 10, 2000, Jewish scholars sponsored by the Institute of Christian and Jewish Studies in Baltimore issued a historic declaration, *Dabru Emet: A Jewish Statement on Christians and Christianity.* This document, affirmed by notable rabbis and Jewish scholars, called on Jews to re-examine their understanding of Christianity.

Encouraged by the work of both Jewish and Christian colleagues, we offer the following ten statements for the consideration of our fellow Christians. We urge all Christians to reflect on their faith in light of these statements. For us, this is a sacred obligation.

1. God's covenant with the Jewish people endures forever.

For centuries Christians claimed that their covenant with God replaced or superseded the Jewish covenant. We renounce this claim. We believe that God does not revoke divine promises. We affirm that God is in covenant with both Jews and Christians. Tragically, the entrenched theology of supersessionism continues to influence Christian faith, worship, and practice, even though it has been repudiated by many Christian denominations and many Christians no longer accept it. Our recognition of the abiding validity of Judaism has implications for all aspects of Christian life.

2. Jesus of Nazareth lived and died as a faithful Jew.

Christians worship the God of Israel in and through Jesus Christ. Supersessionism, however, prompted Christians over the centuries to speak of Jesus as an opponent of Judaism. This is historically incorrect. Jewish worship, ethics, and practice shaped Jesus's life and teachings. The scriptures of his people inspired and nurtured him. Christian preaching and teaching today must describe Jesus's earthly life as engaged in the ongoing Jewish quest to live out God's covenant in everyday life.

3. Ancient rivalries must not define Christian-Jewish relations today.

Although today we know Christianity and Judaism as separate religions, what became the church was a movement within the Jewish community for many decades after the ministry and resurrection of Jesus. The destruction of the Jerusalem Temple by Roman armies in the year 70 of the first century caused a crisis among the Jewish people. Various groups, including Christianity and early rabbinic Judaism, competed for leadership in the Jewish community by claiming that they were the true heirs of biblical Israel. The gospels reflect this rivalry in which the disputants exchanged various accusations. Christian charges of hypocrisy and legalism misrepresent Judaism and constitute an unworthy foundation for Christian self-understanding.

4. Judaism is a living faith, enriched by many centuries of development.

Many Christians mistakenly equate Judaism with biblical Israel. However, Judaism, like Christianity, developed new modes of belief and practice in the centuries after the destruction of the Temple. The rabbinic tradition gave new emphasis and understanding to existing practices, such as communal prayer, study of Torah, and deeds of loving-kindness. Thus Jews could live out the covenant in a world without the Temple. Over time they developed an extensive body of interpretive literature that continues to enrich Jewish life, faith, and self-understanding. Christians cannot fully understand Judaism apart from its post-biblical development, which can also enrich and enhance Christian faith.

5. The Bible both connects and separates Jews and Christians.

Some Jews and Christians today, in the process of studying the Bible together, are discovering new ways of reading that provide a deeper appreciation of both traditions. While the two communities draw from the same biblical texts of ancient Israel, they have developed different traditions of interpretation. Christians view these texts through the lens of the New Testament, while Jews understand these scriptures through the traditions of rabbinic commentary.

Referring to the first part of the Christian Bible as the "Old Testament" can wrongly suggest that these texts are obsolete. Alternative expressions— Hebrew Bible," "First Testament," or "Shared Testament"—although also problematic, may better express the church's renewed appreciation of the ongoing power of these scriptures for both Jews and Christians.

6. Affirming God's enduring covenant with the Jewish people has consequences for Christian understandings of salvation.

Christians meet God's saving power in the person of Jesus Christ and believe that this power is available to all people in him. Christians have therefore taught for centuries that salvation is available only through Jesus Christ. With their recent realization that God's covenant with the Jewish people is eternal, Christians can now recognize in the Jewish tradition the redemptive power of God at work. If Jews, who do not share our faith in Christ, are in a saving covenant with God, then Christians need new ways of understanding the universal significance of Christ.

7. Christians should not target Jews for conversion.

In view of our conviction that Jews are in an eternal covenant with God, we renounce missionary efforts directed at converting Jews. At the same time, we welcome opportunities for Jews and Christians to bear witness to their respective experiences of God's saving ways Neither can properly claim to possess knowledge of God entirely or exclusively.

8. Christian worship that teaches contempt for Judaism dishonors God.

The New Testament contains passages that have frequently generated negative attitudes toward Jews and Judaism. The use of these texts in the context of worship increases the likelihood of hostility toward Jews. Christian anti-Jewish theology has also shaped worship in ways that denigrate Judaism and foster contempt for Jews. We urge church leaders to examine scripture readings, prayers, the structure of the lectionaries, preaching and hymns to remove distorted images of Judaism. A reformed Christian liturgical life would express a new relationship with Jews and thus honor God.

9. We affirm the importance of the land of Israel for the life of the Jewish people.

The land of Israel has always been of central significance to the Jewish people. However, Christian theology charged that the Jews had condemned themselves to homelessness by rejecting God's Messiah. Such supersessionism precluded any possibility for Christian understanding of Jewish attachment to the land of Israel. Christian theologians can no longer avoid this crucial issue, especially in light of the complex and persistent conflict over the land. Recognizing that both Israelis and Palestinians have the right to live in peace and security in a homeland of their own, we call for efforts that contribute to a just peace among all the peoples in the region.

10. Christians should work with Jews for the healing of the world.

For almost a century, Jews and Christians in the United States have worked together on important social issues, such as the rights of workers and civil rights. As violence and terrorism intensify in our time, we must strengthen our common efforts in the work of justice and peace to which both the prophets of Israel and Jesus summon us. These common efforts by Jews and Christians offer a vision of human solidarity and provide models of collaboration with people of other faith traditions.

Signed by members of the
Christian Scholars Group on Christian-Jewish Relations

Norman A. Beck; Mary C. Boys, S.N.J.M.; Rosann Catalano; Philip A. Cunningham; Celia Deutsch, N.D.S.; Alice L. Eckardt; Eugene J. Fisher; Eva Fleischner; Deidre Good; Walter Harrelson; Michael McGarry, C.S.P.; John C. Merkle; John T. Pawlikowski, O.S.M.; Peter A. Pettit; Peter C. Phan; Jean Pierre Ruiz; Franklin Sherman; Joann Spillman; John T. Townsend; Joseph Tyson; and Clark M. Williamson

IRVIN J. BOROWSKY

Afterword

It is an honor to have the opportunity to reflect on the fine collection
of essays by the brilliant and dedicated Christian scholars represented in
this volume. I am privileged to count several as personal friends, and
proud that the American Interfaith Institute, which I founded some
twenty-one years ago, has published the work of more than half of them.
The accounts of their fruitful encounters with Jews and Judaism are moving and enlightening.

Over the years, my own encounters with Christian scholars and leaders have been gratifying. Working with both clergy and laity has enriched
my life and deepened my appreciation of Christianity. Most enlightening
has been the exploration and study of that majority version of Christianity which has been ridding itself of the last vestiges of anti-Judaism.

Since the early days of the American Interfaith Institute, we have
seen the remarkable tapestry of bold research and dialogue that has given
birth to new relationships and understanding among Christians and Jews.
It is thrilling to witness, and it is humbling to be part of this splendid outreach. But encounters can also have their dark side. It is, therefore, key
that I mention aspects of a number of passages in the New Testament
that are, I believe, both frightening and harmful.

Imagine, if you can, what it would be like for a young Jew to hear or
read, for the first time, passages such as those quoted immediately below.
Even worse, think of the harm done as an impressionable young Christian
has his or her portrait of Jews shaped by these same verses:

1 Thess 2:14-16: ". . . the Jews, who killed the Lord Jesus and the prophets. . . . They displease God and are hostile to all men. . . . In this way they always heap up their sins to the limit. The wrath of God has come upon them at last" (NIV = New International Version).

John 5:18: "Therefore the Jews sought the more to kill him [Jesus], because he not only had broken the Sabbath, but said also that God was his Father, making himself equal to God" (KJ = King James).

John 8:44: [Jesus to "the Jews"] "Your father is the devil, and you choose to carry out your father's desires" (REB = Revised English Bible).

John 19:7: "The Jews answered . . . , 'We have a law, and according to that law he ought to die because he has claimed to be the Son of God'" (NRSV = New Revised Standard Version).

Matt 27:25: "And the whole people [the Jews of Jerusalem] said in reply, 'His blood be on us and on our children'" (NAB = New American Bible).

Acts 23:12: ". . . the Jews held a secret meeting at which they made a vow not to eat or drink until they had killed Paul" (NJB = New Jerusalem Bible).

I have included in each case the source of the translation to indicate that the problem transcends any single version.

Matthew 27:25 and John 8:44 are the most challenging texts. Almost certainly, they have done the most damage. But throughout the New Testament there are literally dozens of other passages, many in John and Acts, in which "the Jews" appear as enemies of Jesus and as antagonists of what became Christianity. Clearly, it is texts such as these that helped to create the "teaching of contempt" for Jews and Judaism that has contaminated nineteen centuries of Christian history. I am convinced that one cannot account for the Nazi murder of six million Jews, including one and a half million children, without that teaching and without the traditional translations of those texts.

Since the *Shoah,* both Protestant and Catholic churches have officially stated their sorrow about the Christian mistreatment of Jews over the centuries. Further, as Professor Merkle notes in his introduction, they have repudiated traditional anti-Jewish teachings and affirmed the continuing validity of God's covenant with the Jewish people. Many have added an affirmation of the lasting contributions of Jews and Judaism—to the world and to Christianity itself, something brought out forcefully in these essays.

But what about the New Testament texts that I have cited above? The degrading of any group such as Native Americans, African Americans, and Jews, at least in the print and electronic media, is now widely rejected. But these New Testament texts are still read, and even proclaimed in churches. Is nothing to be done?

Many sympathetic Christians are aware of the problem, but feel they have no right to change texts which they believe to be "sacred," "inspired," "the Word of God." When one notes that translations are not sacred or inspired, the standard reply is that the translations must be accurate and not too free. Is providing explanatory notes, in fine print, usually visually far removed from the troublesome text, the best we can do? Surely not.

I was pleased to have had an involvement with the ten-year project of the Translations Committee of the American Bible Society, which resulted in the excellent translation called the Contemporary English Version (CEV). Their effort produced an accurate version which renders, in clear English, that which the first century C.E. authors intended to communicate. The CEV's translators have been sensitive to words and phrases which would be likely to mislead or to distort the meaning for today's reader. Thus, when in John's Gospel, Jesus' enemies are called "the Jews" without qualification, it can lead the unprepared contemporary reader to think that it means all Jews. This, of course, cannot be so because Jesus himself, his mother, and his disciples were all Jewish. The translators of the CEV considered each context, and correctly referred to "the leaders," or "some of the authorities," or "the crowd." Not only are these changes less distorting, but, I would argue, more accurate and effective renderings of the authors' meaning.

My friend Norman Beck addresses this issue in his essay in this volume. He has taken a slightly different approach, using a combination of translation, the imaginative application of various print sizes, and a judicious use of expansion and elaboration to provide appropriate explanatory and clarifying context for many passages. I recommend his *The New Testament: A New Translation and Redaction*. It is a seminal work for our time. Let me add that his suggested new four-year lectionary, which bypasses the most dangerous texts, is a superb tool and must be taken very seriously by Christian leaders.

The approach to translation used in the CEV (technically called the dynamic or functional equivalence theory) has won wide support, and most of its readers have been enthusiastic. Catholics (many of them supporters of the CEV) tell me, however, that administrative agencies in the Vatican are currently opposed to any but the most literal translation. There appears to be little chance for official Catholic approval of the CEV in the near future. It would be good to be proven wrong. Regrettably, many evangelical Protestants seem to have taken a position similar to that of the Vatican. But within a framework of research, education and dialogue, outreach efforts to overcome anti-Jewish translation features will continue to be extended to both groups by enlightened Christians and Jews worldwide.

One hopes for the broadest distribution and use of the CEV. With guidance from trained scholars and time to deal with serious issues, literal translations such as the NIV, the NAB, and the NRSV may be appropriate for academic study. But for personal use and public proclamation, we need the CEV.

Clearly, the issue of translation presented here is significant in that it links history and truth in order to keep vital the faith of tomorrows still to come. Equally significant is the rethinking of Christian faith in relation to Jews and Judaism so eloquently articulated throughout this important book.

Index

Abraham, 45, 105, 107, 117, 189
Ad Gentes Divinitus (Vatican Council II), 152
Adler, Hans, 112
Adler, Rachel, 106, 177–78
Agadah, 141, 142
Anguish of the Jews, The (Flannery), 115, 150
Anti-Judaism/anti-Jewish theology, 17–18, 19, 20, 22, 24, 25–27, 32–33, 41, 46, 63–68, 73–74, 80–86, 92–104, 111–17, 126, 141, 151–52, 157, 163–64, 174, 183, 187, 188
Antisemitism, 19, 20, 24, 41, 46, 63–68, 80–86, 111–16, 135, 149, 151–52, 153, 157, 170, 174, 183, 187
Asbury, Beverly, 5–6
Augustine, 39

Babylonian Exile, 139–40
Bainton, Roland H., 65–66
Baltimore Catechism, 131, 162–63
Baltmann, Rudolf, 112, 124, 126
Barak, Ehud, 159
Barth, Karl, 45, 73, 96–97
Baum, Gregory, 146, 151–52

Beck, Esther, 72
Bernards, Solomon S., 5, 73–74, 75
Bible. *See* Sacred Scripture
Bishop, Clare Huchet, 116
Blancy, Alain, 94
Boff, Leonardo, 121
Bonhoeffer, Dietrich, 1–2, 55, 61
Bonino, José Miquez, 120–21
Brown, Raymond E., 167
Brown, Robert McAfee, 53, 186
Brueggeman, Walter, 40
Brunett, Alex, 137
Buber, Martin, 4, 61, 185, 197
Bullock, Robert, 167
Burbules, Nicholas, 171

Castlelot, John J., 133, 134
Chaverim, 106–07
Christ. *See* Jesus; *see also* Christology, Messiah
Christian Scholars Group on Christian-Jewish Relations, xii, 6, 75
Christology, 47–48, 57, 80, 82–83, 87–88, 145, 152–54
Chutzpah, as component of faith, 107
Civil rights movement, 132–33, 135

Clark, John, 132–33
Community, 119–21, 197–98
Confessions (Augustine), 39
Constantine, 101
Constantinius, 101
Cost of Discipleship, The (Bonhoeffer), 55
Covenant, 45, 60, 80, 97–99, 107, 117,
    140, 147, 153–54, 156, 186, 189–90
Creation, 8–9, 10, 28, 121–22, 124
Crossan, John Dominic, 112–13, 125

Daniélou, Jean, 38
Davies, Alan, 145
Davies, W. D., 123
"Declaration of the Evangelical
    Church in America to the Jewish
    Community," 67–68
Deicide accusation, 98, 121
Deitrich, Donald, 168
Dershowitz, Alan, 67
Dewart, Leslie, 146
Dialogue, phenomenon/process of,
    146–50, 170–72
Die Judenfrage (Greunagel), 26
Dominus Iesus (Vatican), 175

Earth is the Lord's, The (Heschel), 55–56
Easter, 29–30
Eck, Johannes, 63
Eckardt, A. Roy, 17, 20–27, 95, 145, 153
Education, religious, 168–72
Edwards, Mark, 63
Ehrenberg, Rudolf, 60
Elder and Younger Brothers (Eckardt), 95
Essenes/Qumran Community, 10, 11
Eucharist, 119–20
Evangelical Lutheran Church in
    America, 62, 67–68, 86
Evangelical Lutheran Church in
    Germany, 26
Exodus, 30, 120–21

Fackenheim, Emil, 149
Faith and Fratricide (Ruether), 95, 151
Falk, Randall M., 6
Family life, 139–43
Fasching, Darrell, 107
Flannery, Edward, 24, 110–11, 115,
    136, 137, 138, 146, 150
Fleischner, Eva, 137, 146, 154
Forgiveness, 30–33, 60, 123, 159
Fourth Lateran Council, 101

Gamm, Hans-Jochen, 26
Gargan, Edward, 113, 115
Gilson, Etienne, 146
Glatzer, Nahum, 6, 60
Gnostics/Gnosticism, 103, 104
God
    as caring/loving, 28–29, 194–96
    and creation, 8–9, 28, 121–22, 124
    goodness of, 29
    human co-creatorship with, 121–22
    and human suffering, 27–29, 196–97
    incarnate in Jesus, 8–9, 80, 88, 154,
        196
    incomprehensibility of, 174–75, 177,
        193
    intelligibility of, 29
    omnipotence of, 28–29, 121, 196–97
    omnipresence of, 192
    oneness of, 14, 192–94
    as portrayed in the Psalms, 39–40
    question of, 27–30
    reality of, 53–54, 185
    and redemption, 10, 11–13, 29–30,
        46, 58, 105, 190, 199
    and religious pluralism, 18, 48, 88,
        175–78
    revelation of, 18, 33, 48, 119, 148, 154
    suffering of, 28–29, 196–97
    as transcendent, 192
    as Trinity, 9, 192–94

wisdom of, 8–9
Word of, 9, 33, 88, 151, 154, 193
Gospel and the Jews, The (Baum), 151
Greenberg, Irving, 107, 121, 137
Greunagel, Friedrich, 26
"Guidelines for Catholic-Jewish
   Relations (NCCB), 137–38, 188
"Guidelines for Lutheran-Jewish
   Relations" (ELCA), 68
"Guidelines and Suggestions for
   Implementing the Conciliar
   Declaration *Nostra Aetate* (no. 4)"
   (Vatican), 138
Gutiérrez, Gustavo, 120–21

Halakhah, 141, 142
Hals, Ron, 72
Hanukah, 141
Hartman, David, 75, 195
Hasidism, 58, 141
Hellwig, Monika, 146, 194
Herberg, Will, 2–3, 185
Herzl, Theodore, 158
Heschel, Abraham Joshua, 2, 33, 39, 43,
   46–47, 48, 52–56, 149, 166, 169, 185,
   186, 188, 191, 196–97
Heschel, Susannah, 47, 54
Heschel, Sylvia, 47, 54
Higgins, George, 137
Holocaust. See *Shoah*
Holy Land, 158–60, 168
Hope, 11–13, 127
Hotchkin, John, 138
Humor, 127

Idolatry/idols, 33, 87, 107, 175, 191
Incarnation, 8–9, 80, 88, 123, 154, 196
Ingall, Carol, 171
Is the New Testament Anti-Semitic?
   (Baum), 151
Isaac, Jules, 40, 51, 116

Israel, State of, 5, 20–21, 22–25,
   157–60, 168

Janowski, Max, 59
Janzen, Gerry, 104–05
Jaspers, Karl, 64
Jensen, Trudy Rogness, 74
Jesus
   and conversion, 45
   crucifixion/death of, 17–18, 27–28,
      82, 98 188, 190–91
   and forgiveness, 31
   as incarnation of God/God's Word,
      8–9, 80, 88, 154
   Jewishness of, 17, 46, 64, 87–88,
      114, 119, 124–26, 153
   as Messiah/Christ, 12, 13, 44, 47,
      57–58, 80, 83, 87–88, 189
   ministry of, 190
   and the Pharisees, 126, 157
   resurrection of, 12, 13, 27–28,
      29–30, 87, 190, 191
   Second Coming of, 47, 88
   as "sole mediator" of salvation,
      152, 153
   and the Torah, 190
   as way to "the Father," 60–61
   as *zaddik,* 58
John XXIII, Pope, 116, 163
John Paul II, Pope, 116, 117, 121, 155,
   158, 159, 188
Jonas, Hans, 28–29
Josephus, 1
Joshua ben Perahyah, 106
Josiah, 139

Keifer, Ralph, 123
Kelly, Jack, 137
Kelly, Thomas, 138
Kempis, Thomas à, 198
King, Martin Luther, 133

Klenicki, Leon, 149
Kushner, Harold, 149

Laborum Exercens (John Paul II), 121
Lectionary, 85–86, 118
Lee, Pauline, 164
Lee, Sara S., 170–71, 175
Lehmann, Helmut, 64
Letters and Papers from Prison
    (Bonhoeffer), 61
Lewis, B. F., 92
Liberation theology, 120–21, 169
Lichten, Joseph, 137
Lindberg, Carter, 63
Littell, Franklin, 133
Liturgy/liturgical reform, 32–33,
    119–20, 124, 139–43
Locke, Hubert G., 133
Lonergan, Bernard, 146
Long Night's Journey into Day
    (Eckardts), 26–27
Luther, Martin, 40–41, 55, 62–68

Mach, Rudolf, 3
Man Is Not Alone (Heschel), 53
Marcus, Ralph, 4
Marinoff, Shlomo, 134
Maritain, Jacques, 56, 146
Martini, Carol Maria, 117, 119, 125
Marty, Martin, 54, 114–15
Matt, Hershel, 189, 191
Mature Christianity (Beck), 74
McLuhan, Marshall, 146
McSorley, Harry, 146
Melanchthon, Philip, 63
Melito of Sardis, 98–99
Messiah/messianism, 11–13, 44, 47,
    57–58, 80, 83, 88, 189
Messianic Idea in Judaism, The
    (Scholem), 57
Metz, Johann-Baptist, 103

Midrash, 3, 78–79, 148
Mishnah, 1, 3
Mission to the Jews, 25, 26, 44–45,
    46–47, 155–56
Moltmann, Jürgen, 26
Monotheism, 192–94
Moran, Gabriel, 168
Morse, Christopher, 96
Moses, 14, 99, 119
Mukerji, Bitika, 94

National Workshop on Christian-Jewish
    Relations, 6, 75, 137, 138, 157
New Testament. *See* Sacred Scripture
New Testament: A New Translation
    and Redaction, The (Beck), 86
Niebuhr, Reinhold, 2, 3, 20
Night (Wiesel), 42
Nissiotis, Nikos, 94
Nostra Aetate (Vatican Council II), 112,
    116, 121, 133, 145, 152, 188
"Notes on the Correct Way to Present
    Jews and Judaism" (Vatican), 118
Novak, Michael, 53

Oesterreicher, John, 137, 146
Ogden, Shubert, 93
O'Hare, Padraic, 168
Old Testament. *See* Sacred Scripture
On the Jews and Their Lies (Luther), 62,
    64, 66
Orlinsky, Harry, 7
Otto, Rudolph, 53

Parkes, James, 21, 115, 145
Parkes, Dorothy, 21
Particularism, religious, 176–77
Passover/*Pesach*, 29–30, 139–40, 141
Paul/Pauline, 8, 10, 14, 61, 74, 76, 87,
    119, 122, 126, 141
Pawlikowski, John, 137, 146

Payne, Pamela, 100
Pelikan, Jaroslav, 64
People of God, 44–45, 80, 120, 141–42
Perelmuter, Hayim Goren, 57–59, 127
Perrin, Norman, 112, 114, 125
Pfisterer, Rudolf, 26
Pharisees, 74, 78, 123, 126, 131, 157, 163
Pirke Aboth, 106
Pius X, Pope, 158, 159
Pluralism, religious, 18, 48, 88, 127,
    175–78
Prayer, 39–40, 46–47, 60, 140, 142–43,
    178, 197
Preaching, 126, 156–57
Promise of Heschel, The (Sherman), 54
Psalms, 38–40
Purim, 141

Reconciliation, 62–69, 115–17, 123, 160,
    178
Redemption/salvation, 10, 11–13, 29–30,
    46, 48, 57–58, 104–05, 119–20,
    152–53, 163, 190–91, 197, 199
Relativism, 175–77
Religious life, 165–66, 177–78
Rendtorff, Rolf, 26
Repentance, 32, 60, 62–69, 78, 115–17
Revelation, 18, 33, 45, 48, 119, 148, 154
Ritual. *See* Liturgy
Rivkin, Ellis, 123
Rosenfeld, Elsbeth, 21
Rosenstock-Huessy, Eugene, 61
Rosenzweig, Franz, 60–62, 149, 185
Rothman, Murray, 167
Rudavsky, David, 134
Ruether, Rosemary, 95, 146
Rylaarsdam, J. Coert, 4, 92–93, 114,
    145–46

Sabbath/*Shabbat,* 42, 58–59, 139, 140,
    169, 173 198–99

Sabbath, The (Heschel), 56, 58, 169
Secretariat for Catholic-Jewish
    Relations (NCCB), 137, 138
"Sacred Obligation: A Christian
    Statement on Judaism and the
    Jewish People, A," xii
Sacred Scripture
    anti-Jewish materials in New
        Testament, 73–74, 80–82, 83–87,
        151–52
    authority of, 87, 102–03
    Hebrew Scriptures as resource for
        Christian faith, 117–19, 121
    idolatrous approach to, 87
    interpretations/exegesis of, 76–79, 91,
        112, 124–26, 148–49, 157
    and preaching 126, 157
    Psalms, 38–40
    relationship between the testaments,
        38, 54, 76–77, 117–18, 163, 169
    richness of, 118, 133–34
    and tradition, 102–03, 148–49, 151,
        156
Saldarini, Anthony, 168
Saltzman, Murray, 95–96
Salvation. *See* Redemption
Salvation of the Nations, The
    (Daniélou), 38
Sasso, Dennis, 95–96
Schiotz, Fredrik, 74
Schneiders, Sandra, 103, 165, 177–78
Scholem, Gershom, 57, 58
Sexuality, 2–3, 15–16, 122
Shalom, 105
Sheerin, John, 137, 138, 146
Shema, 14, 56
Shoah/Holocaust, 21–22, 25–33, 40–43,
    72, 80, 107, 113, 116, 122, 127, 136,
    149, 150–52, 174
Simchat Torah, 141
Sin, 9–10, 105, 122–23

Sloyan, Gerard, 120
Sobrino, Jon, 121
Soulen, R. Kendall, 104, 105
Spirituality, 56, 118, 119, 124, 141, 169, 177–78, 197–99
Stahl, Samuel M., 75
Star of Redemption, The (Rosenzweig), 60–62
"Statement on Catholic-Jewish Relations" (NCCB), 138, 188
Steiman, Sidney, 95
Stein, Jonathan, 95–96
Steiner, Jean-François, 41
Stendahl, Krister, 44, 122
Stransky, Thomas, 146, 158
Suchocki, Marjorie, 105
Sukkot, 124
Sunflower, The (Wiesenthal), 30–32
Supersessionism/supersessionist, xi, 25, 38, 80–86, 92–93, 97–99, 147–48, 149–50, 163, 169, 173, 186, 189, 190
Synagogue, origins of, 139, 140

Tainted Greatness: Antisemitism and Cultural Heroes (Harrowitz), 63
Tal, Uriel, 94
"Talking Points: Topics in Christian-Jewish Relations" (ELCA), 68
Talmud, 3, 78, 148, 195
Tanakh, 76, 92, 118
Tanenbaum, Marc, 94, 137
Taylor, J. Murray, 90–91
Temple (Jerusalem), 139
Ten Commandments, 14, 77, 169
Teshuvah, 45, 78, 116; *see also* Repentance
That Jesus Christ Was Born a Jew (Luther), 64
Thérèse of Lisieux, 198
Thering, Rose, 137

Thomas, David, 142
Tillich, Paul, 2, 92, 93
Time, sanctification of, 198–99
Tolstoy, Leo, 96
Torah, 13–15, 76–77, 80, 140–41, 142, 185–86, 190, 197–99
Tradition, 102–03, 148–49, 174–78
Treblinka (Steiner), 41
Trinity, 9, 192–94
Troeltsch, Ernst, 93

Unitatis Redintegratio, 133
United States Holocaust Memorial Museum, 6, 67
Van Buren, Paul, 173
Van Dusan, Henry P., 23
Vatican Commission for Religious Relations with the Jews, 117, 127, 148, 183, 188
Vatican Council II, 112, 116–17, 119–20, 121, 132–34, 135, 141–43, 145, 152–53, 155, 156–57, 162–63, 164, 183, 187, 188

"We Remember: A Reflection on the *Shoah*" (Vatican), 116
Weigel, Gustav, 46–47
Weinberg, Dudley, 42
Wiesel, Elie, 27
Wiesenthal, Simon, 30–32
Willaert, Benjamin, 187
Wolpe, David, 195
Works-righteousness, 98–99

Yom HaShoah, 30, 32–33
Yom Kippur, 60, 78
Your People, My People (Eckardt), 95

Zahn, Gordon, 113
Zionism, 20, 158